PRAISE FOR

THE HUNDRED
STORY HOME

"From the beginning of time, I believe it was ordained that Kathy would
have a life-changing encounter with Denver Moore. He believed that
as well. These unexpected encounters ... thrill believers and encourage
doubters to search. Prepare yourself to be thrilled or to begin searching
for your Denver."

—RON HALL, author of *Same Kind of Different As Me*
(movie adaptation, February 2017)

"Compelling, inspiring, funny, and poign ook about
finding your purpose in a meaningful d family
and friendship. But mostly, it's a lo , a mother's
love, a daughter's love, and a beau love."

—KRISTIN HILLS BRADBF Charlotte, N.C.

"Kathy Izard, the remarkable an pion of housing for the
homeless in Charlotte, N.C., gives er gift—her honest, humble, and unforgettable story of the chance encounters and enduring
comments that conceived and sustained Moore Place despite repeated
setbacks."

—KEN GEPFERT, a former editor at *The Charlotte Observer*
and *The Wall Street Journal*

"An extremely powerful testament of courage, determination, and generosity. Kathy invites and challenges us to 'trust the whisper' of God and
to take our own leap of faith. As her story reveals, when we do, our lives
are mysteriously transformed by God's love."

—THE REVEREND CHIP EDENS, Christ Church, Charlotte, N.C.

"In this book, Kathy describes how her father used to say to her, 'You can do anything, Kathy, really anything.' When you reach the last page of *The Hundred Story Home,* you completely agree with Kathy's dad—but equally powerfully, through Kathy's example, you believe you can do anything, too."

— CAROLINE CHAMBRE HAMMOCK, assistant director,
Urban Ministry Center

"From homeless to home seems an impossible journey until you read this compelling true story. The author began by serving soup and ended with finding her soul, while creating an eighty-five-unit apartment building for some of America's 'invisible' people. Amazingly, Kathy Izard will teach you to see—and ask, *Why not do this in my community?"*

— ROLFE NEILL, former publisher, *The Charlotte Observer*

"Kathy Izard tells two compelling stories in one: about her journey toward fulfilling her life's purpose and about Charlotte's journey to finally treating its chronically homeless with compassion and dignity. Each has twists and turns, each has a happy ending, and Izard tells each with a style that will captivate readers far beyond her most natural audience."

— TAYLOR BATTEN, editorial page editor, *The Charlotte Observer*

"Kathy Izard's is a deeply personal story, movingly told. She reminds us that one person can truly make a difference, especially when challenged to Do Good. What a gift she has given us."

— SUSAN PATTERSON, former program director,
John S. and James L. Knight Foundation

"Kathy Izard's candor and bravery in recounting her midlife crisis and her subsequent passion for her work is striking and inspirational. *The Hundred Story Home* is a road map to advocacy, and a touching story of faith, serendipity, and perseverance paying off in a big way."

— SPR

THE
HUNDRED
STORY
HOME

THE
HUNDRED
STORY
HOME

A Journey of Homelessness,
Hope, and Healing

KATHY IZARD

grace press
NORTH CAROLINA

Printed in the United States of America

First Printing 2016

ISBN 978-0-9977784-0-3

EDITING: Fiona Hallowell
PROOFREADING: Diane Aronson
COVER DESIGN: Jon Valk
INTERIOR DESIGN: Karen Minster
AUTHOR PHOTO: Edwina Willis Fleming

Ordering Information:
Special discounts are available on quantity
purchases by corporations, associations, and others.
For details, contact the publisher at

grace press

GRACE PRESS
1235 East Blvd Suite E PMB 126
Charlotte, North Carolina 28203

Kathy@kathyizard.com
www.kathyizard.com

To my Goose,

the First Believer

Sometimes everything
has to be
inscribed across
the heavens
so you can find
the one line
already written
inside you.

DAVID WHYTE

CONTENTS

AUTHOR'S NOTE

The events in this book took place over the course of many years, the majority during 2007-2012. I have reconstructed details to the best of my memory, using journals and emails. Some names have been changed to protect confidentiality. In several scenes, the time element is compressed for the sake of narrative flow, but the stories told in these pages are all true.

PROLOGUE

I had been in this building with my Neighbors well over one hundred times in the past decade, but it was the first time I ever truly saw them.

Surrounding me were exhausted men and women bent from the weight of bulging backpacks and tugging bags that held the remaining contents of a life somehow lost. As I stood facing my guest, people diverted around us, each intent on their own mission, oblivious to mine. It could have been a bus station or train station, but everyone was here precisely because they had nowhere else to go.

This was the Urban Ministry Center in Charlotte, North Carolina, an interfaith homeless service agency. Since 1994, the nonprofit soup kitchen had opened every morning, seven days a week, serving lunch, compassion, and no judgment. For the past thirteen years, every person who ended up on the doorstep was called not a "client" but a "Neighbor." This subtle distinction was made clear to each of the hundreds of volunteers who assisted the shoestring staff. Everyone who sought help at the UMC was treated as if they lived next door. For hundreds of Charlotte's homeless, this was home.

At the time, I didn't really believe in God, but I did believe in leaving the world a better place. The UMC was one of those places where it was easy to do a little good in the world. For over ten years, my family and I had been helping once a month on Sundays, cooking and cleaning in the kitchen. During our four-hour shift we easily served more than five hundred people and we always left feeling a little better about ourselves. Until today, I had never wondered if that soup we served was actually a little hard to swallow.

Along with my kitchen shift, I now served on the board of this nonprofit, and I had given tours of the Urban Ministry Center many times to new volunteers and donors. In the past when I brought visitors through these halls, the reactions were always the same.

Remarkable. Inspiring. Impressive.

But on this day, my guest was impassive. Not speaking. Not moving, just glaring at me intently with a dark stare that communicated a condemnation I could not quite understand. My guest was a man who was formerly homeless himself, now turned coauthor of a book that had been on the *New York Times* bestseller list. I had been excited to show him our Center, certain that he would laud our efforts. I was sure he would confirm how much *good* we did.

In almost thirty minutes of touring the building grounds, however, the man had not asked a single question or made a single comment about our remarkable work for the homeless. Along with our soup kitchen, I had shown him an art studio, community garden, street soccer court, and even a choir room. Each program had been designed to further engage our Neighbors. Yet, not one innovation elicited even a hint of interest from the man I was now leading through the halls. Finally, our uncomfortable tour had ended, and we were standing in the front lobby near the base of the stairs leading to the administrative offices.

I was out of words and out of ideas.

My visitor was the one person I'd given a tour to who I really wanted to impress. His approval meant everything to me. I was sure once he saw what we did, he would be compelled to speak to the exhausted people around me, lifting their spirits with the type of prophetic wisdom for which he had become famous in his book.

His pages had inspired people across the country, and I was sure he would do the same in person.

Defeated, I was about to turn to leave and *this* is when he finally chose to speak.

Finally, there was some emotion in his stony face, and he looked expectantly at the stairs then back to me. Motioning to the stairway in front of us, he asked, "Can we go upstairs now?"

I couldn't believe that now that he finally wanted to see something there was, in fact, nothing to show. My frustration surfaced as I told him, "There are just offices up there, not much to see."

His face flashed a frustration matching mine. We confronted each other, in a standoff. He spoke first.

"Where are the beds?"

"The beds?" I asked, utterly confused.

He must not have been listening. Throughout my tour, I had clearly outlined that UMC was a day ministry, not a shelter. Shelters have beds. The UMC had a strategic mission of providing day services to those on the streets. After being homeless himself, he must know the difference.

As I started the long, complicated explanation of how Charlotte had several shelters where men and women sleep at night, his eyes narrowed to slits that silenced me.

Clearly, *I* wasn't getting *his* point.

Although there was chaos all around us, Neighbors shuffling past, jostling to get in line, calling out to staff, I could not hear anything but his question still hanging unanswered.

What did he mean, "Where are the beds?"

Again, he spoke first, this time with a dagger to my decade of volunteerism.

"You mean to tell me you do all this good in the day
and then lock them out to the bad at night?"

I could not have been more stunned if he had slapped me across the face. It was a stinging accusation. As much as I wanted to defend myself, this mission, this thirteen-year track record, I was shocked into silence.

His point was so obvious.

Were we only doing good in the day when it was easy? All that art, soccer, and counseling were convenient to provide until 4:30 p.m. but what happens after that? As a volunteer, I felt good about myself when I went home but then again, I had a home. Where did the Neighbors go? How did they feel watching us get in our cars and drive away?

Could we really feel good about anything we did in the day when the same human beings who painted in our studio were huddled under highway bridges at night? In all the time that I had been there, I had never once asked myself, *"Where are the beds?"* I had never once thought that "all the good" we did wasn't enough—or even close to enough—if you were the one with frostbite sleeping on cardboard, praying not to be mugged while you slept. I had never once let myself fully imagine the "bad at night."

I knew I had never asked that question because I didn't really want to know the answer. If I had, then I am sure *I* would not sleep very well at night.

He watched me wrestling with the answer to his question. Mercifully, he did not wait for me to come up with a justification, he simply asked the next rhetorical question.

"Does that make any sense to you?"

Of course it made no sense. I felt a rush of shame. I could not answer him. There were no words to say all that I was feeling. No words to convey all that I could now see that I had never seen before.

Then he asked the question I never expected, but, I now know, I had been waiting for my whole life.

"Are you going to do something about it?"

For years after, I stayed awake at night wondering why he had asked *me*: a wife, mother of four, graphic designer, and soup kitchen volunteer. Why would he ask *me* what I was going to do about it? How could I possibly do anything that would make a dent in such a huge problem? Why would he think I could?

But finally, I realized the *real* question was:

Why had I listened?

Mark Twain said, "The two greatest days in our life are the day we were born and the day we find out why."

This is my journey to *Why*.

Why I listened had everything to do with who I was, how I was raised, and experiences from my childhood that I always wanted to forget. In writing this, I realized that everything that had happened in my life connected so I would *listen* in *that* moment.

For all that to happen, there was an enormous amount of serendipity. Coincidence. God-instance. Call it what you want.

All those years ago, I would not have argued with you if you said there is no God.

Today, I would argue you are not listening.

THE
HUNDRED
STORY
HOME

1

Six Candles. One Wish.

*At the end of the day, it isn't where
I came from. Maybe home is somewhere
I'm going and never have been before.*

WARSAN SHIRE

IT WAS THE DAY I WILL ALWAYS REMEMBER IN THE YEAR I WILL always wish I could forget.

Standing on my toes looking over the edge of her large green drafting table, I watched my mom carefully creating ten works of art. She was curled over in concentration so she could work closer to her pencil. We were in the spacious art studio added onto my parents' bedroom of our new split-level home. My family of five had just moved into this four-bedroom house on the last street of a new development on the west side of El Paso, Texas.

The art studio was a twenty-by-twenty-foot room with vaulted ceilings and natural light streaming in the windows. There were two kilns, easels, canvases, acrylic and oil paints, along with cabinets brimming with other supplies. A cassette player and boxes of classical music tapes filled the room with symphonies while we worked. My two sisters and I were probably the only three little girls encouraged to play not house, but Hallmark. For every relative's birthday, anniversary, or holiday, Mom got out the craft supplies and made us create custom cards. Glitter and glue weren't enough; we had to have a theme, an illustration, and a message, just like a real greeting card.

I always thought of this space in our house as my father's love letter to my mom. This was the place he wanted her to thrive even though she had been transplanted to desert soil.

El Paso was my father's hometown and my mother had moved there a decade ago from North Carolina out of pure love for him. All of the houses in our neighborhood were essentially ranch style with added western architectural elements: tile roof, adobe color palettes, and wooden beams protruding over arched windows. Kind of like if you bought the Mexican accent package for Mister Potato Head. Every front yard had a similar landscape scheme of cactus and rocks—except ours. Mom had softened the rocks with the best of her home state, North Carolina, adding rose bushes and Bradford pear trees to our quarter-acre plot. I don't think the local nursery had ever heard of a Bradford pear tree when my mom insisted on special-ordering four.

As I watched her over her drafting table, Mom was deliberate in her work. Delicate fingers with rounded, clear-polished nails pressed firmly to steady the pencil as she meticulously sketched the wording on the outside of ten four-by-six-inch folded-over cards she had cut from white construction paper. This pencil outline was only a rough draft to ensure the letters were centered and evenly spaced.

Next, she took her deep black India ink pen, slowly retracing the lines for the letters to emerge. As she finished one, she moved to the next until all ten cards proclaimed in perfect measured script:

You are cordially invited
to celebrate the sixth birthday of
Katherine Grace Green

For weeks, my mom had poured her substantial creative energies into devising a memorable day for me. Mom never remembered having even a store-bought birthday cake for her childhood birthdays, so she vowed that her girls would always know and remember their celebrations. She began by choosing a theme; everything my mother did had themes. The invitations, games, cake, and party favors all required matching motifs painstakingly penned, painted, and baked for the big day. Mom had decided this special celebration for my sixth year would have a cartoon theme. We had been saving sections of the comics for weeks, so Mom handed me the rounded craft safety scissors to cut out a six-inch-long section of the Goofy strip. I pasted it to the inside of a card and then added typed instructions that informed my best friend, Andrea, she was not only invited to my party but she must come dressed as this particular Disney character. Obviously, there would be prizes for best costume.

Before that afternoon, my mom had already let me pick my character. I chose Linus so I could carry a blue blanket and follow Snoopy (my friend Susie) around. My sister Allyson, who was only a year and a half older than me, was obsessed with Disney princesses and wanted to be Cinderella, so she could wear her blonde hair in a bun and twirl throughout the party in a long blue gown.

My mom overruled this costume, which was not on theme since Cinderella was not a comic strip, so Allyson unhappily dressed as Lucy from the Peanuts gang. My oldest sister, Louise, was twelve years old and already a lifetime away from wanting to come to her little sister's birthday party. Louise agreed to help babysit the partygoers but refused to be in costume, a huge disappointment to my mother who loved to dress us in triplicate for church.

Finally, the day arrived, and I could see from the kitchen window as my friends appeared at our front door. Andrea as Goofy, Nancy as Minnie Mouse, Beth as Beetle Bailey. Mothers and daughters filled our front porch, marveling over the creative costumes of the guests but, mostly, over the ingenuity of my mom.

"Lindsay, I swear, I don't know how you think of these parties!"

"I can't even draw a straight line much less do calligraphy!"

"I don't know how you have the time."

My mother deflected the compliments, gazing down, shyly touching strands of her chestnut brown hair, which were already firmly in place from the beauty shop and Aqua Net hairspray. Inside, she was glowing with pride. Mom may not have been able to receive the compliments but it was all true. She was an integral part of the PTA, an officer in the Junior League, choir member and Sunday school teacher at First Presbyterian Church, wife and mother extraordinaire.

How did she do it all?

The party, as always, was flawless.

When it came time to blow out the candles, my friends pressed against each other to fit around our round kitchen table. The cake was another work of art baked by my mom. She lit the candles while my friends and sisters sang, *"Hap-py-Birth-day dear Ka-thy …"*

"Make a wish!" Mom said.

I hope I get an Easy-Bake oven.

Mom knew that's what I wanted. Tearing into my pile of presents, I spotted the rectangular box meticulously wrapped with pages of comic sections so that even the gift would be dressed on theme. My own Easy-Bake oven.

This was the Best. Day. Ever.

As the last guest left, I could see the exhaustion in my mom's whole body, and I rushed to press my face against her legs, hugging her lower body as we stood in our front hall. The floor beneath us was a Lucite tile that looked like turquoise and celadon shells floating effortlessly in a clear sea.

At that moment, I truly believed my mother could walk on water.

She stroked the top of my wispy dirty-blonde head and when I looked up at her, she absently moved her fingers to straighten my bangs. Mom looked lost in other thoughts as her fingertips touched the fine hairs that didn't need fixing. Shifting her gaze from my hair to the six-foot countertop, Mom walked slowly away from me towards the kitchen to attend to some task I couldn't see. The counter held a green telephone the color of avocados matching all the appliances in the kitchen (stove, refrigerator, and dishwasher), which were custom-painted this same exact shade of green. Beside our house phone was the week's mail piled next to her calendar, note cards, and bible.

Mom held reverence for all three items—two organizing her short-term life and the other her long-term destiny.

She always tracked her duties on three-by-five-inch ruled index cards, making careful notes with a four-color Bic pen, clicking the top to dispense the appropriate color. Mom picked up one of the white cards that ordered her busy world and studied the week's list:

Church— cotton balls Sunday School lesson
Jr League— committee coffee: bake seven layer cookies
Ballet Carpool— Louise & Allyson: Tuesday, Thursday
Kathy— party

Picking up her pen, she drew a line through the last item with only a hint of satisfaction.

"Well, that's done!" she said, trying to convince herself of the victory.

It was January 29, 1969.

Within six months, my mother would be gone for the first time, and it would be sixteen years before all of her would return.

If I'd known, I definitely would have saved my wish for something more magical than an Easy-Bake oven.

My dad never saw it coming. No one did.

My parents' love story was an old-fashioned one that began when they were college sweethearts and academic all-stars. My dad, John Leighton Green Jr., grew up in El Paso, where, in addition to being an all-state tennis player, he set a high school record for the highest GPA ever achieved. Dad did this while skipping two grades and finishing high school early at age sixteen. After graduation, he traveled eight states away to attend Davidson College in North Carolina, where he eventually met my mom, who was attending Queens College thirty minutes away in Charlotte, N.C.

My mom, Lindsay Louise Marshall, went to high school in Winston Salem, N.C., and was equally gifted. Mom was top of her class, an all-state violinist, and a talented painter. She chose Queens because she was "promised" to her high school boyfriend and he had been accepted to nearby Davidson. They agreed going to universities in close proximity would keep their love alive until their inevitable marriage. My mom's parents disapproved of this boyfriend so when they broke up her freshman year, Granddad said simply, "We've been praying for this for a long time."

It was sophomore year when she met my father. Her friend had arranged a blind date and they went to a movie in Charlotte. During this first date, my dad told her he was debating going into either the law or the ministry. My mom, who was rigidly religious and majoring in Christian education, told him flatly, "Anyone going into the law has no business being a minister."

Dad was not deterred by her opinion or that Mom seemed not very interested in him. He arranged a second date and beforehand sent a dozen red roses.

"Do you know why I sent you the roses?" my dad asked.

"Why?" my mom asked.

"Because I love you!"

"Well, I am not sure how I feel about you."

Dad didn't give up.

Growing up, I used to be teased by my sisters about making a "Dad" face when I was really concentrating. A wrinkling of the brow, a narrowing of the eyes, and a clenching of the teeth. I can imagine my father making a "Dad" face in his dorm room at Davidson, trying to decide how he would get this soft southern beauty to love him.

On Valentine's Day, they went on a special date and Dad was prepared. This time, he brought his bible and read aloud to her from 1 Corinthians 13:

And now these three remain: faith, hope and love.
But the greatest of these is love.

She thought it was the most romantic thing anyone had ever done for her and that night told him, "I love you, too."

They saw each other every weekend and then one night, in a corner of the Davidson Kappa Sig house, Mom said, "You know I have no idea where El Paso is!"

"Why don't you marry me and then you won't have to wonder," Dad replied.

That was how Mom found herself transferring to the University of Texas, El Paso, in January of her junior year. My dad had graduated and was completing military service at Fort Bliss outside El Paso. Mom would finish her degree in Texas and they would marry that summer. When they were packing her things in the dorm, Mom's

English professor had chided my dad, "Don't you take her away from Queens until she graduates. She has one of the best minds I have ever seen."

Neither of them listened.

They married on June 9, 1956, the day after my father's birthday, because he said it was the best birthday present he could ever have. On their first anniversary and every anniversary and Valentine's after, Dad would send another dozen red roses and they would read 1 Corinthians aloud to each other.

Fully in love, Mom resolutely finished her studies at UTEP. During that drive to her new home 1,663 miles away from North Carolina, I am sure Mom thought hard about what she had done for love. The name "El Paso" refers to "The Pass in the Mountains," and the city itself wraps around the soaring but treeless Franklin Mountains. Cacti and tumbleweeds are commonplace, and there are seemingly more signs in Spanish than in English in this border town.

As foreign as El Paso looked, my mom will never say she had regrets. My father was the answer to her prayers—the promise of a life filled with God, love, family, and service. She couldn't have foreseen the turns it would take. My father switched from divinity school to law school; he worked long hours towards his partner track at the law firm; and Mom appeared unstoppable in creativity, in motherhood, and in civic responsibility. But that new home they had saved for years to buy would become the setting for a much different story.

We would try to piece together later what exactly had happened. That year of my perfect cartoon party, 1969, would be the year my mother's brilliant mind shattered for the first time—a blindsiding collision that left all of us with collateral damage.

2

Do Good. Love Well.

*Finding a sanctuary, a place apart from time,
is not so different from finding a faith.*

PICO IYER

BOTH MY FATHER AND MOTHER WOULD TELL YOU IT WAS THEIR faith that allowed us to survive that crash at all.

My parents were devoutly Christian, each from a long line of Presbyterian ministers and missionaries on both sides. My family went to church not just every Sunday but almost all day Sunday as well. There was Sunday school, then Big Church service, then afternoon youth group, and youth choir.

Every week in Big Church we sat in the same family pew in the First Presbyterian Church of El Paso. There was no plaque or anything but everyone reserved it for us anyway. We usually sat in the same order, too. First, Poppa, a respected doctor in El Paso for over fifty years. He had delivered babies and then those babies' babies all while serving at the church and on the local school board. He was so passionate about public education that eventually there would be an elementary school named after him, and every child in that school would carry a card to remind them of Poppa's famous motto:

You are as good as anyone; you are better than no one.

Nestled next to him in the pew was Gigi, which stood for Grand-mother Green. I adored her. She had enormous brown eyes set under a cloud of silver-blue hair. When she wrapped her arms around me, she would say my name with a playful twist, "Katarina, how *are* you?" And she truly wanted to know. Always. When she listened, she made me feel as though whatever I had to say was the most vital thought she had ever heard. In her presence, I always felt not merely loved but adored.

We all knew why. Although she was one of five children, Gigi was much younger than her four older brothers. By the time she was five, both of her parents had died, leaving her an orphan whom none of her brothers could care for. Gigi went to live with Grace Walker, for whom I received my middle name.

Grace lived on an estate where she worked as the caretaker of an unmarried heiress. While this was a luxurious setting to sleep in, Gigi grew up in this extravagant home where she was not quite family and not quite servant. She became part of a traveling entou-rage, moving every three months to catch the best climate in each of the heiress's four estates across the U.S. and Canada. With all this movement, Gigi would be in a school three months before she was uprooted again. She grew up with few friends and no sense of family, describing herself a "poor little rich girl."

As a result, Gigi treasured the family she created: two sons, two daughters-in-law, and five granddaughters. My cousins lived in San Antonio so my sisters and I were the grandchildren Gigi spoiled weekly with sleepovers and long lunches. We would each get invited to her house for our own special dates, and Gigi would feed us her famous chocolate mint sticks, a secret recipe she never shared, even when the Junior League asked to put it in their cookbook.

I would curl up next to Gigi on her nubby pink couch and rub my fingers on the raised squares in the sofa fabric as I talked to her. Gigi patiently listened to all I had to say. She would hold my hand and look at me with those round chocolate eyes that gave her, even in her eighties, a perpetual look of childlike wonder. And she was always wondering. Wondering about me, my sisters, and, really, everyone she met. She truly wanted to know about you, where you came from, what your story was, because like her own, she knew everyone had a story worth telling.

Next to Gigi and Poppa in the pew were my dad, mom, and then, the three Green Girls. Mom made me sit next to her so she could pinch my leg to keep me still if I started squirming. It was hard not to squirm in church.

Usually I kept my mind busy by staring up at the dark oak ceiling forty feet above my head and wondering how they changed the light bulbs. The timbers curved up in huge arcs on either side of a central beam and it looked as if I were inside Noah's Ark, which had been flipped upside down. Light bulbs were not supposed to be what I was pondering. I was supposed to be listening to the word of God. But I never felt he was talking to me.

I only behaved in Big Church because I knew the best part of the day, really the best part of my week, came after: lunch at Gigi's. My grandparents' home was tan brick on the outside with thick stucco walls and arched doorways on the inside. Stepping inside was like entering a sanctuary that smelled of roasted potatoes with browned butter. Gigi's weekly offering of lamb, mint jelly, potatoes, green beans with almonds, and angel food cake with caramel sauce was food for my soul. It fed me more than any sermon.

Each Sunday lunch, we would gather at the dining room table while Poppa, who thought education was the most important thing a man or woman could have, always asked about our week, our lives, our future.

Kathy, what's your favorite subject?

Allyson, tell me about your poetry.

Louise, what colleges are you thinking about?

Those Sunday lunches were not fast-food or drive-by affairs. We could easily be at the table for an hour and a half. And really, this was my Sunday school. Poppa discussing his work with the board of education, Gigi's commitment to the Junior League, Dad's service with the El Paso Cancer Treatment Center, and Mom's work with the Girls Club.

Mom used to take the three of us when she drove into south El Paso to do work with the Girls Club. To get there we had to drive along the interstate, I-10, which was bordered on one side with El Paso and Juarez, Mexico on the other. Besides the interstate, the dividing line between the U.S. and Mexico is the Rio Grande. Translated from Spanish, this means "big river," but where it washes into El Paso it is not grand at all. Although the name suggests roaring rapids and vast expanse, the river in most parts of the city is a muddy twenty-five-yard trench. Just as the city curls around the mountain, the river winds its way through the edge of El Paso, creating borders between Texas and Mexico.

This is where the river plays God.

Babies born on the *right* side are brought home from hospitals to homes that had electricity, indoor plumbing, and U.S. citizenship. All those luxuries are unimaginable to babies born on the other side, a mere fifty-yard stretch of water and dirt away. Those babies have Mexican citizenship and the majority goes home to live in shacks constructed of cardboard with dirt floors and lit by kerosene.

Being born on the *wrong* side also meant mothers risked crossing the border to be a maid in El Paso homes, where they could make ten times the wages in Juarez. This meant they left their families and didn't visit or come home for months—if at all. Fathers in Mexico waded thigh-deep in water in order to make dollars a day in construction or landscape maintenance.

Growing up in El Paso, I developed an inner shame that I lived on the *right* side, born to the *right* parents, and afforded the *right* opportunities. It always made me uncomfortable to drive along that interstate and be on the right side of privilege and be helpless about the wrong side.

My father had grown up in that same border city looking at those same views and must have felt the same way. Maybe that's why my sisters and I weren't just raised to *be* good; we were raised to *do* good.

In the early 1970s when daughters were still being raised with the primary goal of becoming wives and mothers, my parents, especially Dad, expected more. He raised us to change the world. His refrain to me was:

*You can do anything, Kathy, really **anything**.*

I never remember a conversation with my father about marrying or having a family. We talked about college, career, and the ultimate goal: leaving the world a better place. Dad wholeheartedly believed each of us would do just that.

It didn't seem to matter to him that we were being raised a little off the grid in West Texas. Dad just accepted on faith that we would all leave El Paso and make an indelible mark on the world.

While I may not have learned much in Big Church, I did take lessons from those Sunday lunches. I believed in two commandments. One from my Dad: Do Good. The other from Gigi: Love Well.

3

No Casseroles for Crazy

Here is the world. Beautiful and terrible things
will happen. Don't be afraid.

FREDERICK BUECHNER

THAT EL PASO LANDSCAPE SO STARTLINGLY CLOSE TO MEXICO
imprinted on me not just an unease of privilege, but also an unease
of the desert.

When there is no wind, deserts appear ancient, solid, immovable.
But deserts are also deceiving. Unpredictable, remarkable natural
phenomena occur there: mirages, flash floods, sandstorms—wicked
sandstorms.

One time in first grade, my elementary school was closed during
the day due to a particularly vicious sandstorm. Our mothers had
been called to pick us up early so we each waited in our classrooms,
several hundred yards from the parking lot, to be taken home.
Teachers formed a human chain to safety, bending in the violent
winds while stretching long ropes in their hands. As our names were
called, we left our homeroom haven to clutch the one-inch-thick
lines leading to the waiting cars and wiping our eyes, stinging from
the swirling sand.

We couldn't see more than a few feet in front of us, and the world
had morphed into a confusing tan curtain that obscured the flying

debris hurling towards us. Stepping cautiously as if we were walking on tightropes instead of holding ropes, we clung to each other, uncertain what the next step would bring.

The morning had been clear with no warning that this dramatic school rescue would unfold. No way to predict. No way to be watchful.

Looking back, what happened in my own home felt remarkably similar.

It was the spring of 1969, three months after my perfect birthday, and although there had been signs that week of trouble, we had not seen them. It began harmlessly, gentle winds in Mom's head swirling her thoughts slowly, mixing and turning like Betty Crocker batter. She must have felt them and tried to put her world back in order. Her first line of defense was always those three-by-five-inch notecards and her four-color pen. As careful as a meteorologist tracking the currents, she would try to reassemble her thoughts in logical order with her perfect penmanship:

Groceries
>   Orange Juice
>   Pepperidge Farm Bread
>   Rice
>   Jolly Green Giant Green Beans with Almonds
>   Chicken

Carpool
>   Tuesday— Jazz and Ballet, Louise, Allyson
>   Wednesday— Piano, Allyson
>   Thursday— Ballet, Kathy

Cards
>   Anniversary (Johnson)
>   Birthday (Karen, Anne)

Clear. Careful. She would make no mistakes. Her home, her daughters, her friends all needed tending. Dinner to be made. Carpools to track. Cards to send. There were always the cards. No matter how she was feeling, my mother was anchored in her Hallmark habit. Buying and sending greeting cards was always a staple of her domesticity, and a grounding force in her day. We had to make cards in the art studio, but my mother purchased all of hers from Hallmark. Each week she would faithfully mail greetings to mark birthdays, anniversaries, and major holidays for countless friends and relatives.

Allyson and I were playing in our downstairs den. Allyson was my in-house buddy and first best friend. Her imagination was limitless, and we would be fairy princesses or magic pixies in kingdoms and faraway places.

We had a small overnight-size suitcase where we kept our treasure collection of doll evening gowns, daywear, swimsuits, and accessories. We could spend hours stretching the sparkling fabric over the impossibly perfect plastic figures and easily losing time in the magical land where our orange shag den carpet became a beach in faraway islands. One afternoon, the "sun" we created from the den lamp was so bright it actually burned a hole in Barbie's skull when we mistakenly left her basking against the bulb all day.

Louise rarely played with us anymore, and on this day she was upstairs with her two best friends whispering secrets we couldn't fathom. Louise was the exotic animal who lived in the bedroom next to mine but never spoke to me. She sprayed herself with Jungle Gardenia perfume, and went on dates with handsome cowboys, and I desperately wanted to be exactly like her. Or at least have her notice me.

Looking up from the wonder of Barbieland, I could see my mom outside in the backyard garden. The upside-down nest of her beauty-shopped hair was just visible in the rosebushes as she moved intently through the leaves, oblivious to the thorns. Mom held clippers in her hand, but she had no clear purpose in the bushes, except she was speaking earnestly aloud as she moved. I stood up to see if she was discussing something with the neighbor.

There was no one there.

Allyson and I cracked the back door to listen to what my mom was saying and to whom she was saying it, but her forceful jumbled dialogue had no apparent human audience. She moved earnestly from bloom to bloom speaking her truths to the beloved roses.

We froze watching her, knowing it wasn't right. Mom at times appeared to see our faces, visible between the den curtains but she looked through us with no apparent recognition.

"We need to get Louise," Allyson said, her eight-year-old self fully aware a grownup was in order and Louise was twelve, which qualified.

As we rushed up the den stairs towards the kitchen, we were confronted with other signs of disarray. We tried to decipher and find clues in the trail: a frozen orange juice concentrate can opened on the kitchen counter, apparently spilled and forgotten for the old hatboxes taken down from her bedroom closet and left opened and abandoned for the garden shears she now held in her hands in the backyard. Mom was meticulous, but now the house was a tornado of her confusion.

We pounded on Louise's door, and reluctantly she opened it a small crack to peer at us with disdain. "What?!"

"It's Mom! Something's not right," Allyson cried. Even as she spoke she was beginning to sob, and I stood behind clutching her arm, nodding and crying in agreement.

Louise rolled her eyes. Allyson, the fairy princess extraordinaire, was known to be predisposed to drama and obviously was not being believed.

"Really, Louise, you have to see!"

Louise looked from us to her friends behind her and said with utter confidence, "I'll be right back."

She followed us down the hall, stomping heavily in exasperation, but when she saw the floor of my parents' bedroom strewn with the orphaned hatboxes, Louise froze.

"There's more," Allyson assured her, glad in some small way that her drama was justified.

We hurried down the front stairs, pausing to see the orange juice dripping over the counter and pooling onto the faux redbrick linoleum kitchen floor, creating a confusing stain of warning and danger.

The most obvious sign was on Mom's desk on the kitchen counter. Her index cards had become a true weather report of what was happening in her head. The perfect script turned illegible and unintelligible.

Store

Lyrics Songs

Silver– hide

Lucille Snoopy

The handwriting was not her perfect penmanship, but rather the scrawl of a stranger desperate to capture messages and whispers from unknown origins. Now her notecards were overflowing and unable to contain all the thoughts pouring from her brilliant brain.

"Where's Mom?" Louise asked urgently, staring at this unfamiliar handwriting and finally coming to believe what we were saying.

"With her roses!" Allyson cried.

We hurried down the short flight of split-level stairs into the den. Mom was still visible outside, moving in small circles through the bushes and speaking rapidly to her planted children.

We watched together, the Green Girls, trying to understand why Mom was there but not there. *How could this be our mom?* My mom noticed when a hair was out of place on my bangs but now this woman didn't even see me, didn't even seem to *recognize* her three daughters.

I looked pleadingly at my big sisters for answers but there were none. Mom's behavior had no context. She seemed to have come untethered from us, and, as the winds sucked her away, was now a fast-forward voice spilling from a body I no longer knew.

Louise knew whatever this was, whatever we could not name, needed a kind of help three children could not provide.

Pushing us out of the way, Louise ran across the den and took the small flight of steps in two desperate leaps. Ally and I held hands, racing behind her to see what she would do. Louise grabbed the avocado phone line in the kitchen, pushing the buttons from memory.

"Gigi? It's Mom. I don't know what's wrong but you need to come—now!"

We huddled together waiting for Gigi, and watching Mom, who was oblivious to the drama that had been unleashed.

Eventually, Gigi would arrive and convince Mom to come inside, and Dad would rush home from the office. Shaken with sorrow and confusion, he helplessly held Mom's hands, speaking words of love to a stranger who seemed not to hear him. Poppa met them all at the hospital with his thirty-year-old cracked black leather medical bag, but there was nothing inside that could heal my mom.

Mom stayed at the hospital that night and did not come home for a long time. It was the first of many nights my mother would endure on a psychiatric ward, which in the 1960s offered restraints but no real respite and certainly no remedies.

I retreated that night to my secret hiding place at the top of my closet. By stepping on the shelves below, I could climb up to the top, which was a U-shaped platform above my clothes. The space was just wide enough for six-year-old me to sit on and tall enough for me to sit up with my feet dangling over the edge. Cushioned with pillows and my baby blanket, it was my indoor tree house where only my stuffed animals were allowed. I curled up on the shelf and hugged Snoopy, wondering if we would ever see my mom again.

I tucked my animals tightly around me as I sobbed into Snoopy's neck. My life had been so idyllic, so secure. I remembered that perfect day hugging my mom's knees after my party, oblivious that she could ever be torn away. I had never felt this type of sorrow or loss, and I had no idea how I would ever be safe from this again.

The suddenness of her affliction was shattering to us all.

When she came home after several weeks, Mom was deflated, lifeless, and slept, it seemed, for almost as many days as she had been gone. My sisters went to camp that summer, and I went to stay with my aunt and uncle in San Antonio. At the time, I thought it was just a vacation with my cousins, not understanding that my mom still couldn't care for us.

That hospital visit was the first of many. Sometimes, I would not see her for weeks. Gigi, Poppa, and Dad would whisper in the kitchen.

Exhaustion.

Fragile constitution.

Lindsay always tries to do too much.

But with each episode the worry deepened. Poppa, a general practitioner, eventually consulted psychiatrists and psychologists. In the early 1970s, these doctors had trouble naming it and put words on symptoms with no clarity.

Nervous breakdown.

Schizophrenic form psychosis.

It would require the right doctor, the right medicine combination, and the right diagnosis, bipolar disorder, to bring all of my mom home to us. It would also take sixteen years.

During that agonizing period, each time as inexplicably as Mom went away, she would return.

With each recurrence, however, a little more of her had blown away.

And each time a little more anger built inside me.

Why did she need to sleep so much? Why didn't she just wake up?

When Mom unraveled so did my family. She was the thread that pulled us tight, and each time she left for a new treatment or hospital stay, we frayed a little more.

A maid, Maria, came to live with us from Juarez, crossing the river illegally and staying for weeks at a time before risking to go back to visit her own two children. Maria had been trained as a secretary in Mexico, but she made more money in the U.S. as a housekeeper. She was diligent at keeping our house, folding our laundry perfectly and making our beds so it always looked as if everything was in order. But Maria couldn't care for us. She spoke no English so we could only pantomime our needs to her. I had begun learning Spanish that year in first grade, but I never found a good translation for, "I want my mom back."

Gigi's house became my safe haven. More than the Sunday lunches, it became the place I felt at home. Between the chocolate mint sticks and the pink nubby couch, I found the place of comfort that would wrap me in reassurance. Our house, that perfect split-level ranch my parents had saved for to hold our dream family, became only a container that held our sadness.

When Mom was depressed, the symphonies that had soared from her classical cassettes were silenced. The art studio would be shuttered and dust collected on her paintbrushes as she slept, trying to outlast the darkness that settled over her for months at a time. It seemed to me there was no pattern to when or if she would wake from each of these mental hibernations, but when she did the signs were clear. Mom was creative only when she was balanced or even slightly manic.

Throughout elementary school, I tried not to be needy. Dad was overwhelmed with his law practice and negotiating this new world of mental health with my mother. I packed my lunch, walked to school, made all As, and walked myself home. My parents' bedroom door became a sign I monitored closely. It was the first thing I checked when I came in from school. If her door was open when I got home, I knew I would find her painting in the studio or tending to her roses. If after school it was closed, I would know to get my own snack and she would wake up in time to make dinner. Mom always made dinner. It was the one task she never gave over to Maria. The one that still meant she was the mother in this home.

But seeing her bedroom door closed when I came home started to feel like an open wound that would not heal. I wanted her to want to wake up and ask me about my day. About the boy who had teased me on the walk home. About the play I was going to be in. About my plans to sleep over with Andrea on Friday night. I couldn't understand where my cartoon party–planning mom had gone and why she wasn't trying harder to come back to us.

Each time she slept though something important made the wound more raw. I still had the hope that we would all go back to the family we had been. I wanted desperately for her to be the superhero mom she used to be, but with each break that ended in a hospital visit our old life felt more like a TV show we used to watch. Someone had switched the channel in our lives from *Brady Bunch* to *Twilight Zone*, and we couldn't find the remote control to get it back.

Because there was no way to know, no way to predict when she would become manic, irrationally I began to believe I could have an effect on her mental wellness. If I was good, Mom wouldn't go in the hospital. If I said the wrong thing or disappointed her, I was convinced that *I* was the reason for her depression.

Throughout middle school I tried to be good by earning top grades, playing on all the teams, and writing for the school newspaper. It also meant I could leave the house at 7:30 in the morning to walk to school and not come home until dinnertime. The wound raw with hope for our family began to harden over. Over time, it was a scab of resentment that left me unable to forgive. Even when Mom was awake and cooking dinner or working in her studio, I found reasons not to talk with her. In my mind, I rationalized it as self-preservation. If I didn't let her in, I couldn't lose her again.

By high school, I was numb to the scar in our family. I kept collecting As, and added to my resume Student Council representative, National Honor Society, editor of the yearbook, and Homecoming Queen. I wanted my dad to be proud of me and he didn't need anything else to worry about. He needed to be able to say his Green Girls were the outstanding progeny expected from the All-American couple, even though the perfect family he thought we were going to be had come undone.

Though we now had a name for this thing that had stolen our promise, manic depression, we still did not name it. We did not talk about it all. My Dad. My sisters. My grandparents. We didn't comfort each other, crying about our devastating loss or cursing the diagnosis. We didn't sit around the Sunday lunch table with Mom's empty chair, trying to console each other or trying to make sense of it. We didn't really even admit what was happening. We simply carried on. Dad went to the office every morning. We went to school, and all three of us were expected to do very well.

I never talked to my teachers. I never said I had done my home-work after visiting my mom on a psychiatric ward. I never admitted to my friends that the reason they weren't invited over to my house was because I was afraid they might see my mother asleep in the middle of the day or, more unexplainable, manic.

I, like my family, simply became immune to it. I could no longer cry when my mom went to the hospital. She just did. I could not get excited when she came home. She would go back. The only cure for this pain was simply not to feel, not to hope. Expectation for her returned wellness was the only true pain. Accepting what was and hoping for nothing more was the only way to move through each day.

By high school, I needed small escapes from this dysfunction and I found it by secretly rebelling at night. I would sneak out of the house to join friends smoking pot and drinking beer at the river. Some weekend nights we might drive over the border to Juarez to party in clubs that only asked for our American dollars and not our IDs. Taking shots of tequila, I could forget every feeling I had about my mom, my dad, the loss of our once-shining promise of a family. I didn't have to be good. And it felt incredibly freeing to be bad.

Andrea, aka Goofy, was still my best friend twelve years later. Together we rebelled at night, me escaping the crazy in my home and she escaping the cancer in hers. Her father had been battling prostate cancer, and her mother was trying to keep the family busi-ness going while radiation burned new holes in their life. It was striking to see how her family was supported as her father suf-fered. Their family was inundated with help, especially from their small Lutheran community church. Friends swarmed the tragedy with cards, meals, offers of compassionate support. I often went to Andrea's church on Sundays after spending the night, and always her mother and father were surrounded with love and concern. They called her father by name in the prayers and asked for his healing.

It always struck me how, unlike Andrea's family, we were not inundated with help. Throughout those sixteen years searching for a cure for my mother's mind, our fellow Presbyterians didn't bake and didn't write. Whether Mom was sick or not, the Green family still went to church every Sunday, smiling at the friends around First Presbyterian Church, saying hello but not speaking our truth.

Our congregation didn't swarm us with support not because they didn't care, but because they didn't know.

We never told them.

Mental illness doesn't work like cancer.

There is no Hallmark card for, "I'm sorry your loved one is bipolar."

There are no casseroles for crazy.

Over the years, I watched Poppa, Gigi, Dad, and Mom all bow their heads in church, and there was less and less sense I could make of it. When I sat quietly in the pew beside them, I wasn't drawing on my program or gazing at the ceiling anymore. I was studying the profiles of my parents and grandparents as they bowed their heads in prayer.

What exactly were they praying for?

I had no idea. But from where I was sitting, God had not answered any of them nor was he delivering us from this evil.

4

Headed for Home

Don't forget—no one else sees the world
the way you do, so no one else can
tell the stories that you have to tell.

CHARLES DE LINT

IT WAS ALMOST MY LAST YEAR OF HIGH SCHOOL BEFORE ANY
doctor could begin to explain what had happened to my mother's brain
and the two keys to successfully live with a bipolar disorder. One, Mom
would always need daily medications to balance her brain chemistry,
and two, she would need to valiantly fight each day to stay sane.

He explained it like this, "When the mania begins it is as if there
are three TV stations and two radio stations all playing in her head
at the same time with her own thoughts. She has to constantly try to
turn them down and figure out what she is really hearing. You are
lucky your mom is so smart and that she can determine what is real.
Most people can't—or they give up trying."

By my college years, almost all of Mom had returned, as well as
her early promise of a life of service, church involvement, and even
classes to obtain a master's in art. Battling for sanity had swallowed
almost two decades of her life—time she calls her *Lost Years*. Even
after she was well, we held our collective breath, hoping not to tip
the fragile balance that kept her with us.

It was a struggle I was not fully ready to appreciate. Although my mom was back, I didn't really welcome her home into my heart. At twenty-one, I could still revert to my six-year-old self, hurt that she had left after my perfect cartoon birthday and effectively left us wandering in the desert.

It wasn't rational, I know. She couldn't help it. As the doctor explained, she fought valiantly. But those unpredictable winds scared me.

Throughout college and for years after, my calls home became the barometer, instead of the bedroom door. I learned to hear in my mom's speech how things were on her end. Rapid-fire, staccato sentences signaled possible mania. Slow, deliberate questions meant the fog of depression. Both triggered a slow dread of what might be next. *Hospital stay? New medication?* My heart would pick up the pace with worry. My mom's mental health never deteriorated again as badly as it had during my childhood, but it was always a lurking threat.

While I understood what the doctor had explained, I just didn't trust medicine or Mom's own determination to be whole. While Gigi and Poppa's home had been a refuge, I still felt like my own home was irrevocably broken. I loved my parents and my sisters, but I felt somehow cheated out of the life we were meant to have. My self-reliance learned in elementary school was now almost pathological. I didn't want to depend on anyone for anything. If I craved that perfect home and family, I was going to have to build them on my own. And I was not going to look for a future in El Paso, or even the state of Texas.

It was January 1985, and I had worked every summer taking extra classes along with a part-time job at a design firm so that I could graduate early from the University of Texas at Austin. At twenty-one, I was eager for adventure and desperate to leave the state I had always lived in. Watching it recede in my rearview mirror, I was not even a little bit sad.

Thirty years after my mother's odyssey from North Carolina to El Paso, I was making that exact trip in reverse. Texas, Louisiana, Mississippi, Alabama, Georgia, North Carolina, the states crawled by as I headed from the Texas desert to the green of Charlotte for my first job out of college as an art director with an ad agency. I was hoping it was the Promised Land.

I wasn't trying to trace my parents' college path in moving to Charlotte; a job offer in the same city where my parents had met was random. It was also random that I had ended up with a B.S. in advertising. I had started out going to UT Austin undergraduate fully intent on continuing on to UT law school—my dad's alma mater after he gave up on the ministry.

In my mind, the law degree would prove to my dad I was as smart as he always said I was, and I would do great things as a lawyer. My sophomore year, I took an intro to advertising class on copywriting, thinking it would be an easy A—I needed a high GPA to get into law school. Watching my mom develop themes for parties and designing our own Hallmark-style cards for our relatives in the art studio turned out to be the same skills needed for mastering copywriting. Advertising was apparently in my DNA.

The years spent in my mother's art studio also meant I could draw reasonably well, so I switched my major to the graphic design track of the advertising program, run by Dr. Leonard Ruben, an original Mad Man. He had worked on Madison Avenue in its heyday and moved to Austin to teach young, naïve college students about the ruthless world of advertising.

"Concept, people, concept!" Ruben would yell at us. "What is your big idea? Why should I give a damn about your product?"

There were twelve of us my senior year in the advertising program, and Ruben hammered this message in all of us daily, hourly.

What is your big idea?

Ruben didn't care as much what it looked like. He said it didn't matter how much you polished up something; it could look good, feel good, but every ad concept had to have that intangible thing that separated it from everything else. *The big idea.*

Each week, Ruben would bark our orders to us: *Full-color magazine two-page spread for a food product. Go.*

This was twenty years before Apple computers and Adobe software would revolutionize our industry and make typefaces and photos magically appear on a page to complete such an assignment. In the eighties, it was a much different process. We all learned quickly what this task meant: pick a real-world product, write a hundred headlines before the perfect *aha holy grail* moment of *concept* crystallized, create a visual that succinctly paired it with a memorable tagline, draw the visual, and hand-letter the headline in a precisely rendered version of one of the famous typefaces: Garamond, Helvetica, or Times Roman.

Typically, we would have three days to dazzle him. To find the *big idea* on every project week after week. By the time I had been in the program a year, I forgot all about my law degree and my dad's approval.

I wanted Dr. Ruben's approval.

On the mornings that assignments were due, we would file into the classroom and pin our layouts to the wall with silver thumbtacks. Each ad campaign was our silent offering to please the Ad God. We would sit in the class waiting patiently for the arrival of our messiah, hoping today would be the day we would be chosen and blessed.

Gruff, bearded, and chain-smoking, Dr. Ruben would arrive. No words or sermons, he would unceremoniously begin the ritual. He would study our layouts one by one, slowly drawing in smoke and exhaling an impossibly long time later. As he contemplated, we didn't speak. We didn't dare. We would only know that he liked our feeble attempts at advertising genius if he moved on from a page, stepping to the next layout without comment. Sometimes, he would just shake his head in slow disgust and rip one page viciously to the floor. He saved his worst punishments for those concepts he felt completely lacked any redeeming value or the cardinal sin, no big idea.

For those offending layouts, he would first take a long pull in on his Marlboro before taking his cigarette, and carefully touching it to the edge of the paper. We would draw in our breaths, the whole class watching in horror as hours of work slowly curled and burned to extinction. Ruben never showed emotion as these offending, fragile, yet failing ideas—concepts that took days to execute—quietly disappeared forever in a burning, disappointed ash.

In the early days of the program it happened to me over and over. *"Where's the concept, Green?"* he would bellow.

After being publicly burned in front of my classmates, I would slink away in humiliation. But slowly, I got it. We all did. And job offers waited at the end of this pilgrimage. All my classmates went to Dallas or New York, taking jobs with large creative agencies with dozens of copywriters and art directors vying internally for projects.

I was determined to leave Texas and terrified of New York, so I looked for other options—smaller cities with "hot" agencies that were getting noticed. I wanted quality of life along with the opportunity to do great work. Minneapolis, D.C., Charlotte. Each had some award-winning firms and I got offers in D.C. and Charlotte. I took the offer in Charlotte. Ruben shook his head in disgust. *"No big ideas there."*

I was driven to prove to Ruben there *were* big ideas in Charlotte—*mine.*

Charlotte in those days had a Mayberry feel—it seemed everyone knew each other and said *Hey!* In the beginning when strangers were friendly, I assumed they knew my parents. Then I realized it was just what people in the South did. Warm didn't just describe the weather; it characterized the way of life. People genuinely cared about talking to each other.

In 1985, a little more than 300,000 people lived within the Charlotte city limits, but it was already becoming a financial center that would grow to 2.5 million people in the metro region a decade into the twenty-first century. The same reasons I was attracted to Charlotte were drawing thousands of others: jobs, low cost of living, good quality of life. Unlike my advertising-school friends who shared cramped walk-up apartments in New York City, I could rent a brand-new one-bedroom apartment in a complex with a swimming pool. A ten-minute commute along tree-lined streets brought me into a laid-back downtown that consisted of a few dozen towers.

Starting my job, I was in heaven. It was everything Dr. Ruben's stories had promised—photo shoots, filming with TV crews, deadlines, and brainstorming. I felt glamorous at twenty-one with my own client roster and being responsible for creating regional and national campaigns. I had been trained well and the work was exhilarating to me. When clients reviewed layouts and haltingly suggested changes, I had no problem with criticism. No matter what a client didn't like, at least they weren't lighting my ideas on fire.

Three months into my new job, I had barely looked up from my layouts. I only knew a few people in Charlotte and my one friend was the boss's daughter, who worked in the marketing department. It was ten o'clock on a Thursday night, and I was still hunched over my drafting table, painstakingly arranging the type on a full-page newspaper ad for a soft drink company that had to be ready in the morning. My one friend had invited me to a party, but I had declined, saying I had to work. I was at my drafting table when it hit me: *I should go to that party.*

Turning out the light above my worktable, I grabbed my keys and headed to my car. I felt bold and independent. I felt like the girl who had driven 1,600 miles to build a new life. On the drive over, I turned up the radio and felt almost a humming inside. *My adventurous life as an adult was beginning.*

By the time I arrived at the backyard party, my resolve was slipping. As I approached a small white house, the beach music blared, and a mob of friends danced the dance of a happy keg crowd in the dark. The yard was filled with strangers who all seemed to know each other from attending college at Chapel Hill or Duke. I was a transplanted Texan with no real connection to any of them.

By this time, I had reached the edge of the fence surrounding the yard and a spotlight was on the gate in front of me. Tentatively, I put my hand on the latch. If I left at this point, no one would notice. But I had already walked into that circle from the porch light, and it seemed my defeat would be too painfully visible.

I opened the gate and went in. Although I was with dozens of people, I was completely alone. I could barely enter because of the crush of guests but vowed to chug one beer, pretend to look for the bathroom, and leave.

Searching for the keg, I saw him. One tall figure, three inches above the rest of the crowd, facing sideways—a profile to my stare. Beer in his hand, he looked a part of the crowd but still somehow separate. Maybe it was his height that set him apart but it felt like something more. He turned and I was caught staring. I didn't look away. I wanted him to see me. When he did, I felt almost a shock. I didn't know him, but somehow I felt like I recognized him. Like we had always known each other.

"Beer?"

He startled me when he spoke. I didn't think he was feeling the same cosmic experience, but I think he knew someone had to break this awkward staring.

As he filled a clear plastic cup for me, I discreetly sized him up.

Blue-and-green-plaid button-down shirt. *Conservative choice, probably banker.*

Loose Levis. *A mistake in Texas—real guys there only wear Wranglers, but I was learning to adapt to this southern choice.*

White Converse sneakers. *Really? I was a boots-only girl when it came to guys, but I was going to need to make exceptions if I was ever going to meet a man in Charlotte.*

He handed me my drink and I prayed he wouldn't walk away. I had no obvious island of friend safety to move towards. I probably looked as desperate as I felt—I've never had a poker face. His lips moved, asking a question, but he was 6'3" to my 5'3", and I had to stand on my toes to hear him a foot above me.

Somehow, with him leaning over and me stretching up, we talked for two hours without hesitation or interruption, oblivious to the crowd that moved around us.

It was way past midnight before I remembered the unfinished layout on my drafting table and reluctantly drove home to my apartment, thinking about him all the way.

I knew nothing about him except that I wanted to know *everything* about him.

We had made no plans to see each other, but he had mentioned in our awkward shouting conversation that he exercised after work every day at the YMCA.

The next day after work, I joined the Y.

Somehow, I had to get a date with this guy because I could not stop the thought going through my head. A thought as crazy as the impulse that had brought me to that party would not stop whispering: *That's the guy I am going to marry.*

Two weeks and fourteen aerobic classes later, I finally saw him again. He crossed in front of my car in the Y parking lot as I was leaving, holding his suit in one hand and his briefcase in the other.

Checking the rearview mirror, I confirmed that I looked awful. My face was red from the workout, my brown hair plastered to my forehead with sweat. Not my best look, but I'd take a chance because I might not ever see him again.

I slowed down as he moved towards my open driver's window, and I tried to be casual but my heart was pounding. "Hey!"

He bent down to look in. "Oh, hey?" A little confusion and then flicker of recognition. "It's *you*!"

Obviously, he had not been thinking about me the way I had been obsessing about him. At least he could recognize my face if he couldn't remember my name. *Did he even remember that he had talked to me for two hours?*

I tried to act like I had not been desperately seeking him since that night. "Yeah! We met at the party didn't we?"

"Yes!" Obvious relief appeared on his face now that he could finally place mine.

A prolonged, painful moment passed.

Finally, he spoke. "You wouldn't want to have a beer with me, would you?"

We had a beer, then dinner, then another dinner and then dinner every night for six weeks straight.

As crazy as it seemed, after only forty-two days of knowing him, I said *yes* to Charlie Izard's proposal, blurted out over a late-night bottle of wine with no ring, and as unplanned as our whole improbable meeting. We were married within the year. Although I was happier than I had ever been, I also clearly remember a moment of panic at our rehearsal dinner, looking at his friends and family thinking, *Oh my god, everyone here invited by Charlie knows him better than I do.*

5

A Heart with a Hole

Making the decision to have a child—it is
momentous. It is to decide forever to have your
heart go walking around outside your body.

ELIZABETH STONE

I DIDN'T JUST LOVE CHARLIE FROM FIRST SIGHT, I LOVED HIS whole family, too. It seemed by moving to North Carolina, I had accidently stumbled into the life I was looking for.

Charlie came from the type of big boisterous family I had always envied. He was the middle of five children his mother had delivered in six years. Boy, girl, boy, girl, boy. His parents were next-door neighbors in Asheville, N.C., but were eight years apart so really did not know one another growing up. They rediscovered each other years later, and their five children eventually became part of a large family on both sides. There were so many cousins, uncles, and aunts that Charlie had to draw a family diagram for me when over fifty of them arrived in El Paso for our wedding.

Charlie moved twice growing up before his parents settled into a picturesque gray clapboard on two acres of gorgeous gardens in Rye, N.Y. when he was six years old. The first time I visited this childhood home I felt like I had entered the pages of a magazine ad for family nirvana. While I sat in their cozy kitchen, his mom was cooking a lavish sit-down dinner of family recipes, his father breezed in and out depositing fresh-picked vegetables, and a golden retriever and two dachshunds wagged for attention at my feet. On the wall next to the dinner table, was a framed illustration drawn by a friend depicting Charlie's family. In it, children played silly games in the driveway, animals ran pleasantly amuck, and his parents were hilariously and lovingly orchestrating the chaos.

Studying that drawing filled me with a kind of longing I couldn't quite name. Looking at all that carefree love and laughter spilling out of the characters, I could see the enormity of what my family had lost. After that first manic episode, I had always felt a sense of danger growing up in our house with calamity approaching at any moment. We were always wary and watchful for the next time Mom's mind would threaten to sweep away our security. To witness in Charlie's home this slice of normalcy brought a sense of peace and safety that felt luxurious. It seemed in finding Charlie, I had also found an entire family. Although it was a place I had never been, it felt like I had come home.

I wanted to study it. Bottle it. Whatever had made that house a home, I was determined Charlie and I would re-create it for our family-to-be.

Three years after our wedding and three days before my twenty-sixth birthday, our first daughter, Lauren Lindsay, was born, followed seventeen months later by her sister Kailey. We decided one more child would create the perfect family of five, but I was having trouble getting pregnant this time, so my ob-gyn ordered an ultrasound to check for a cyst.

"Yep, there's two," said the ultrasound tech, who was not supposed to say anything to patients.

"Two what? Two cysts?" I asked.

"Two babies!" he said as if I was an idiot.

"Two babies? I'm not pregnant."

"You are now," he said, "with twins!"

Fraternal girls, Maddie and Emma, completed our family of six. With the twins born, Lauren and Kailey never needed to play with dolls again. They had live ones. With one sister for each of the older girls, there were endless games and possibilities. Maddie and Emma grew up being dressed up in outlandish costumes, carried precariously on piggyback, and offered potions of twigs, leaves, and mud concocted in the backyard by their older sisters. They were a growing, laughing pack with seemingly one body, eight legs and four hearts. One call, "*Laurenkaileyeammamaddie!*," could bring them thundering down the stairs to dinner, a twin dangling from each older sister's arms.

Looking at the four of them still sometimes caught me off guard. That they were ours. That we had created this blonde bundle of beautiful girls.

Their antics and giggles began to re-create in our own home the drawing on Charlie's family's kitchen wall. This was the family I had always wanted and now we lived in a picturesque home ourselves, around the corner from Queens College (now Queens University), where my mom had first gone to school and met my dad.

Over time Charlie and I settled into a rhythm of the daily basics needed to care for a family of six by dividing and conquering the duties. Although I chose to stay home, I didn't want to give up on a career, so I started a graphic design business out of our house, designing logos and brochures during naptime or after the girls went to bed. We used plenty of babysitters but I wanted to be the one they came home to. I wanted to be there when they came home from school and ask them about their day. I promised myself our house would be different. It would never break. It would be like the *before* in my childhood home. I would keep my girls safe and we would be whole always.

I remembered how Gigi had so easily curled up with us on the couch to hear our problems. It was the most natural thing in the world for her to listen and love us. But I realized it was very hard for me. I just wanted to fix things for my girls so they didn't have to cry or feel sad *ever*. Watching one of my daughters feel pain was agonizing to me. I had no idea that being a mother was so heart-wrenching.

Maddie and Emma had been born six weeks premature, with Emma coming in a little over six pounds and Maddie barely registering five pounds. While Emma was a chubby little baby, Maddie remained much skinnier and smaller than her sister. At first we weren't concerned because Maddie was achieving every developmental milestone before Emma—smiling, standing, crawling. She was a tiny bundle of energy who never sat still and hated to nap. When she finally would fall asleep at night it was a pass-out slumber like someone had pulled her power cord. But at their nine-month checkup, Maddie weighed only fourteen pounds and the pediatrician was alarmed.

"She is meeting the criteria for failure to thrive syndrome," he told me after checking her chart.

We'd been watching Maddie for the past few months, ever since her doctor had noticed something unusual with her heartbeat at her sixth-month checkup. He held the stethoscope to my ear and said, "You hear that? That soft murmur?" he asked.

I put the ear pieces in and listened. There was a distinct but faint "whoosh" accompanying Maddie's heartbeat. He put the end of the stethoscope on Emma's chest and I listened to her. Only a strong, solid beating could be heard in her chubby chest as she grabbed the end of the stethoscope and tried to chew on it.

"I am pretty sure Maddie has a hole in her heart," he said.

The technical term we'd learn was atrial septal defect (ASD). Basically there was a "hole" in the wall that separated the top two chambers of Maddie's heart. Babies are born with this opening and it is supposed to close within weeks or months after birth. If it remains open and is small, it won't cause symptoms. But the larger the hole, the harder the heart and lungs have to work to repump blood that is flowing the wrong way.

"Maddie is basically running a marathon sitting still," he explained.

A consult with a cardiologist confirmed our pediatrician's diagnosis, but he suggested waiting a few months longer to see if it would close on its own. If not, Maddie would need open-heart surgery.

At nine months old, Maddie was scheduled for surgery. The cardiologist and our pediatrician assured us this operation was the "appendectomy of the heart world." While open-heart surgery sounded terrifying to Charlie and me, the doctors were much more confident in this fairly routine cardiac surgery. But the fact was, they would be opening the chest of our tiny baby girl, stopping her heart, making the repair, and closing her back up.

Maddie would have two scars—one the entire length of her chest and a smaller one from the drainage tubes. The scars she could live with, but I wasn't sure how I could live if Maddie didn't. If this didn't go well, how could I ever look at Emma and not think of her other half? How does any mother survive the loss of a child?

Charlie and I had been lucky so far in creating our family with four healthy, beautiful girls. I had never fathomed something going wrong. Motherhood had been easy thus far. But this, this was agonizing. There was nothing we could do for Maddie. Nothing I could do to fix her. Working hard, being self-reliant were my go-to skills and not being able to control the situation or the outcome was paralyzing. Maddie had a hole in her heart and I clearly did, too.

"You might try some prayer," Dad suggested on the phone.

"I wish I thought that would work, Dad, but I don't," I told him.

"I know. I wish you did, too," he said. "I'll try some for you."

"Thanks, Dad," I said. "I am just not sure God listens."

"You'll see someday," he said. "You may not think he does, but I absolutely believe it's true. God might not send you exactly what you expect but he's always with you."

Maybe God heard Dad because Maddie's surgery was successful. By day three she was sitting up eating pancakes with her fingers and day four she was discharged. As a toddler, Maddie would proudly point to her tummy and call her scar her "stripe." Her energy level continued to be exuberant as well so Charlie nicknamed her "Tigger."

One month after her open-heart surgery, we celebrated Maddie and Emma's first birthday. Our family of six was whole once again. Our four girls squished together in the kitchen as I brought out a zebra cake, Charlie's favorite now made for each of our girls. It is not cake really but thin chocolate cookies covered in whipped cream and refrigerated into gooey goodness. The twins wriggled and laughed unable to blow out their candles, so Lauren and Kailey did it while the younger sisters watched in fascination.

No one needed to make a wish, so many had already come true.

6

Soup and Salvation

One sees clearly only with the heart.
Anything essential is invisible to the eyes.

ANTOINE DE SAINT-EXUPÉRY
The Little Prince

BEING A MOM MYSELF AND SEEING HOW DIFFICULT IT WAS TO respond to all the logistics and emotions of girls began to soften a bit that stone in my heart. It was humbling to realize just how difficult it was to be a mom with a working, albeit sleep-deprived, brain, much less one battling depression and mania.

I thought about how my parents had worked to do things in the community even while raising three daughters and struggling with Mom's chronic illness. Throughout it all Dad had volunteered, served in the church, and run his legal practice.

Charlie worked as an investment wealth manager so he worried constantly about how we would afford four kids and how we could plan for their futures. I worried constantly about how we would raise four *good* kids. How I would teach the two commandments I learned from my family: *Do Good* and *Love Well*.

Church was not a place I wanted to revisit with our girls. All those hours spent trying to sit still in the pew felt like wasted time and merely the penance in order to be rewarded at Gigi's dinner table. I never felt like the sermons were meant for me and certainly did not believe church had molded any part of my character. Now that I had a choice, I was not going to force religion on our daughters. Charlie and I felt in control of our own fate, working hard to be self-reliant to get what we needed.

No outside prayers required.

In Charlotte, we had no excuse not to find a church because it is a city where it was easier to opt into religion rather than opt out. Charlotte is sometimes called "The City of Churches" because there is a house of faith on nearly every corner and Sunday mornings they are all in session. In the eighties and even today, most stores opened only after 1 p.m. on Sundays because sales were too slow until church let out.

The most Christian thing our family did on Sundays was go swimming at the YMCA indoor pool.

One day while juggling four towels and the twins' floaties, our little wet herd was leaving the Y when Lauren stopped to study a framed portrait by the front door.

Obviously realizing the painting was of someone important, she asked earnestly, "Mommy, who's that man?"

It was Jesus.

I could feel the shudder of disappointment from Mom, Dad, Gigi, and Poppa. In an effort to ensure our daughters could at least name this iconic biblical figure, we began attending a church: First Presbyterian Church of Charlotte.

We'd been going only a few months when I was reminded of one reason I had abandoned organized religion—getting dressed. My mom would have had our girls with perfectly combed hair tied with ribbons, matching smocked dresses, and tights with no holes.

I was struggling to get my four daughters into shoes. Inevitably, Lauren and Kailey would descend the stairs every Sunday in wrinkled skirts, rumpled blouses, bare legs, and tattered rainbow flip-flops even though it was thirty-two degrees and sleeting outside. By the time I would wrestle Maddie and Emma into tights, I would have screamed *and* made them cry. I knew our girls needed some moral education but there wasn't a sermon anywhere that could save me on Sundays from this weekly fashion exhaustion.

It was a small ad in the church bulletin that offered divine inspiration:

**Volunteers needed for the
First Presbyterian soup kitchen team!**

**Every fourth Sunday morning, all ages welcome!
Contact the Volunteer Coordinator Office.**

Finally, something I could work with—a place where only blue jeans were required.

I signed up our family to work one Sunday a month from 8 a.m. to 1 p.m. The volunteer coordinator told me we would be helping at Charlotte's Urban Ministry Center (UMC), which served the homeless. Our duties would include preparing soup in the thirty-gallon pot, making hundreds of sandwiches, and then serving lunch. This would be perfect, I thought. We could all get out of sitting still in a church pew and still Do Good each Sunday.

Driving to the UMC for the first time, I was confused by the directions. They said to get off the interstate and turn right but that appeared to be a dead end. Charlie turned where I told him to turn but did not accelerate. There was only about a hundred yards of street ahead leading directly into a chain link fence. There was no building that we could see, only dozens of people standing, sitting, even sleeping on the sidewalk.

"Are you sure this is right?" Charlie asked.

The UMC opened their gates in the parking lot at 8 a.m., but dozens of people were already waiting to be let inside early to use bathrooms or just get out of the cold. It was difficult to distinguish faces in the crowd because gray hoods and worn black layers obscured age or gender. Possessions were lugged in plastic bags, rolled in suitcases, and carried in backpacks. Lives reduced to what some Americans bought in a single trip to the mall.

The first look at all this was shocking. In answering the ad in the church bulletin, I was expecting a more feel-good opportunity. Homeless Lite. The girls were staring in disbelief out the minivan window as well. They had never seen extreme poverty so up close and personal. Our house was in an affluent neighborhood of Charlotte. For the most part, all of their lives had been spent within almost a three-mile radius. This was not only out of our zip code, it was definitely out of our comfort zone. Charlie looked at me, silently communicating, "Are you sure?"

I nodded and we pulled forward slowly so as not to hit one of the many bodies spilling over the sidewalks. As we got out of the car, Emma grabbed my hand and Maddie grabbed Emma's. Lauren and Kailey walked close to their dad, glad for his 6'3", 200-pound show of strength. I am not going to lie. I was nervous. It felt mildly dangerous and reckless to be bringing our girls here. What if someone pulled a knife? I wanted to help someone and show my girls the value of community service, but I didn't want to actually risk getting hurt in the process.

An effusive woman with frosted gray hair and red lips met us at the front door of the depot.

"Hey! Y'all must be the Izard family!" she gushed. "I am Beverly and this is my husband, Roy!" I recognized them from the few times we had been at First Presbyterian Church.

"We are so glad you are here to help! Now tell me who's who with these pretty girls!"

With Beverly breaking the ice, we all relaxed a little. She led us into a commercial kitchen where a thirty-gallon soup pot was already simmering with a vegetable stew. Roy had an apron on and was gently stirring a lumpy, bubbling red liquid.

"So what kind is it?" Kailey asked him.

"All kinds!" he said brightly. "Ever heard of the story "Stone Soup"? It's like that. We put in a little bit of everything and sometimes we don't even know what's in there!"

Beverly handed each of the girls an apron to put on. "Now, Lauren and Kailey, you girls look big enough to use knives so why don't you help me chop fruit for the salad, and you little girls can make peanut butter and jelly sandwiches with your mom and dad."

We moved to the stainless steel island where dozens of bags of white Wonder Bread were stacked next to a huge silver bowl. Inside was a gloppy purplish, brownish concoction.

"Ew!" Maddie said. "What is that?"

Emma nodded, concurring with Maddie's disgust. Maddie usually spoke for the two of them.

"The peanut butter and jelly!" Beverly said. "We go ahead and mix it together to save time. You know we only have a couple hours and 600 sandwiches to make!"

As we spread the goo, we learned a lot.

We would be serving lunch for anywhere between 400 to 600 people. This happened 365 days a year, all made and served by volunteers. The UMC never missed a day. Over the years there had been ice storms, power outages, even a blizzard or two, but the Center had always opened 8:30–4:30, *every day*.

Homeless people don't get holidays off and neither did the Center.

During the weekdays, there were more volunteers who came to help provide services beyond lunch. Counseling, showers, laundry, and mail. I never thought about it, but where did you shower if you were homeless? Where did you get your mail? In Charlotte, apparently hundreds of people used 945 North College Street as their address.

Beverly let us know that our day, the fourth Sunday of the month, was one of the biggest days for lunch crowds because it was at the end of the month when food stamps and incomes ran short.

"Do people need a ticket to eat?" Lauren asked.

"No, honey, anyone who comes here gets served free no questions asked," Beverly said. "And we call everyone Neighbor just like your neighbors at home. We are just here to help all our Neighbors who need it."

At 11:30, Roy rolled up the steel window cover over the six-foot-long counter separating the dining room from the kitchen. "Come on girls, let's go welcome our guests," he said.

All four girls scooted after him to unlock the door. Roy stood out in the parking lot next to the line and shook hands with a couple of the regulars he recognized. Roy called out down the line, "Y'all bow your heads and we will say a little blessing."

Lauren, Kailey, Emma, and Maddie stood close to his side as he prayed.

"Dear Lord, bless this food to our use, and us to thy service and make us ever mindful of the needs of others. Amen."

A chorus of *Amens* rippled down the line.

Lauren came running back from the blessing. "Mom! You are not going to believe how many people are out there! I hope we have enough food!"

Slowly people came through, quietly accepting a tray. Lauren and Kailey sat on stools so they could see over the counter, and we filled and pushed the trays towards them as fast as we could. Maddie and Emma were on dessert duty, putting two cookies or a cupcake on each tray. Charlie was in charge of reinforcements, fetching dessert items from the back and making more sandwiches as we ran out.

Lauren and Kailey served with sunshine. "Have a nice day! Hope you enjoy!"

Some Neighbors silently slid by not making eye contact, but a few bantered brightly. "Thank you, darling!"

One wild-eyed gentleman was particularly memorable. "Hey pretty girls, how are you?"

He had matted white hair, a sunburnt face, and a Harley Davidson tattoo not on his neck or hand but *on the middle of* his forehead. *Directly on* his forehead over his eyes. It looked like he had taken a Budweiser label off a beer bottle and stuck it to his forehead. But this was a motorcycle logo and it was permanent. He balanced a small boom box, more of a radio really, in one hand as he took his tray with the other.

Lauren and Kailey stared at him in wonder.

"Hi? Have a nice day?" Kailey eeked out.

"You know what my name is, darlin'?" he asked them.

"Harley?" Kailey guessed.

"Nope! It's Chilly. Chilly Willy! Cuz I'm a cool guy! The coolest there is! The coolest you'll ever meet!"

By now he had all my girls' attention as Maddie and Emma dropped their cookie duty to get a closer look. Now that he had a bigger audience, Chilly Willy really started hamming it up.

"You want to hear me sing? I can sing real good." And he started a particularly bad rendition of the Charlie Daniels Band's "Long Haired Country Boy." As Chilly howled the lyrics of getting stoned in the morning and drunk in the afternoon, it was obviously his anthem.

"Thank you, Chilly," a man interrupted him. He had graying hair and a gray mustache, making him look older, but he was probably in his late forties. He wore glasses with thick black frames that gave him a serious look, but he joked easily with Chilly Willy. "Let's save the Grand Ole Opry for another time. We have a line of people here who want to get their lunch."

"Hey, Dale!" Chilly gave the man a huge hug and turned to my girls. "This here's the boss man, I got to do what he says. He's a preacher, too. Jesus loves you, Dale!"

"He loves you too, Chilly, now eat that lunch," Dale said patting Chilly gently on the back to send him on his way.

Dale Mullennix, we found out, was the executive director of the Urban Ministry Center and had been since the day it opened. He was living a very comfortable life as a minister at a suburban church in the Myers Park section of town where we lived until he was asked to leave to take on this job. Business and faith leaders had worked together in 1994 to make UMC more of a full-service center for the homeless, not just a kitchen open at lunch. This new mission would need a director, and Dale had been asked to be the first leader.

"Thank you all for coming out today!" he said to us, shaking each of our hands. It was obvious he knew Roy and Beverly and he chatted with them for a while. Dale then moved into the dining room, going table to table and greeting most everyone by name.

"Hey, Rose, how you doing today? Sam, how's the foot?" Dale said to a man limping. He handed out hugs and handshakes like everyone was a good friend.

How in the world did he know everyone? How could he keep all the names straight?

I had spent the last four hours almost hiding behind the lunch-counter window. That stainless steel counter provided an easy dividing line between the volunteers and those we were serving. I don't think it was designed that way but I was taking advantage of it. I was still a little uncertain about the Neighbors we were serving. Keeping my distance felt like a safe bet. If I got closer I wasn't sure what would happen.

What if someone asked me for money? Should I give it to them? What if someone started telling me their problems? How would I help them or fix anything for them?

I felt really sorry for everyone there but it also felt incredibly complicated and overwhelming. If I got to know someone, I was afraid I'd feel responsible for doing something about their situation.

How did Dale go home and not want to take everyone with him?

Finally it was time to clean up and the girls were giddy.

"That was so *fun*, Mom!" Lauren said

"Can we come back tomorrow?" Kailey asked.

In the car on the way home there were more questions.

"Mom, can a food stamp mail a letter too?"

"Dad, how can a man have a gold chain but no house?"

"Why did that nice lady have a black eye and no front teeth?"

Until I came to the UMC, I somehow thought that injustice was exclusive to border cities. I had not considered the right and wrong sides of our own U.S. cities or how disparity develops. That first visit to the soup kitchen began a slow realization that less than three miles from my comfortable Charlotte home was clearly a very divided existence.

Month after month that education evolved. Over time, I took Beverly's job and became the Fourth Sunday Soup Kitchen Captain for the church, recruiting our daughters' friends and families to join this accessible alternative to church. For the most part, Lauren, Kailey, Emma, and Maddie's friends were all children who lived similar,

comfortable lives. I loved that the UMC was interfaith, where people of all religions and no religion served the homeless together.
Here, our kids weren't hearing bible stories but they were learning
life lessons. Neighbors did not have to hear a sermon or accept a
certain religious doctrine to be fed.

I liked that I didn't have to accept one either.

While I'd never found religion in a pew, each Sunday in the soup
kitchen made me feel a little closer to someone I wanted to be. Each
month at the end of our shift, I could take off my apron, hug my
girls, drive out the gates, and feel I had done a little something good
in the world.

For a long time, that was enough.

<hr>

Homelessness remained an abstract concept for me until our den
ceiling started to leak. I called our plumber, Jimmy, who had been
working for us ever since he had re-plumbed the entire first house
Charlie and I bought as newlyweds. Over the years he had become
a trusted provider and friend. Jimmy had been upstairs all morning
looking for the source of the water dripping into our den. He came
into the kitchen before lunch and apologized. "I need to go meet my
brother at Freedom Park and give him some money."

"Just tell him to come here," I offered.

"You don't understand," he said, dropping his gaze to the floor
and shifting his feet uncomfortably. "My brother *lives* in the park."

He was right. I didn't understand. Freedom Park was less than
half a mile from our house, and we went there all the time for the
girls' soccer games and to ride bikes. His brother *lived* there? Did
Jimmy mean in a nearby house?

He saw my confusion and clarified with visible shame. "He's homeless."

Jimmy tried to explain the unexplainable.

"My brother did something bad when he was seventeen and went to prison. When he got out, he was never quite right. I don't know what happened in there but it must have been awful. We've tried to have him live with my mom or with me but he just can't. He wanders off for days and nothing seems to help. He calls me so I can give him money when I can and a radio ..."

"A radio?" With that clue, I connected the dots. "Jimmy, is your brother that guy with the white hair and tattoo on his forehead? Chilly Willy?"

Jimmy nodded, cringing at the street name. "His real name is Larry. William Larry Major. He's my brother."

I had no idea what to say. I had never thought about the families of the homeless. When I served soup to Neighbors, they seemed disconnected from everyone else. Sometimes we served families with children, but the vast majority appeared alone. No family. No apparent connection to the world.

"I worry he is going to die out there and we won't know," Jimmy confessed.

Of course he did. How could anyone ever stop worrying if their brother or sister was sleeping unprotected on the streets every night? When the phone rang, did Jimmy always imagine it was the police? The coroner?

Since that very first meeting when I had served Chilly Willy soup, I never thought that he had a given name: Larry. I never thought about who his family was or how he ended up in a soup kitchen, a twenty-four-inch-wide stainless steel counter between us. Me on the *right* side, Chilly Willy on the *wrong* side.

"Everybody in town knows him, and when they don't see him for a while they call and ask me if he's dead. I have to call the police stations and hospitals to find out if he's still alive," Jimmy admitted, tearing up.

I couldn't say anything to help Jimmy but I started looking for Chilly Willy, just so I could be sure and tell Jimmy I had seen his brother, Larry, and he was not dead. That gap was closing between me and *them*. It was beginning to be more difficult to keep my distance from the problem.

Chilly Willy was William Larry Major.

He had a brother, a family, and a story behind how he had ended up on the streets of Charlotte.

And like my mother, Larry had people who loved him and worried about him all the time.

7

Failure Is Not an Option

*It's not hard to decide what you want your life
to be about. What's hard, she said, is figuring
out what you're willing to give up in order
to do the things you really care about.*

SHAUNA NIEQUIEST

———————

I DECIDED EARLY ON IN MY LIFE THAT FAILURE WAS NOT AN option. I usually threw in the towel when failure was even looking possible.

I generally felt there were two reasons to quit. One, if failure was probable, like piano playing. Allyson had innate, unfathomable talent that I couldn't possibly measure up to so I begged my mom to let me quit Mrs. Wade's piano school after only two years. The second reason I felt it was acceptable to quit was if the work needed to attain success was not fun. This is why my tennis career ended.

Dad was not a gifted athlete growing up. In Texas, football was the only real sport for boys but Dad was too small to be a star player. Gigi and Poppa needed to find something he could excel at beyond the classroom and they found it on the tennis court. Dad practiced religiously, realizing this was his avenue to not only avoid teasing at school but eventually his ticket to the prestigious Davidson College. Dad loved the game and wanted his three daughters to love it, too.

Teaching us tennis began as his way of giving Mom a break on the weekends after he kept long work hours during the week. With this sport he was so accomplished in, Dad didn't just explain the strategy, he eventually used it to impart his wisdom.

Every Saturday, Dad had his standing doubles foursome with the same guys at the El Paso Tennis Club. In the mornings, Dad would play doubles and then come home to play tennis with his three girls in the afternoon. Dad kept an overflowing hopper of tennis balls in the trunk of his blue Ford El Torino, and we'd drive to the public tennis courts where he'd patiently hit to each of us.

"Swing *through* the ball, Kathy! Swing *through* it!" he would yell from across the net.

As it became apparent that I had been blessed with the most hand-eye coordination of the Green Girls, these group outings thinned as first Louise and then Allyson happily dropped out. Saturdays became my father-daughter alone time and I loved the weekly one-on-one attention from my father.

We would plow through a basket of balls and then pick them up and start all over.

Forehands. Backhands. Volleys. Finish with serve.

"Everything in life is about hard work, Kathy! Hard work and practice!" he would yell across the net as he fed me balls. This was his chance to not only mold my game but my character as well.

While I never tired of the time with my dad, my love of tennis began to wane—it was just so difficult to be really good at it. But Dad believed I could be great.

"That's *it*! That's *IT*!" Dad called out with pride as one of my forehands zinged with intention on a cross-court winner.

I had stuck with tennis because I was reasonably good at it and because it gave my dad so much pleasure. But to win tournaments, I realized, was going to take a lot of work.

At my father's insistence, I entered the citywide competition in the girls thirteen and under doubles category with my friend Susan. Her father worked at the same law firm as my dad, and they loved to compare notes on their daughters' swings and stats. Much to my surprise, but not to my father's, Susan and I won. Instead of trophies, we were each given small silver medals meant to be necklaces as symbols of our achievement, and our names were printed in the newspaper the next day.

"I told you! I told you!" he exclaimed, grabbing me in a bear hug that lasted a full minute. "You can do anything, Kathy! Really, *anything*!"

The crushing press of affection was unmistakable pride and his smile lasted until bedtime and beyond.

At breakfast the next morning, he was full of plans.

"We can start playing on Sundays after church before you go back for youth group. I can get the club pro to give you some lessons, too. I think he can help your serve."

It took almost a full year of those extra lessons before I worked up the courage. The disappointment would be crushing for him but I couldn't take any more. I hated tennis.

Dad was sitting at his desk in the den when I got up the nerve. Framed behind him on the paneled wall were many of his proudest achievements: Davidson College Salutatorian, University of Texas Law School Top of Class, El Paso Outstanding Man of the Year, Commendation of Service El Paso Cancer Treatment Center Board of Directors. To his right were the bookshelves that held some of his favorite tennis trophies. They spanned decades from the twelve and under City Championship to Texas State Doubles Over Forty-Five Division. My heart was in my throat as I approached him and in my hand the precious medal that meant so much to him. I reached for his hand, pressing it into his palm.

"Dad, you are right, maybe I could do it," I confessed. "I'm sorry, I just don't want to."

It would be twenty-five years before I picked up a tennis racquet again.

I could feel his disappointment in me every Saturday when he'd come home from his men's doubles game at the tennis club. Instead of rushing inside for me and heading to the park with his hopper of balls, he'd sit heavily on the den couch.

What I didn't realize until much later was that our weekly practice sessions were about so much more than tennis.

Without the excuse to take me to play, we were each forced to be in the house on Saturdays. He'd hint around the edges of conversation but he was never good at small talk with us. If there wasn't a court full of sunshine, he was a little lost on teaching life lessons.

I know there was so much he needed to tell me, and really so much we should be talking about. But back in that house that held all our secrets and sadness, Dad just couldn't find the words.

It wasn't until I was in my forties that I realized how much my dad and those tennis lessons really meant. It was 1997 and it was supposed to be a very good year.

The twins were turning three, Maddie's scars from her heart surgery had healed and I thought medical worries were behind us. Infant twins plus two older girls had been a challenge but now Maddie and Emma were both toddling happily while I cooked dinner.

I was stirring a big pot of meat sauce for spaghetti when the phone rang. Emma was at my feet chewing on the Tupperware cup that had held the intended snack of Cheerios, now spread across the hardwood floor in forlorn Os. I could hear Maddie scuttling around her indoor track created by pretending she was in a race car zooming from the kitchen, den, and living room, all of which were fairly devoid of furniture.

My Buddha Baby and Tasmanian Devil.

My week's To Do list was on the phone by the counter. I refused to get a Bic four-color pen and I never used three-by-five index cards, but my organizational strategies were exactly like my mom's: make lists. I had learned to design for clients at night or nap time, but the days were reserved for the logistics of carpools and life.

Dinner— make sauce
Soccer— Lauren & Kailey 4pm
Brochure— revisions Wednesday
Museum— gala invitation design Friday

With a small smile of satisfaction, I crossed through "Make Sauce." I loved crossing things off. Sometimes, if I didn't have the item on my list but it was a task I accomplished, I would write it down after I had done it just to have the small rush of crossing it off.

The phone shrilled insistently again, demanding to be noticed. I glanced at my watch. I had exactly twenty-four minutes before I would need to load up the twins in the minivan, get to the bus stop, and hurry Lauren and Kailey into the car so that we could be at two soccer practices both starting at 4:00 and on fields ten minutes apart. Lauren and Kailey's snacks, water bottles, socks, and cleats were already in the backseat, preloaded for maximum time efficiency.

Stepping carefully over Emma, I finally reached the phone on the fourth ring. "Hello?"

I had put a fourteen-foot cord on the phone so I could talk, cook, and serve the two high chairs simultaneously.

"Hey, it's Dad."

I checked my watch. *Weird*. My dad never called this early.

After years of never leaving the office before 6 p.m., he was gearing down at age sixty-two, looking towards full retirement. This was also why 1997 was going to be a great year. With my mom's health steady, my parents were going to travel to all the places they had dreamed about. They had checked off some on their bucket list—primarily Melbourne, Paris, London, and New York. These four destinations were not just to tour these famous cities but also to attend every one of the Tennis Grand Slams: the Australian Open, the French Open, Wimbledon, and the U.S. Open.

With this Tennis Grand Slam goal achieved, the catalogs on Dad's desk were now of train travel across Europe and Mom wanted to go to China. That was my first thought when I heard his voice— *Mom*. Over the years when the phone rang at odd hours, the dread would creep up with the first ring.

Was it a manic episode? Did I need to fly home?

But as the years passed without incident, I tried not to automatically assume a hospital stay every time the phone rang. With the right diagnosis and medicine, now all it took was a tweak of milligrams and a rest before the new combination held her steady.

"Is it Mom? Is she okay?"

"Actually, it's *me*, Kathy."

What? Dad was a relative picture of health. He had several back injuries from tennis and was being monitored for a blood condition that I had never bothered to learn the name of because my Dad assured me it was benign.

"I have cancer."

How could that be? Dad didn't smoke, didn't drink, didn't swear, exercised, ate well, wore sunscreen, went to church, paid his taxes. How could cancer possibly have come to his door? He served on the

Board of the Cancer Treatment Center to *do good* not because he *had* cancer. *This must be a mistake.*

"What kind, Dad? Is it bad?" I was struggling to think. I readily absorbed bad news about my mom. We all worried about my mom. We had experience with that. I had no idea how to process this.

"It's leukemia—acute myeloid leukemia."

Today, I would have immediately gone to the Internet and found out this was not great news. His original blood condition was called myelodysplasia and in 30 percent of cases it developed into leukemia. An aggressive leukemia. But in 1997, I had to rely on Dad's information and he was characteristically upbeat.

"We are going to MD Anderson in Houston. Their doctors are the best and you know me—I will fight this!"

He left off the "and win!" but it went without saying that he believed he would.

He always won. He worked hard. He practiced. He never gave up. Winning was the natural, logical outcome to perseverance.

*You can do anything, Kathy, really **anything**.*

I hung up the phone, shattered. This was not going to go well. I could feel it. My To Do list stared up at me from the counter. What had seemed a week full of purpose with easy mark-through tasks was instantly trivial in the context of this overwhelmingly bad news.

I grabbed the pen and added to my list:

Research Acute Myeloid Leukemia

Word of Dad's diagnosis spread quickly—El Paso is basically a small town. Unlike my mom's illness, we didn't hide the cancer. We talked about it. The Presbyterians and all my parents' friends showed up strong. This time they all knew. This time we told them.

Cards. Casseroles. Compassion. We were inundated.

Dad and Mom spent nine months in Houston from the end of 1997 and the beginning of 1998 so that he could receive an experimental treatment that we learned was his only option. This trial therapy would consist of taking his blood marrow cells down to zero and building them back up again with the hope that the new marrow would not have the cancer cells. Dad would live in a sterile environment at MD Anderson, and my mom would live in the hotel attached to the cancer center.

Dad's new home was a twelve-by-twelve-foot sterile room with a hospital bed. He was confined there twenty-four hours a day connected to tubes on rolling IV poles he could push around his cell of hope. A five-foot glass window wall on one side allowed him to see visitors and my mom. She was his constant companion on the other side of the glass, reading and needlepointing.

In order to cheer up this hospital home, our girls made cards for "Poppy" and "Lili" that mom taped to his window on the world. Dad would proudly point to the artwork, telling the nurses about each of his four granddaughters.

His airless prison had no natural sunshine and no way to escape to a tennis court, but this was his only shot. Dad asked hospital staff to bring an exercise bike into his solitary confinement and he would pedal furiously watching TV—football games, basketball games, and tennis tournaments, depending on the sports season.

Louise, Allyson, and I rotated weeks visiting them in Houston and it was like space travel to a cancer planet. Tunnels and walkways connected everything, including the hotel, so entire days could go by without feeling heat, cold, or wind. Even though this world inside MD Anderson was a constant seventy degrees, the forecast always seemed gloomy. Too many bald heads hidden by scarves and too many hollow-eyed children who should have been playing on swings not pushing poles with bagged fluids.

While I had been to visit on psychiatric wards, I was unprepared for the distinct difference on cancer wards. So much of the disease of the mind happens on the inside with so much invisible to the eye. With cancer and disease of the body, so much was plainly visible. Weight loss. Hair loss. Hollow eyes. Gaunt skin. There was no question who were the patients and who were the caregivers. But in both cancer and mental illness, I learned, families' hopes held on to pills and protocols that took far too long to reverse the course of suffering.

I always worried I would arrive on one of those visits to Houston to find Mom battling extreme depression or mania. Yet during those agonizing months, she was the strongest, best version of herself. The one who had dazzled in college, planned my gorgeous wedding, and created old-fashioned paper dolls for her granddaughters. Dad needed her in this medical crisis and Mom was steady and fully present. She seemed to summon an uncommon strength in order to be there for Dad as he had always been there for her. Mom became an expert in AML blast cells and CBC counts, always a calm but insistent advocate when a nurse was late with pain medication.

Witnessing this new side of my mother meant in some strange way that I enjoyed those visits to Houston. It may have been the first time in decades we really had a conversation. Mom and I would go to dinner each night, escaping the medical compound in search of chile con queso (for me) and a good crab cake (for her). We found ways to distract ourselves from the ever-present worry, but the conversation usually circled back to Dad and God.

"Are you worried?" I'd ask.

"Your dad and I have a strong faith," she'd answer, which did not really answer the question.

We never talked about *what if.*

Since we'd never talked about her living with manic depression, we certainly were not going to discuss her living without Dad.

Each day, my parents waited, prayed, and read the bible just like on their first Valentine's Day date.

And now these three remain: faith, hope and love. But the greatest of these is love.

Now more than ever, for my father, the greatest of these was faith.

"My white count is not good, but I told the doctor it will be better by the end of the week," Dad would assure me.

His uniform of optimism was a T-shirt that another patient had given him, which proclaimed on the front, *"Never, never give up!"* He preferred it to his hospital gown and would tell every visitor that cancer was not getting him this young.

At the end of that first trial, the doctors had told my parents that research indicated 60 percent of patients responded to treatment. My dad was not one of them.

The oncologists told Dad he could repeat the same treatment. More living in Houston. More tubes. More weeks in the glass bubble.

In the second round of treatment, research showed that nearly 80 percent of the unlucky 40 percent who did not see results in the first trial would achieve success in the second round. My dad was not one of them.

He went home to El Paso, a little more shaken in his belief that a medical miracle might occur. Since he had worked so diligently all his life for his law firm, for the church, for the community, he had delayed time for himself. Cancer had arrived unexpectedly with his retirement package. Dad would not concede that it was possible all his plans to see the world might not happen. The train trip across Europe might not ever leave the station. Doctors advised him to save his strength but he kept playing tennis with his regular Saturday foursome, only he didn't run for every ball. When doctors said it was impossible to get on a plane to New York for Allyson's wedding given his white blood count was so low, he stubbornly walked the bride down the aisle anyway.

Over the years, I had been forced to imagine many times what it would be like to lose my mom. Each hospital visit always led my anxiety down the rabbit hole of what would happen if she did not come home, or if this time she came home irrevocably damaged. I don't think I ever really established a contingency plan for that possibility, but I had allowed myself to consider that and imagine surviving it.

Not this.

I had never imagined losing my father. While my mother had always been somewhat of a question mark in my life, Dad was the exclamation point. He was solid and steady. He anchored my being. He encouraged me, believed in me, and dreamed for me dreams I didn't even have for myself.

I was his mini-me. From the "Dad" face I made to the logical workings of our minds, we understood each other. To not have my father in my life would mean disconnecting from my source of strength and that was a possibility I could not fathom.

Even if I did not want to think about it, Dad began to make plans for that eventuality. Even though I was the youngest daughter, he let me know he was leaving me in charge not only as executor of his estate, but all of Mom's ongoing legal and financial affairs. Although I had never gone to law school, Dad said he trusted me to handle it all with my logical mind and Charlie's financial savvy. Just as he had for his clients, Dad meticulously planned everything. There was a five-page document with every account, investment, and obligation listed with his specific wishes spelled out. One afternoon when I phoned to check on him he said he was even writing his obituary.

"Dad! Stop! That's morbid!" I told him.

"No it's not! I'm just at the good part about the loving wife and three daughters!"

Even as he carefully planned for the end, I think he had a secret hope that it was all just a test of his faith. Maybe if he just believed and prayed, there would be a miracle cure. As he grew weaker, Dad's anger flashed.

He had lived a good life. He had been a good servant. Why was this happening?

He wouldn't yell at God but he could yell at Mom.

She didn't yell back—at God or Dad. Whatever she was thinking, she kept to herself, and remained resolutely caretaking and soothing.

But the greatest of these is love.

I did not share my father's hope that God would intervene. But I was unreasonably hopeful because my dad's resilience and optimism convinced me he would have years ahead of us still.

He just didn't look sick. He still played tennis. There was no way he could die.

Not even a year after his first symptoms began, I called to check on him on a Saturday morning and he admitted he wasn't feeling well.

"Are you going to call your doctor?" I asked.

"No, I'm sure it is just the hot dog I ate at the UT El Paso basketball game last night," he said, before adding, "it won't kill me."

It did.

My dad, John Leighton Green, Jr., died that night, November 15, 1998, at sixty-four. It had been just ten months and ten days since we were introduced to leukemia.

I had many months to contemplate this, to prepare for this moment. I guess that is the small consolation with cancer. You have time to begin to say what should be said and try to make up for all the moments that will be stolen from you. Six weeks before he died,

I had met my parents at Dad's favorite beachside resort in La Jolla, California. Many summers growing up, my family had rented a home there, and I spent that week with him and my mom revisiting all our favorite places. By then, I had taken up playing tennis again and Dad challenged me to a match. Even in his weakened state, he easily won both sets. Dad still had a mean dropshot. Throughout our match, he grinned mischievously as he forced me to chase balls on the baseline before sending a wily short shot for a winner.

I wished I had used that trip, that court time to say more. With the court full of sunshine between us, I wish I had called joyously across to him, "You are the best, Dad!"

On the change-overs as we sipped water, I should have whispered, "You were always there for me, Dad. No matter what happened to Mom, I always knew I would never be left alone."

And when he won that last set, I wished I had jumped across the net and given him a bear hug and a victory grin that would have lasted until the next day.

I didn't. Like so much of our relationship, we didn't say all that we could have. We talked about ways to improve my forehand or his remarkable dropshot. We talked about nothing that mattered. We acted like there would always be more games, more matches.

We didn't capture those precious minutes, holding tight to the knowledge that we would never, ever be in this game of life together again.

I may have been thirty-five, but with my father gone I felt abandoned. I had always known, in every sandstorm, Dad was on the other end of the rope steadfastly holding tight. I had always known in my bones, he would never, ever, let me go. I wasn't sure what it meant to be in this world without his circle of safety. Throughout my mother's Lost Years and after, there had always been that irreplaceable father-daughter love in my life. That one person who not only kept me safe but imagined I could do the unimaginable. That one person who looked at me with such a mix of pride and joy that in his presence it was impossible not to radiate it back.

I gathered my girls to tell them. Lauren was eight, Kailey six, Emma and Maddie, four.

"You all know Poppy has been sick and that he has been in the hospital a lot." I couldn't keep my voice from cracking. Lauren didn't know what I was trying to tell her but she knew it wasn't good.

"But he's going to be okay, right, Mom?"

There was no lying on this one, no making it better, no softening it. As much as I never wanted my girls to be sad or hurt, there was no fixing this. I touched her blonde head and started crying. "No, honey, I'm sorry. He won't be okay. Poppy died last night."

I'm not sure Kailey, Emma, and Maddie fully grasped the situation but they knew if Lauren was crying, they should be crying, too.

Laurenkaileyemmamaddie. One body, four hearts.

Emma must have been thinking about her other grandfather's garden overflowing with vegetables in Rye, N.Y. Tagging behind Charlie's dad, the girls had all seen vegetable plants alive and abundant in the summer become lifeless, dormant stalks in the winter. The next summer those same dead plants would once again be magically living and leaning with the weight of new growth.

"Mommy, Poppy will grow back—right?" Emma asked.

I had known my dad's cancer would never allow him to see his four granddaughters grow into women. Four graduations at which he would never applaud. Four weddings at which he would never dance.

But I really, truly believed there would be more time.

For his birthday four months before, I had given him a brown leather journal, and on the front I had embossed the words *Poppy Talk.*

Dad was going to write his story and impart all the wisdom he wanted his granddaughters to know.

Mom told me that in his last night in the hospital, Dad had instructed the nurse to put the IV in his left arm to make sure he could use his right arm to write. He had more stories to tell. More he needed to say.

Now, he would never finish. *Laurenkaileyemmamaddie* would never know what he had wanted to tell them.

There was so much Dad had tried to tell me, too, that I could not hear. I wanted to listen now. I wanted to play tennis with him now. I was ready to play the game now. I wanted him to see that I could work hard at something important and *never, never give up* until I succeeded. Dad had loved me and kept me safe for *something*. He had believed in me so fiercely not just as a wife and mother but that I was meant to Do Good.

*You can do anything, Kathy, really, **anything**.*

He had imagined the unimaginable for me. The only way I could ever feel surrounded by his love again was to prove he was right.

8

Working My Way Home

If the path before you is clear,
you're probably on someone else's.

JOSEPH CAMPBELL

YOU CAN DO ANYTHING, KATHY, REALLY, ANYTHING.

That thought haunted me after Dad died.

What could I do that mattered?

At thirty-five, I was an accidental tourist in my own life. I had done so many things on impulse—the move to Charlotte, meeting Charlie, getting married. I had no idea how to make an actual life plan. My dad had a plan and it had been too late. His plan had been to work diligently until his retirement and then do all things he dreamed about. His travel, his train trips were all going to happen in his golden years. But it had been too late.

What if I was too late? What if I had waited too long to start my life?

I had built the family I had craved and a career I reasonably enjoyed but as far as any dreams, I had none. My father's death dislodged my complacency. Something inside began to stir, urging me to think differently. I was not comfortable anymore to just let my life happen to me. I needed to *do* something, risk something, but I felt stuck.

It was like I couldn't even get up from the couch. Somewhere with three pregnancies and the baby weight that never completely went away, I had become sedentary. My girls knew nothing about my former athleticism and self-sufficiency. It was Charlie they played basketball with, even though I was on a team for years in middle school. It was Charlie they went to even simply to open a jar, thinking Mom had no muscles, no toughness. I'd given them no reason to think otherwise.

Four months after my dad died, Charlie went on a heli-skiing adventure in Canada with his brothers and a cousin. When he planned the trip, I had not been even remotely jealous because it sounded awful to me.

Subfreezing temperatures. Terrifying slopes. No thanks.

My one condition if he went was I asked Charlie to call me every night from the satellite phone so I would know he had not died hurling himself off a frozen precipice.

That first static-filled phone call, Charlie gushed with excitement, "*That* was the best day of my life!"

But then the next night he was even more effusive. "I know I said yesterday was the best day but *today*! Today was the best day!"

Each night, he was progressively amped up like a man drunk on gallons of Red Bull Happiness. I may not have been jealous about a heli-ski trip, but his newfound exhilaration about life and testing his physical limits, *that* I was looking for.

Charlie came home energized about his life, making me even more desperate to plug in to mine. I thought about taking a trip that summer that might jumpstart me back to someone I wanted to be. It was during a third-grade after-school meeting for Kailey's class that I finally found the spark. Sarah Belk, the mother of one of Kailey's friends, provided it. I overheard her talking to a few other moms.

"I am going on a weeklong horse pack trip in the Wind River Range with three of my kids!" she said. "We will be riding horses and sleeping in the wilderness in tents!"

Horses? I loved horses but had not ridden since summer camp when I was in third grade. I turned to look at Sarah. We didn't know each other well, except that our daughters had played together since kindergarten.

"Sarah, that sounds amazing! When are you going?" I interrupted.

"This summer! You *so* should come!" Sarah's face lit up as she spoke to me. Her brown eyes were inviting and her hand gestures welcoming. "It's going to be so fun and even better if our girls can hang together!"

My heart skipped a beat. *She was asking me to come?*

For the next few days, I fantasized. Maybe this would wake me from my midlife hibernation, but could I do this? *Could I pitch a tent? Could I stand not showering for four days? Could I ride a horse not just for an hour, but all day?* When I was a girl that horse camp had been one of the best summers I could remember. I had even won the barrel race, and Charlie always thought that trophy was the most random yet impressive of all my childhood possessions.

Charlie was all in before I was. "You should do it!"

"But I barely know Sarah."

"So? She wouldn't have offered if she didn't mean it, and Kailey is great friends with her daughter."

That was how I found myself in the summer of 1999 with Lauren and Kailey, riding horses up a mountainside with Charlie home watching the twins. Sarah was riding ahead with three of her five children following our leaders, a married couple, Abie and Grant Beck of Pinedale, W.Y. When we met, Abie hugged me like a long-lost friend and I felt immediately like we were. She was in her uniform that never changed in the week we were together: long-sleeve denim shirt over a maroon T-shirt, patched jeans, roper boots, and a dark green baseball cap with her fifteen-inch-long brown ponytail swinging through the back. Although we were not that far apart in age, we were worlds away in body type. My sedentary mom-jeans life was evident next to her well-earned, rock-hard body.

Abie had been up since 3:30 a.m. preparing for our five-day trip. In those early morning hours, Abie had already fed and saddled nine horses and five mules, and packed provisions for the fifteen meals she would cook on the trail. I watched in awe as she expertly crowded everything into fifty-pound saddlebags, hoisting them with ease and tying them securely to the mules.

Having introduced us to our horses an hour before, Abie was now leading us up 9,000 feet into the Bridger Wilderness. Lauren rode a blonde palomino quarter horse named Tucker, Kailey a brown-and-white paint with eerie blue eyes thus called Angel Eyes, and my horse was a leopard Appaloosa named Joe. Third-grade summer camp had been a long time ago, and I shifted uncomfortably in my saddle trying to find the muscle memory of horseback riding. My girls were giddy with enthusiasm, clearly amazed that their mom was actually going on this adventure with them. Sarah was much more outdoorsy than I was and clearly had no qualms about what was ahead.

"Isn't this awesome?" she gushed. "I am *so* glad you all came!"

The ride did not disappoint as we wound our way up the mountain single file on narrow trails through the woods and crossing streams. It would take all day to reach our campsite beside Big Trapper Lake and we stopped only briefly for lunch. We dismounted at the lakeside, hot, tired, and—those of us over thirty-five—very sore. Abie and Grant busied themselves with building a fire and cooking dinner for nine, leaving Sarah and me to unpack our own gear. Lauren, Kailey, and I shared one overstuffed duffle and it took all my strength to lug it under a stand of trees. Pulling out the tent, I looked over to Sarah to see if she knew how to do this, but she looked up at the same time, a mess of tent poles falling out of her hand.

We made eye contact and Sarah raised her eyebrows and scrunched her lips in a clear mother-to-mother silent sign of "No idea, but don't tell the kids." Kailey saw me struggling and stepped forward to take charge. She had always had spatial abilities and once assembled a bike rack while the rest of the family watched helplessly. Sarah and I smiled with pride, watching our five kids solving the tent puzzle.

"I think this goes in the middle!"

"No, look, these hook together and form the sides!"

As our tent city began to rise, the buzzing started.

We swatted away one, then ten, then hundreds of swarming mosquitoes, blackflies, and horseflies, all attacking at once our exposed flesh. The kids thought it was funny at first making a game of swatting and running away, but the pests pursued. We tried covering every inch of skin with long-sleeve shirts, hats, bandanas, and bug spray but the onslaught was relentless. The huge blackflies particularly liked the back of our necks, and I noticed with horror that each of my girls had not only red welts but blood oozing from the bites. They were not happy. It seemed our grand adventure was going to be a four-day debacle.

We quickly ate dinner and ducked into the safety of our tent, saying good night to Sarah and her kids. I was truly regretting ever saying yes to this. Lauren and Kailey were trying to be brave but they looked miserable and exhausted.

Once inside our tent, the buzzing faded and we zipped up the front to keep the invaders away. The temperature had cooled and we pushed our sleeping bags together. We each had brought journals and started writing and drawing pictures of our day.

"Remember that stream we had lunch by?" Lauren asked.

"We could see all the fish!" Kailey said.

"I loved swimming where I could see all the way to the bottom! I felt like a mermaid!" Lauren added.

The heat and the frustration of the last two hours melted away as we remembered the good parts. The horses were now roaming freely outside our tents, grazing quietly. They had cowbells tied around their necks and they sounded like a living wind chime, louder and softer as they moved through the fields.

We salvaged that day and then the whole trip. I did things I never thought I could and used muscles I had forgotten I possessed. Braving fifty-degree water for a bath; carrying buckets of water half a mile for morning coffee; using a two-man saw for firewood while drinking red wine out of a metal mug. My inner child was awakened too as we built forts worthy of a dozen beavers and played charades while roasting marshmallows around the campfire at night. As Grant told us every night, "The best thing for the inside of a man is the outside of a horse."

My real awakening, however, came on day three.

We were making our way to the highest point of our trip, lovingly referred to as "Grant's Peak" by Abie. I had become a pro the last few days of riding with only one hand on the reins so I could take photos of the incredible scenery. I had shot three rolls of film already on this morning ride, each time thinking, "*this* is the most spectacular shot" only to be mesmerized over the next ridge. We ate lunch around a campfire with the 11,000-foot Grant's Peak on our left. Abie was going to lead us on a hike to the top while Grant offered to sleep in the field with the horses.

Looking nervously at the peak, I wasn't sure I could make it because it looked like something out of *The Sound of Music*, only with more boulders. Lauren, Kailey, and Sarah's kids sprinted ahead, scurrying easily across the rocks while Sarah and I trudged behind.

"Oh, Lordy," Sarah said—her favorite southern expression coming out as we sweated, climbing over each gray obstacle.

It was a steady uphill climb made easier at times by giant rocks making a virtual staircase to the top. Just short of the peak, we encountered a vast snowfield. Our kids dressed only in their T-shirts and jeans slid across it, pretending to snowboard in their cowboy boots. Clouds were gathering so we hurried to the "Top of the World" as Abie called it. That view from the top must have been part of Charlie's exhilaration when he came back from heli-skiing in Canada. There is something in witnessing a 360-degree view of nature's most impressive creations that stays in your soul. In every direction we looked, peaks and layers of gray rock mixed with deep green forests, nothing man-made in sight. We cautiously crept to the edge, peering down to admire the different, stunning vistas.

By now the clouds were thick and angry-looking, and we scrambled down trying to beat the storm. Booming thunder rocked the sky as we made our way towards Grant and the horses. He had already gathered them under an eighty-foot clump of pine trees and we huddled together hoping it all would pass quickly. The trees provided cover for the next thirty minutes while hail bounced around us. The day had started out a beautiful seventy degrees, so we were unprepared for the sudden thirty-degree temperature drop and the steady rain that followed the hail. As we put thin raincoats over T-shirts and jeans, the realization set in. We were a two-and-a-half-hour wet horseback ride from camp and this storm was not stopping.

We saddled up for the long, slow slog ahead. During the next two hours, I fantasized about a lot of things. *A truck to come pick us up. A lodge to rise up in the distance. A longer raincoat.* None of them magically appeared. The girls were soaked and hung their heads towards their horses as the unending rain dripped off their baseball caps. An hour into the misery, I had an even darker realization. Even when we made it back to camp, there was no cozy lodge, no warm shower, and not even a fire, since all the wood was now as wet as we were.

Kailey must have been thinking the same because she turned in her saddle to look back at me and wail, "I'm so cold, Mom, I can't go anymore."

Fearing mutiny from all the kids if one buckled, I channeled an inner general voice I didn't know I had. "You *will*, Kailey. We all will because we have no choice."

Although it felt cruel to be so harsh, I really didn't have an option—there was no way out of this but the long ride home. Expecting sympathy, Kailey looked stunned not to receive a more motherly rescue solution. She whipped around in her saddle and hunkered into a silent wet lump for the rest of the ride.

When we finally sloshed into camp, our kids were all so frozen to their saddles, we had to help them off their horses. Their jeans were soaked stiff with water so once they dismounted, they had to waddle back to the tents. Our canvas home didn't hold much for warmth and comfort. Lauren, Kailey, and I had all pared down to one shared duffle for the trip so pajamas and an extra jean shirt were the best we could find. I zipped Lauren and Kailey into their sleeping bags and we shivered side by side, waiting for the circulation to return to our fingers and toes.

When we could finally feel our extremities, I tried to think how to entertain them without leaving the tent. "Have Dad and I ever taught you to play poker?"

We turned on our battery lantern and pulled out the cards, and I began a tutorial in Texas Hold'em. As we shuffled and dealt cards, Lauren began singing, and we became our own jukebox belting out all the words we could remember to our favorite Dixie Chicks and Shania Twain songs. We finished the evening with a rousing round of "Man, I Feel Like a Woman."

The funny thing is, I really did finally feel like a woman. A strong, capable, I-can-do-anything woman. Beginning with the biting bugs on our first night to this day's epic wet journey, the trip was exactly as I had hoped. I'd never be the same. Before I came on the trip, I felt I had been sleepwalking through my life. Going through safe motions, never risking, never questioning my choices.

I had heard Dale Mullennix speak once at the Urban Ministry about serving the homeless. Dale said one of his volunteers told him he was "ruined for life" after working there. After serving in the soup kitchen, this volunteer said he would never look at a plate of food the same way again. Having witnessed at UMC the reality of having nothing, he would always be incredibly grateful for everything.

After this week, I felt the same. I'd never look at my bed the same way again. Or my shower or a rainstorm. All week it had taken so little to be happy. A campfire. A sunny day. Chocolate in my trail mix at lunch. And I knew that when I looked at Lauren and Kailey, I would now know they could handle anything.

I was ruined for life and grateful for it.

Charlie met us in the airport at the baggage claim. When our duffle came up, I instinctively stepped in front of him and hoisted it easily off the belt as I had been doing all week.

"Whoa!" he said laughing. "What happened out there?"

"I think I found myself," I answered.

"I didn't know you were lost."

"I truly didn't either."

That trip created a new restlessness inside me. I was not going to sleepwalk through my life anymore. I vowed to push myself physically and mentally. That meant my career, too. Graphic design wasn't challenging anymore and I wanted to quit. Economically, that was hard to justify. I had a great business with good clients who paid me well. I had a home office, and I could easily design brochures when the girls were at school. I set my own hours and could make any after-school carpool or activity work. I was always there to ask about their day when my girls came home from school.

But I also had been working with a lot of nonprofit clients recently. Arts organizations. Education groups. I would sit in a meeting with those clients and be fascinated by their work. Not my work. *Their* work. We would strategize how to market new programs or how to raise money for a project. I'd develop marketing materials to help sell their ideas and then be envious of the work they would be implementing when my design work was over. I didn't want to just be Graphics Girl; I wanted to do something that mattered.

It didn't seem feasible to go back to graduate school with our four daughters still in high school and middle school. Even if graduate school was an option, I had no idea what exactly I would choose to achieve the elusive something *that mattered.* Flipping through course catalogues, I didn't even know which departments to browse.

Psychology? Sociology? Business? Nonprofit Management?

I wandered the aisles of Charlotte bookstores hoping my purpose might leap out from the pages and reveal itself.

My shelves at home were soon filled with books on midlife career changes, nonprofit management, and nonfiction meant to inspire. Anne Lamott. Brene Brown. Even *Oprah* magazine encouraged me to live the life I'd dreamed—but I felt stuck again. The options were so vast I was paralyzed looking at the horizon of my future.

How would I know what I was meant to do? I kept waiting for that *aha* moment like the one when I met Charlie and I had *known* he was the one. My moment of purpose would surely just arise now that I was intentionally searching for it.

But it didn't.

I kept busy with work and volunteering while I waited for my life to find me. I joined the boards of several organizations in Charlotte, including the Urban Ministry Center. Although I'd spent a decade volunteering there, I had already determined the Urban Ministry Center was *not* the place to find my purpose. I was certain my one true thing would be something I could solve. To do something that mattered meant I would find something I could fix—something that needed my innate problem-solving abilities, creativity, and logic. It was clear to me homelessness was not something I could do anything about.

Homelessness was simply too unsolvable.

Other issues eluded me as well. Health. Education. Poverty. There were so many causes, but I wasn't sure if there was a fight I was willing to take up. And I certainly was not going to try anything where I might *fail*.

The closer I got to an empty nest, the more anxious I became about it. As Lauren and Kailey went off to college and Emma and Maddie prepared for high school, I could feel the hole opening up inside me.

If I wasn't *Laurenkaileyemmamaddie*'s mom, who was I?

Other than raise my family, what had I done to justify my dad's extraordinary faith in me? His wild hope that I would change the world. What had I done to *Do Good*?

You can do anything, Kathy, really anything.

But honestly, I couldn't think of a thing.

It was ironic really.

For almost twenty years, I had been a student and producer of ideas. To solve a marketing problem for a client, I was trained to study a problem and distill it down to a single, simple solution. A logo.

A headline. A tagline. Dr. Ruben had drilled it into my being during my college advertising boot camp.

But now *I* was the client. I needed an idea. And I could not think of a single one. Not one thing I felt capable of accomplishing that would *matter* in this world.

I could hear Dr. Ruben's criticism.

"Where's the concept, Green?"

It was true. Even though I was studying it, looking for it, hoping for it, I had no single, simple, solution for my purpose.

Where was the big idea for my life?

9

Circled by Safety

The only important thing in a book
is the meaning that it has for you.

W. SOMERSET MAUGHAM

AS IT TURNED OUT, A BOOK DID HELP ME FIND MY WAY TO MY
big idea, but the answer revealed itself not on the page but in person.

In February 2007, my sisters and I were flying to El Paso to convince Mom to move out of our childhood home into a retirement community. It was a decision we knew would not be received well.

Right before my father died in 1998, I asked him if we should move Mom to Charlotte so she wouldn't be alone in El Paso. Dad smiled, shaking his head. "She won't go; she is stubborn." He was right. Even though Louise and I lived on the East Coast and Allyson in California, Mom was happy in the home she had been in since 1968.

In the nine years my father had been gone, Mom, now seventy-two, handled her sudden, early widowhood with incredible strength and independence. She was comfortable in the haven that was our childhood home, but my sisters and I weren't comfortable with her being there.

While she was still relatively young to move into senior living, there were the obvious signs that the house was becoming a burden—needed repairs gone unnoticed—and the subtler signs that four bedrooms were a lot to keep up with. Most of all, the two flights of stairs were a constant threat of potential danger. If she fell, how long would she lie there before anyone knew? Neighbors who had been close friends had all moved away, replaced by strangers we couldn't call in an emergency. My sisters and I each lived two plane rides away from the next emergency.

Louise, Allyson, and I agreed to fly in Valentine's weekend for a family summit. Over the years we had developed our roles in the family dynamic. Louise had surprised us all and become a minister. As the spiritual advisor among us, she tended to connect with Mom on theology and church dynamics. Allyson was now a university professor of dance in California, still well versed in music and all forms of art. Mom always turned to her for discussions on painting or her passion for the Santa Fe Opera. I still handled all the legal and financial details, so this idea of moving into a senior living community had been dropped into my job jar. While my sisters were going to be there for support, my role was to outline the financial need for moving to an independent-living apartment. Mom was not going to be a willing participant.

As I headed to the airport for this mission to move, I picked up a book Mom had recently told me about, *Same Kind of Different As Me* written by Ron Hall and Denver Moore. Honestly, I only chose it to read on the plane because Mom had told me she was reading it on the recommendation of my uncle and cousin in San Antonio. I hoped reading it would give me something to talk about with my mom besides retirement homes.

Because of my volunteer work at UMC, Mom knew I would be interested in this true story where the central characters meet in a Fort Worth soup kitchen and the inspiring friendship that developed. Ron Hall, one of the coauthors, and his wife, Deborah, were volunteers at the Union Gospel Mission soup kitchen when they met Denver Moore, who sounded much tougher than Chilly Willy or any of the Neighbors I had met at UMC. I was also intrigued with the book jacket promise that Denver's real-life story had changed the way Fort Worth treated their homeless neighbors.

I settled into my seat and the seven-hour journey to El Paso, and I was soon lost in the story. The narrative talked a lot about soup kitchens and homeless people—something I thought I knew a lot about after ten years in the UMC kitchen. But I never thought about it from the Neighbor's point of view. Just mine. Volunteering there made me feel good and like I was doing some good.

But was I?

Denver's voice was strong throughout the book. And it was clearly meant to make the reader feel uncomfortable:

You is blessin' folks with your dollars and service, but a dollar bill and plate of food ain't changin' a life. That takes love.

Wasn't that what I had been doing all these years? Donating money? Serving soup with a smile. But how many people was I *truly* helping? How many people did I really know? I surely hadn't loved anybody. I had not even bothered to learn a single name until Jimmy let me know Chilly Willy was William Larry Major.

In the book, Ron Hall didn't want to be at the Fort Worth Union Gospel Mission either. He had only gone because he had cheated on his wife and he thought that would be a way to make amends—follow her passion to the soup kitchen.

But once there, Ron had allowed himself to truly know and care for one person—Denver Moore. As crazy as it might seem, Ron and Debbie had invited Denver to come into their home, their lives, and after that, nothing was the same.

Could I do that? Not a chance. There was no way I was inviting a homeless man home with me from the UMC. I had a husband, four daughters, a business, and a busy life. I wanted to do some good, but I was not going to do what Ron and Debbie did—move a homeless person in to live with us.

I finished the book midair and closed the cover. It had unnerved me. I had been restless the last few years searching for something and now it felt like this book was speaking to me whether I wanted to hear it or not. Could my yearning and this book somehow be related?

That was ridiculous.

I did enough. I showed up to make soup once a month. It was my church and I was faithful.

I shoved the book in my bag and tried to forget it.

When my sisters and I all arrived in El Paso, we gathered in our family living room, Mom sitting on the blue velvet couch, listening to the three of us outline our concern for her well-being. We talked about finances and safety and stairs, and she remained quiet until she couldn't contain the reservoir of misery.

Slow tears leaked out as she spoke. "I never want to be a burden to you girls so if you think this is the right thing… " Her voice drifted, unable to form a defense in the face of her three strong daughters.

I shifted uncomfortably and tried not to look at my sisters. We had all agreed. This move was necessary to be sure Mom was safe. It was all very logical. I had not let myself consider it would be emotional as well. Her sadness was gut-wrenching.

There were few senior-living options in El Paso, and we had lined up an appointment that afternoon to tour available units at one of the best. It had independent living as well as assisted living on a hillside campus in west El Paso. Mom's favorite apartment was a ground-floor two-bedroom home with a patio that overlooked the valley below. The view from her new living room would be far better than the one she currently had at home and we signed a contract on the spot.

We all pretended this was a great outcome, but the sad resignation on my mother's face was unmistakable.

Allyson, always Mom's emotional support, hugged her tightly. I hung back watching my sister comfort Mom, unable to let myself empathize the way Allyson could. My long-held strategy of numbness where my mother was concerned remained. I thought I could be stoic and steadfast. Dad would want me to be the solid support in this situation, wouldn't he? It made perfect financial sense to sell the house and use the gain for Mom's long-term needs. I knew Dad would have agreed.

Mom's clearly broken spirit presented a different side of the argument. We may have found a way to have our mother live with more safeguards, but she obviously was not feeling secure.

On the plane ride home, I reread portions of Ron and Denver's book. A new passage jumped out at me:

Most people want to be circled by safety, not by the unexpected. The unexpected can take you out. But the unexpected can also take you over and change your life. Put a heart in your body where a stone used to be.

Flying out to El Paso, I had been sure that we were doing the right thing. Mom needed to move *now*. Everyone said you needed to move a parent before something terrible happened—a broken hip, a stroke. Once that happened, you wouldn't have your choice of places to move—only the places that would accept your parent with their physical limitations.

In my mother's mind, however, we had not circled her with safety. We had just made her homeless.

When I returned from El Paso, *Same Kind of Different,* its message, and the authors were still haunting me. I kept hearing the same thought whispering over and over.

Invite them to Charlotte.

I had no idea where that thought was coming from. At a UMC board meeting a few months back, we had discussed the need for a fund-raising event but I had no authority to plan one.

The day after I returned from El Paso, however, I found myself Googling Ron Hall's contact information, which popped up easily on the book's website. Without much thought, I composed an email to Ron, introducing myself as a board member of the Urban Ministry Center *(true)* and asked if he would consider coming to North Carolina for a planned fund-raiser *(false).*

I pressed "send" and immediately regretted it.

What was I thinking? I hadn't even mentioned this idea to Dale Mullennix, who would be justifiably upset with my unauthorized invitation to book a speaker for a nonexistent event.

Full of guilt, I stared at the screen where my lie had been launched into cyberspace. I hoped Ron didn't read emails or, if he did, that he would delete mine, knowing I was a fraud.

No such luck. Twenty minutes later, a reply from Ron blinked in my in-box.

> **Yes, we do accept speaking engagements.**
> **When is your event?**

Good question. When was my "event"?

The screen waited patiently for an answer.

I could feel perspiration begin to form as I typed a lie:

**I need to get with my committee but
hold the second week in November.**

The next day, I sheepishly walked into Dale Mullennix's office with a copy of Ron and Denver's book. My greatest salvation lay in the fact Dale was an ordained minister, so I assumed he would be kind when I confessed to booking a speaker without authorization.

Dale had served as a traveling evangelist and campus minister before landing in Charlotte's affluent Myers Park Baptist church and then, the Urban Ministry Center.

His brother had died as a child, and the love his small Baptist church had extended to his family during that unimaginable loss became a driving force behind Dale choosing to major in religious studies. In seminary, Dale was far more outspoken and questioning than his fellow divinity students. With his profound and vocal disappointment in fundamentalist religion, a fellow student asked Dale why he still wanted to be a minister. Dale had no idea how providential his answer to that question would be when he answered, "I want to be pastor of the Last Chance Baptist Church."

I am sure he never imagined that sarcastic comment would come surprisingly close to describing his current job at the Urban Ministry Center.

Entering Dale's office, I hoped he remembered enough of his pastoral roots not to yell at me for overstepping my authority and virtually booking Ron Hall and Denver Moore.

My interactions with Dale up to this point had been limited to when I volunteered in the soup kitchen or during board meetings, so we didn't have an extensive relationship. From what I knew of Dale, he was not intimidating, more likely to tell a joke or send a witty email than quote the bible.

After some small talk, I started bumbling through an explanation of *Same Kind of Different As Me,* noting what a huge following it had in Texas. I tried to interject some spiritual references, mentioning the book was in some weird way *"a calling to me."*

Dale shifted uncomfortably in his chair, not exactly sure where I was going with this. Truthfully, I didn't either. He folded his arms across his chest, dropping his chin in a secret glance at his watch. I know now this is his classic "I'm trying to be patient as a pastor with you" body language.

I cut to the chase. "Ron agreed to come and we just need to pick a date!"

Dale was a little stunned. "He's coming to Charlotte? Did I miss a board meeting where we voted on this?"

I pressed to stop his panic before he shot me down completely. "I will handle everything. We can make it a 'friendraiser'—you know, to introduce people to the Urban Ministry Center."

I was making it up as I went. "We could do a lunch and invite people to hear Ron and Denver to help them understand homelessness. We could ask a church to use their space for free."

Dale was nodding with a poker face.

I am sure he was weighing the UMC's mission and wondering how this idea fit in. Dale's divinity background helped him understand that the Center really serves two groups of people. The first group, obviously, is those on the streets who need not only the soup but showers, laundry, medical care, and counseling. The second, less obvious, group UMC serves is volunteers like me.

In 2007, this interfaith agency had a small paid staff of fewer than twenty but an army of 4,000 volunteers. Some came once a week and some once a year. But each volunteer would tell you the same thing: they always get more than they give. There was something about the UMC campus that helped you leave each time feeling a little changed. Over the years, Dale had learned that when volunteers approached him with their ideas to teach yoga, start book clubs, or organize a choir with the Neighbors, he should just say *yes* and leave the rest up to God.

Neither of us was sure what we were agreeing to, but I left his office with a skeptical *yes*.

A few days later, I gathered with three friends, including my horseback adventure buddy, Sarah Belk, in a restaurant booth to celebrate Angela Breeden's birthday. Sarah and I, forever bonded by our saddle sores, had stayed good friends. She and her five children now also volunteered in the soup kitchen with us every month. Sarah had an amazing ability to gather people to a cause. Everyone genuinely adored Sarah, and if she asked somebody to do something, people usually said *yes*. Since her family worked in the soup kitchen, I hoped Sarah might be interested in helping me with this event I had spontaneously started. Sarah caught on immediately.

"Ooh, Kathy, this sounds like a great book and a great idea!" she said, even though she had never even heard of *Same Kind of Different*.

Everyone at the table agreed and it became infectious.

"I'll run the bank!" Angela offered.

"I'll host a party for Ron and Denver!" said Kim Belk, Sarah's sister-in-law.

"We can order a bunch of copies and give them to our friends to start firing people up!" Sarah said.

No one at the table had ever orchestrated something like this, but we had all helped with church and school events. We were all nervous to tackle it alone, but felt that together we might be able to pull it off.

We set the date for November 14, 2007, and since this was just before Thanksgiving, we brainstormed a title for our luncheon: "True Blessings." The idea was to create an inspiring event before the holidays with a "true" message about homelessness from Ron and Denver. We wouldn't charge anyone to come. We just hoped the day would be so moving that friends would write checks to help cover the cost of food and the expenses of getting the famous authors here from Texas.

"We'll get friends to be table hosts and each host will bring nine of their friends for a table of ten and we will sell it out!" Sarah said.

Sarah was right. As we passed out the book to friends, more and more women offered to help. Word spread about our planned "church lunch," and we easily surpassed our original goal of twenty-five table hosts. With only weeks to go, almost one hundred hosts had pledged to bring over one thousand guests. It was overwhelming. We switched from a church space to a hotel ballroom that could accommodate the massive crowd. This mounting attendance also meant escalating food costs for what we had originally planned as a "free lunch."

Although our strategy to get people to attend was paying off, True Blessings had become a true nightmare for me. When I sent that random email to Ron, I had certainly not envisioned orchestrating such a complex event. Since we were all novice event planners, we had only one paid sponsor for $10,000 to cover the costs, which wasn't nearly enough. This meant if people didn't donate that day, my wild idea to invite Ron and Denver was about to cost the UMC a lot of money.

Why had I ever sent that email? What had I been thinking, imagining that I could pull this off?

The weekend before True Blessings, Sarah and her husband, Tim, invited Charlie and me to attend a "Forty Years of Service" fundraiser for Outward Bound. To coincide with the theme, the event was honoring a founding member for his forty years of service to this outdoor leadership program. Since our big event was in just five days, Sarah and I took note of everything from centerpieces to donor envelopes. It was an incredibly professional and well-planned event. We could only hope ours would go as well.

At the end of the night, it wasn't the event details that stuck with me, it was the evening's message that was unforgettable.

A video presentation along with speakers recounted how the honoree, Rufus Dalton, had left an indelible mark on the organization. It was amazing how forty years of directed effort from one individual had profoundly affected Outward Bound.

I thought about all my scattershot efforts in the past fifteen years. Along with the UMC, I had volunteered at our girls' schools and at various community agencies. I had provided free graphic design and advertising for a variety of nonprofits. All of that volunteer service had the short-term benefit of making me feel useful but nothing felt lasting or vital. I had tried bouncing from opportunity to opportunity looking for my purpose, but maybe that was the reason I hadn't found something that mattered—I had never stayed at one thing long enough.

As we drove home, Charlie commented, "That was pretty amazing—forty years that guy has worked on one cause."

"I know! Makes you think," I agreed.

"So what would your forty-year thing be?" he asked.

Neither of us had an answer, but I knew for me it would not be event planning. I would finish whatever crazy notion had made me spearhead this True Blessings lunch and after it was over, I would begin looking for my true forty-year thing.

I felt beyond inspired that evening; I clearly felt my clock ticking.

My father had died at sixty-four. I might have only nineteen years left to do something that really mattered.

10

Going for a Ride

Let us do something while we have the chance!
It is not everyday that we are needed.

SAMUEL BECKETT
Waiting for Godot

I PICKED UP RON AND DENVER ON WEDNESDAY, NOVEMBER 13, 2007, at the Charlotte airport, trying to appear confident.

After imagining this day for months, I was excited to meet in person the two men who had changed my perspective on homelessness. But the dynamic duo I had read about was not living up to their press. The pair billed as having an amazing and "unlikely friendship" arrived for our event in a silent feud. In the car on the way to lunch, Ron explained the rift.

A couple nights before, there had been a fund-raising dinner in Texas where they were honored guests. Former first lady Barbara Bush had read their book and invited them to "A Celebration of Reading" promoting literacy.

News of this high-profile engagement shocked me, as I had no idea they were in such demand when I sent my email six months before. Ron laughed, telling me Denver's famous quote about the Texas event: "*I done gone from livin' in the bushes to eatin' with the Bushes. God bless America, this is a great country!*"

Although Denver had now been off the streets for years, he had still not lost his habit of wandering off when it suited. The night of the big event for the first lady, Denver had been seated at the head table with former president George Bush. Denver, however, had other ideas rather than dine with the POTUS emeritus. During dinner, Denver had gotten up from the table and simply walked home.

As Ron related all this on the drive from the airport, he was obviously still fuming that he and the Secret Service had spent hours searching for the missing honored guest.

Denver, listening in the back seat, shot back, "Mr. Ron! I lived on those streets for years! You think I can't find my way home?"

If I wasn't worried enough about our event, now I started to panic. If a president couldn't hold Denver's attention, what chance did a bunch of moms have of getting him to attend our luncheon? That very night we also had a cocktail reception planned so volunteers who had invested so much time in planning True Blessings could meet Ron and Denver before the big day.

Now it seemed evident one of our highly anticipated guests of honor might actually choose not to attend.

As if to amplify my concern, Denver promptly disappeared at lunch.

Sarah, Angela, Kim, and all our True Blessings team met on the patio of a restaurant to welcome Ron and Denver to Charlotte. Shortly after we ordered, however, Denver got up and walked off down the busy street. Angela's eyes grew wide—and she has saucer-size brown eyes anyway. She looked at Denver's figure disappearing down the road and then back at Ron in alarm. "Is he coming back?"

Ron laughed. "He will. Eventually."

"I hope so," said Kim. "I have a hundred people coming to my house tonight who want to meet him! My dad is dying to shake his hand and my mom wants his autograph!"

We made small talk with Ron while waiting for our food, but Angela's leg bounced anxiously as she monitored the street for signs of Denver's return. With obvious concern, she checked her watch, and as each minute ticked by her eyes grew wider in silent alarm. By the time our sandwiches arrived, Denver's dark figure could finally be seen moving slowly up the sidewalk towards us.

"Oh, thank God," Angela said, pointing to the reappearing Denver. "Now really, ya'll, what are we going to do if he wanders off during the luncheon tomorrow?"

She was right, and I had no idea what we would tell one thousand people if one of our promised guest speakers failed to show. I had very detailed lists to make sure everything went off smoothly. Denver disappearing was not something I had a contingency plan for. I made a mental note not to let him out of my sight again if at all possible.

After lunch, I delivered Ron and Denver to their hotel, making plans to see them later at Kim's house. I was panicked by the thought only one would actually show up, but I trusted Ron to deliver Denver.

Two hours later, I was unloading boxes of programs for the luncheon to the hotel ballroom where True Blessings was going to be held. My palms started to sweat when I noticed Denver out in front of the hotel, with Ron nowhere in sight.

How could Ron have left Denver alone to just wander off again?

I hurried over to make sure he didn't escape. Denver was leaning against the hotel's stone façade, and he did not appear to immediately recognize me as the same woman who had picked him up hours earlier at the airport.

"White folk look alike," he would say.

Cloaked in black shirt, black sport coat, black slacks, and signature black hat, he looked ominous. I took it as a warning sign he was preparing to slip into Charlotte's downtown and avoid the tedious meet-and-greet schedule ahead of him. I needed to think quickly to keep Denver from disappearing. Out of desperation, I tried to find out where he might be headed.

"Denver, you need a ride somewhere?" I asked.

He studied me before answering. "You got homeless people here?"

Relieved at his simple request, I nodded and asked, "Sure, do you want me to take you there? We can go to the Urban Ministry Center."

Why hadn't I thought of that before?

Of course, I should show Denver the Urban Ministry Center; it was the perfect plan. Inspiring scenes from his book *Same Kind of Different* ran through my head. I imagined taking him to the soup kitchen where Denver would surely motivate some grateful Charlotte homeless person. Denver would be motivational. *Transformational.*

Denver thought a minute as if considering the same scenario in my head but looked down at his formal outfit. "I need to change. They won't listen to me like this."

I wondered who he was talking about but decided not to ask.

Turning towards the revolving doors, Denver was suddenly blocked by bellmen carting luggage. I waited for Denver to continue through the doors to change clothes as he had intended. Denver, however, had made a full stop in the doorway, seeming to reconsider this plan. Slowly, he turned around to stare intently at me. It seemed Denver had just received a message only he could hear. It was unnerving.

"Didn't you want to change?" I prodded, eager to keep him on mission.

My mission. My timetable.

"No," he said, his eyes narrowing as he spoke. Denver silently studied me. Before adding, "Maybe I'm not supposed to be talking to *them*."

I had no idea what he was talking about.

Denver stepped towards my minivan, apparently ready to go the UMC as he was, wearing his coat and hat. As he opened the door, I reached in to move the thick folder of notes and lists filling the passenger seat. With this herculean task of lunch for one thousand, I had put my organizational skills into overdrive filling two pages of a yellow legal pad with items to check off by category and day.

Wednesday
    Airport— 11:45 American Airlines
    Lunch— Patio Reservation for 8
    Programs— Deliver to hotel
    Reception— Kim's house
      Pick up patron bags
      Nametags
      Check food and wine delivery
Thursday
    Volunteers— 4 groups (Pre, Table Captains, Sign-in, Bank)
    Email Assignments

As I got behind the wheel with my lists in my hands, I felt Denver examining me. I looked from his stare to my overly exact schedule, and back. My anxiety clearly outlined in those lists looked a little ridiculous to me, now.

"Denver, I've got every minute of today scheduled but this ride is not on the schedule," I confessed.

Denver nodded as if he already knew this and then flashed a grin I had not seen since he arrived.

"We are going for a ride!" he exclaimed. His emphasis on "ride" exaggerated in a long, southern drawl.

Throwing that folder with all my lists, all my worries, all my anxiety in the back seat, I laughed and agreed, "We are going for a ride!"

It occurred to me then, as it does now, that although I was driving, only Denver knew where we were headed.

We arrived a few minutes later at the Urban Ministry Center in the middle of the afternoon. Lunch was over but there were still crowds moving between buildings on campus, waiting to do their laundry, get mail, or see a counselor. As we walked towards the buildings, I was already explaining about all we did for Charlotte's homeless. I was sure Denver would be impressed.

He wasn't.

Leading Denver on a tour of the Center, I proudly gave a monologue about all of the UMC's innovative programming. In the art room, dozens of paintings by homeless artists were on display. The works were vibrant in color, rich in texture, and layered with meaning.

Denver passed them without comment.

Neighbors weren't flocking to Denver either. I had been certain Neighbors would somehow recognize this formerly homeless man, now celebrity author, and swarm us when we arrived. But everyone ignored us, intent on their own mission—surviving the day. In his dapper sport coat and hat, no one seemed to consider Denver had anything in common with them, least of all a shared history of homelessness. For his part, Denver wasn't even trying to connect his story with the homeless waiting in line.

Where was the wise man from the best-selling book?

It continued to become increasingly uncomfortable. As my tour dragged on, we passed photos of our soccer team hanging on the walls. All our players competed locally and internationally while still enduring homelessness. Visitors always remarked upon the commitment to the team in the face of this obstacle. Again, Denver had no visible display of emotion as he studied the players' proud smiles in these photos.

Moving outside the building, we came to our vegetable patch. It was at the end of the season but Neighbors were tending collards and kale alongside volunteers. Witnessing this side-by-side interaction always sparked conversation, but Denver peered only briefly over the fence before walking back into our main building.

Trailing behind him, I couldn't understand why Denver didn't think what we were doing was as extraordinary as most visitors did. It was maddening to think how an hour before I had imagined a much different scene, sure that Denver would change someone's life at the UMC. My fantasy had been to see him wrap his arm around one of our Neighbors and whisper something utterly profound. In all honesty, I was also hoping to receive some message as well. Some praise for my ten years of dedicated volunteer service for the Neighbors.

His silence was disturbing. Was there a message in that? Was Denver communicating by not speaking? I remembered another of his quotes from the book:

> *If you really serious 'bout helpin' somebody, crawl down in the ditch with 'em, bandage up their wounds, and stick with 'em until they is strong enough to crawl up on your back and get out.*

Weren't we doing that and more? All of our art, soccer, and gardening programs as well as services were designed to build relationships with Neighbors and restore dignity. Most cities had just soup kitchens and limited services, but in our thirteen years, the UMC had developed extensive programming far beyond this basic first-aid response.

Yet Denver had not asked a single question, made one comment, or expressed a word of admiration about our innovations.

What had happened to my book hero?

I had wanted him to be motivational. *Transformational.* I had brought him here to change somebody's life.

That email. The luncheon. This tour. It was all supposed to **matter.** I thought that was what the little voice had been telling me. I thought I was finally doing some good, but Denver was not helping me execute my master plan.

How could I have been so misguided? Why had I listened to any of it?

Frustrated, I turned to leave.

This is when Denver finally spoke.

Motioning to the stairway in front of us, he said, "Can we go upstairs now?"

Now I was angry. I couldn't believe Denver finally wanted to see something when there was, in fact, nothing to show. "There are just offices up there, not much to see."

Denver looked from the stairs to me, and then back again. All these years later, I still hear his question, and the ones that followed it, as clearly as I did that day:

"Where are the beds?"

"The beds?" I asked, utterly confused.

As I started the long, complicated explanation of how Charlotte has several shelters, Denver's dark face silenced me.

Clearly*, I* wasn't getting *his* point.

> *"You mean to tell me you do all*
> *this good in the day and then lock*
> *them out to the bad at night?"*

His accusation left me feeling gutted.

During the decade that I had volunteered at the Urban Ministry Center, I had never once asked myself, *"Where are the beds?"* I had never once let myself fully imagine the *"bad at night."*

I knew in that moment I had never asked because I didn't really want to know.

For ten years, I had allowed that twenty-four inches of stainless steel counter in the soup kitchen to keep me on the safe side. Not knowing and not asking kept me on the comfortable side, and I didn't have to get uncomfortable about the other side. Just like growing up, I was once again on the *right* side of privilege, feeling ashamed about what was happening on the *wrong* side.

Denver patiently allowed me my discomfort. He watched me silently wrestle with my new awareness before quietly asking:

"Does that make any sense to you?"

Of course it made no sense. I was flooded with shame.

Denver's next question would change the trajectory of my path forever. The one that I know I had been waiting for and looking to answer ever since my Dad died nine years before.

"Are you going to do something about it?"

Me? I wanted to look behind me to see exactly who he was talking to but there was little doubt. Denver was staring at me and only me. I had come here for Denver to talk to someone else. To be prophetic to someone else. To transform someone else. I was going to witness *that* miracle.

Now, Denver was talking to me—just me.

What was I going to do?

I was a graphic designer, a married mother of four, and a soup kitchen volunteer—and I had fallen into that mostly to avoid taking my family to church on Sundays.

What could I possibly do about homelessness?

In that moment, I could no longer bear being on the "right" side and no longer not care about what happened on the "wrong" side. I could no longer bear the shame of knowing Denver was right about "the bad at night." There was only one answer.

Yes.

I would have to do something.

Now that I saw, I couldn't *not see.*

"Do I need to say anything else?" he whispered.

My "no" was barely audible but we both heard it loud and clear.

I don't even remember leaving and going back to my minivan. I didn't feel wholly a part of this world, the one where "*we do all this good in the day and then lock them out to the bad at night.*" But I also wasn't part of the world that did anything about it. I didn't even know where to find that place. I had the same sense of shame I felt when I went home to El Paso and looked at those shacks in Juarez on the wrong side of the river.

It was a big, impossible problem. It was not something I caused. It was not something I could do anything about. I had no *big ideas* about how to solve it. But after meeting Denver, I felt completely and totally responsible. Whether I wanted it or not, Denver had just made homelessness my personal mission.

Only hours ago, I had been so proud of all we did at the Urban Ministry Center, but now through Denver's eyes it all seemed inconsequential. We were providing everything the homeless needed to manage their homelessness but we weren't actually solving anything. We were just making them more comfortable in their excruciating discomfort.

Steering the car back to the hotel, I tried not to look at Denver but his words were still ringing in my ears. Denver's insistence that I not look away from this problem had overwhelmed my old conscience at the same time it forced me towards another staggering possibility.

The silence settled between us. I had totally forgotten why we went to the UMC—to keep Denver from wandering off before the cocktail party.

Instead, he had wandered into my life and hijacked my conscience.

I couldn't think of anything except Denver's four questions unforgivingly cycling over and over as I drove him back to the hotel.

From the passenger seat, Denver was studying me and interrupted my panic. "You know, you don't have to be scared."

Scared? Was he talking about the reception in a couple of hours or the one thousand-guest fund-raiser in the morning? Now, both seemed completely irrelevant.

"The beds," he explained reading my mind and sensing my rising anxiety. "It's not that hard."

Really?

Did Denver actually think I might be some magical carpenter who could make beds appear for all of Charlotte's homeless?

How many homeless were there anyway?

I had no idea.

He kept talking, adding cryptically, "They already know they are coming."

"Who?" I asked, still reeling from the magnitude of his assignment.

At this moment, we arrived back into circular drive of the hotel.

Denver stared at me with utter certainty as he said, "The people who are going to help you—they already know they are coming."

And with that, Denver opened my car door and walked away.

11

My Forty-Year Thing

The best way to find yourself is to
lose yourself in the service of others.

MAHATMA GANDHI

DENVER HAD SHOWN UP FOR THE RECEPTION THAT NIGHT AND acted like nothing happened. I did, too. Frankly, I wanted the whole thing to go away. I wanted the True Blessings event to be over and for Denver to go back to Texas, and then I could go back to designing logos and serving soup. I didn't mention my conversation with Denver to anyone.

But I didn't sleep very well that night. I tried to tell myself that I was nervous about the luncheon. *Would people donate? Would we be able to afford our catering bill much less have any profits to help the homeless?*

The truth was, I was just beginning to realize, Denver had ruined me for life.

After a restless night not sleeping, I arrived in the hotel ballroom early and with all my lists to set up for True Blessings. My daughters were out of school for the day to help and my sister Louise had flown in that morning from Washington, D.C. Months before when I told her about True Blessings, Louise couldn't wait to book her ticket. I wonder now if she sensed something big was going to come of it even before I did.

There were dozens of volunteers assembling centerpieces and putting out programs when Dale entered the vast ballroom. Full of excitement for the day, he headed straight for me and I resisted the urge to hide under a table. What if Denver said something on stage today about the UMC *doing good only in the day and locking them out to the bad at night*? I really needed to have a serious discussion with Dale about what this all meant—this charge from Denver to do more. Dale was the one who actually needed to do something about this bed problem—that was his job.

With True Blessings only one hour away, there just wasn't time for a full discussion, so I started to give Dale a small warning about what might happen today.

"Dale, I took Denver on a tour of the UMC yesterday..." I began.

"Really? That's great, what did he think?" Dale looked eager to receive the same affirmation of purpose that I had been expecting when I took Denver on that fateful tour.

"Well, that's the thing. He really wasn't impressed. He thought we should be doing more," I hesitated as Dale's face fell. "He told me we should build some beds and talked about locking them out to the bad at night..."

I was skipping too many of the details, unable to convey the intensity the encounter. My words were not nearly as compelling as Denver's *call* had felt. How could I express how what I thought I knew about helping homelessness had been transformed in the past eighteen hours? Denver's message was clear. I knew what he was saying and now fully believed that we should do more. I just needed someone else to listen. I needed *Dale* to listen to Denver.

As I floundered to find the right words, Dale tried to track my point, "Beds? Do you mean housing?" He was trying to connect the dots. "But that's not what we do, Kathy. Remember our board discussion last month? We developed a strategic plan and we did not add *housing*."

"But maybe we should? If you had heard him yesterday, Denver was so ..."

We were interrupted by a volunteer's question, and I never really tried to follow up. I didn't know how to re-create the scene from yesterday. It had been so incredibly profound, life-changing really. *Transformational*. Words failed and I simply couldn't do it justice.

I allowed Dale's logic to sway me in the moment. Dale did have a point. There was a very rational and strategic plan for the Urban Ministry Center, which I helped draft through several board meetings.

Housing was not on it—anywhere. Building beds was simply not in our mission statement.

Dale and I would need to talk later because hundreds of guests were beginning to fill the room. My only concern now was if Denver, who was supposed to inspire the crowd to give to the UMC, instead told a thousand people we weren't actually doing a very good job.

Ron Hall spoke first and entertained the crowd with stories of his unlikely friendship with Denver. He was an engaging speaker and masterful storyteller. You could tell he was just as comfortable in front of hundreds as he would be entertaining a friend in his living room. His stories were captivating the crowd, but I couldn't pay attention, worrying about what Denver might say next.

Would Denver be the wise man from the book or the silent judge from our tour of the Urban Ministry Center?

As Ron finished, Denver mounted the stage with all the fervor of a Southern Baptist preacher. Once more, he was dressed in his signature black outfit, including his hat. To me, he looked like a dark, impending storm cloud. I closed my eyes, expecting the worst, but

Denver reached the microphone and began a gentle rain of inspiration.

Denver was his best self, stepping off the pages and bringing to life quotes from their book and gospel songs. His voice began softly and built to a crescendo that was part prayer and part song. Although the room was filled with people from all faiths and no faith, no one seemed to be squirming at his evangelical tone. It wasn't forced; Denver was an authentic presence who felt larger than life. The crowd had gone reverently silent. Lunch was forgotten as we all were now in Denver's church and he was delivering a sermon.

His preaching peaked when he bellowed, "Charlotte, y'all need to do more! Y'all need to build some beds!"

I'm glad I couldn't see Dale's face in that moment. Some in the crowd seemed a little confused. Beds? Had Denver just said *build beds*? The many UMC volunteers in the room knew we didn't have a single bed. Those who were hearing about the UMC for the first time, however, seemed to take it in stride, not understanding this would be an incredible mission shift.

A longtime donor, Dave Campbell, seated next to Dale, leaned over and asked, perplexed, "Are you launching a capital campaign?"

Dale whispered back truthfully, "I have no idea what he is talking about."

Denver continued preaching, even though our event timekeeper was frantically signaling that his time was up. Denver dismissed her saying, "I see you but I's got more to say!"

It didn't seem to matter that Denver ran on a little long because when the one thousand guests did leave, they were buzzing about what felt more like a tent revival than fund-raising lunch. It didn't take long to realize everyone gave with such generosity that the spirit must have moved the audience as well.

A small group of us led by Angela gathered in the next room that we had set up as "the bank" to open piles of pledge envelopes. We gasped as we pulled out checks for $500, $1000 and even one pledge card promising $50,000.

Angela showed me a check she was holding, and we both teared up.

It was one of the largest we received, and it was signed by Charlie.

I was stunned. In all the planning I'd forgotten to discuss what our personal pledge would be. Charlie and I had never given a gift like that to any charity. It was beyond generous and given our four girls and mounting tuitions, it was a little crazy.

Picking up the phone to call him, I could hear him smiling on the other end. Although he hated receiving surprises, Charlie excelled at giving them. "I was proud of you," he said simply.

Everyone involved with planning True Blessings was realizing our gamble had paid off. Our free lunch had just raised over $350,000 in one hour.

It was astounding. In the thirteen-year history of the organization, UMC had never even held an event and never received pledges of this magnitude. Nonprofits all over Charlotte regularly held fundraisers for the arts or children's causes but not to help homeless people. What exactly had Ron or Denver said to inspire so many? In all my nervousness, the last two hours were foggy and I couldn't remember a word that had been said.

But like everyone there, I had felt it.

I had thought after True Blessings was over and the months of planning complete, I would feel a sense of relief and enormous accomplishment. But exactly the opposite was true. At 9 p.m. that night, I was restless.

More restless than I had ever been in my entire life.

True Blessings had been over for eight hours but Denver had "charged" me the afternoon before. I had not mentioned that conversation except to Dale, mostly because it felt crazy. Why was I continuing to hear the words of a formerly homeless man from Texas tell me that I should become personally in charge of housing for the homeless in Charlotte?

It sounded as unlikely as building an ark and I definitely wasn't Noah.

With all the stress of planning the past few months, maybe I was having some kind of breakdown. Maybe this constant voice I was hearing was the start of something I had feared for most of my life— voices like my mom used to hear.

Maybe none of it was real. Maybe I had imagined Denver's conversation yesterday.

I hadn't told anyone what had happened, but it was time to confess.

Charlie, Louise, and I were in our den recounting True Blessing's highlights. While we had discussed almost everything about the past two days, marveling at the financial success, I still hadn't mentioned my personal epiphany with Denver. I didn't want either my husband or my sister to tell me I was delusional.

If one of them could understand the prophetic conversation with Denver, I thought it would be Louise—the family minister. At age thirty-two, Louise had shocked us all with the revelation that she was going into the ministry and was accepted to Harvard Divinity School. My father was beside himself with pride.

At the time, I truly didn't get it.

Seminary? Louise?

She had been down several career paths, yet I had not seen God in any of them. But Louise said unabashedly that she felt called and was certain of this next move. She graduated from Harvard and had served in congregations in New York and, now, Washington, D.C.

Charlie was more like me, agnostic. I imagined his reaction would be one of rational cynicism. Without saying it aloud, I already agreed with him. It felt ridiculous to believe that Denver, so full of faith, had come to life from the pages of a book to speak to me— someone of no faith.

What would Charlie say if I admitted that I thought the actual meaning of the past few months and this entire True Blessings event had been so I could meet Denver? That the nagging voice to bring the two authors here had actually been meant to be so that Denver could give me a personal message to quit my job and house homeless people?

It was nutty.

And because of my family history of mental illness, it felt mildly dangerous to believe it had actually happened.

I felt the conversation would go better if Louise, the minister, was in the room to back me up. She had felt a call once, so she might be able to verify this call from Denver or dispel it.

Hesitantly, I began telling them the story of how I had taken Denver on a tour that didn't go as planned. I finished with Denver's insistence that I "build beds."

They were both silent.

Louise spoke first. "So you feel Denver had a message for you?"

No judgment exactly, more of a question of surprise. She knew me well enough to know I was not one to talk about faith, spirituality, or religion. That was her department.

Listening to her say that aloud, I couldn't answer her question. Hearing Louise voice it, I knew it was insane. I would forget Denver ever said anything. I would forget I had ever heard anything.

Charlie and I went up to bed, and we were brushing our teeth, standing side by side at the double sinks, looking at each other's reflection in the mirror.

He is seriously worried. He thinks I am crazy.

Silently, we each finished and held each other's gaze in the mirror. Charlie broke the tension.

"You know the funny thing? I'm not sure Louise got it," he paused. "But I did."

I wanted to cry with relief. I could breathe.

The one person who mattered most didn't think I was crazy.

Looking back, I realize Charlie, the agnostic, was the first believer. For whatever reason, he could tell this was not a random thought or an unwanted voice in my head. He clearly seemed *not* to be questioning my sanity.

That night, if Charlie had called me foolish or made one of his excellent rational arguments, I am sure I would have dropped the whole idea. At that moment, the dream of doing something was too fragile. Honestly, I really wanted someone I trusted to talk me out of it.

All it would have taken was a little loud logic to silence that brief whisper of purpose.

Instead, Charlie remembered our evening only a week before at the Outward Bound fund-raiser and asked the perfect question, "So is *this* going to be your forty-year thing?"

It took forever to fall asleep that night as I played out scenes in my head.

Was I really going to quit my job to try to work on homelessness?

Was I finally going to stop being Graphics Girl?

Did I have a choice?

I couldn't shake Denver and his questions, not that day, not that night, not the next, not ever. His words did more than make sense. They began to sketch a road map for a forty-four-year-old life that had lost direction. I had no idea why Denver had asked me instead of Dale or anyone else at the UMC, *"What are you going to do about it?"*

But it was beginning to feel like everything in my life had been lining up so I would understand Denver's message intuitively in that moment and be willing to answer *Yes.*

Now I could not help but see that locking people out to the bad at night was even crazier than a graphic designer thinking she could do something about it.

The next morning I picked up Ron and Denver to take them to the airport. Ron was thrilled about the total amount of money raised—one of the largest fund-raising events outside their home state of Texas.

As excited as I was about all the money True Blessings had raised, my mind was on something much bigger. I wasn't sure Denver remembered that I was the one he "took for a ride." He had met so many of us in Charlotte that I was fairly confident he still had me confused with another white woman. As far as I knew, Ron had no idea Denver had "charged" me to do something about building beds two days before.

As they got out of my minivan with their suitcases, I took a chance, pulling Denver aside before he walked into the terminal. I had to talk to Denver once more before he left. I needed to know if our conversation was real or imagined. My heart was pounding.

"Denver, can I ask you something?"

He stopped and gave me another one of his intense, unnerving stares.

"If I do this," I asked, searching for the right words, "if I build the beds, can I name it after you?"

Denver looked back at me with clear understanding. He didn't ask *what beds?* He didn't hesitate and or ask what I meant.

Denver knew exactly what I was talking about.

"I would like that," he said.

Denver then paused to consider before adding, "But you better hurry because I'm old."

12

Home Tour

I do not understand the mystery of Grace.
Only that it doesn't leave us where it
found us and never lets us go.

ANNE LAMOTT

DRIVING HOME FROM THE AIRPORT, MY MENTAL WHEELS WERE
spinning. I had just promised Denver not only to *do* something about
the beds, I also pledged to name the place after him. I was getting in
deep, and I didn't really even know what I was promising. What exactly
was I agreeing to build? Bunk beds? Dormitories? Houses? I couldn't
even picture what it was I was now supposed to begin working on.

My sister Louise was not fazed by these questions and she certainly was not bothered by the fact that in my mid-forties I was
contemplating completely changing my life. The night before when
I was confessing my strange experience with Denver, Louise's silence
wasn't signifying she doubted what I was feeling. She was remembering her own out-of-body experience years before that had sharply
changed her path.

At thirty, Louise had already established her career as a teacher
and modern dancer in Chicago when she began to question her own
life. She found herself looking for answers in a Unitarian church
very different from our family's Presbyterian roots but at the same

time immensely comforting. It was as if she had been on a long trip and finally come home. The sense of peace from the hymns and the thoughtfulness of the sermon left Louise fighting back tears, knowing this place had something to do with filling her emptiness.

One day the minister's message seemed explicitly written for her:

You can sit in the pews or read the bible all you want but if you aren't doing anything with your faith, what are you really doing?

She knew the whisper she had been hearing over and over in her head that she tried to ignore was telling her the one thing she needed to hear: *You are going to be a minister.*

It had been more than a little inconvenient to listen. She had to completely disrupt the life she had planned but was fully on a new course she never anticipated. Now Louise was not only an ordained minister but also had been involved for years in community organizing in D.C. and New York. Through many social justice projects, Louise had become familiar with housing options and organizations. While I still wasn't sure if I had promised Denver bunk beds or buildings, Louise started telling me about national housing leaders I could contact for information.

It seemed laughable, really. I couldn't even believe we were talking about this. My expertise was typefaces, magazine ads, and brochures. Housing and homelessness were subjects I didn't even understand well enough to know the questions I needed to find answers for.

Louise knew where to start. "You should call Roseanne Haggerty with Common Ground in New York."

Haggerty grew up outside Hartford and was only seventeen when her father died, leaving her to help her mother take care of her seven younger siblings. In the 1980s, Roseanne Haggerty went to New York after graduating from Amherst College, and she volunteered at Covenant House—a homeless teens' charity—on 43rd Street in Times Square. Each time she walked there, she would pass the homeless sleeping in doorways on the same block where a multistory building, the Times Square Hotel, stood vacant. It made no sense to her that this available shelter was going unused, while on the same block, people were homeless. Roseanne kept thinking *someone* should be able to put the two together.

One day, she realized that *someone* might just be her.

Roseanne launched Common Ground in 1990, and her organization became a leader in a program called permanent supportive housing that combined the support services of counselors directly with housing units. It was at the forefront of a growing movement known as "Housing First." The idea was that in order to end homelessness, organizations needed to shift the way people thought about helping.

Instead of expecting homeless people to "earn" their housing by becoming sober, Housing First philosophy advocated for moving a homeless person directly off the streets into an apartment and then providing them with the counseling, medication, and addiction treatment they might need to succeed. By having counselors work in these same housing complexes where formerly homeless tenants lived, services were easily accessible and success more likely.

Research showed this new approach was a game-changer for ending homelessness. Men and women who had been homeless for years and thought to be unreachable had dramatic improvements once they had consistent sleep, food, and medicine.

Roseanne was an early pioneer when she convinced city, state, and federal funders to use low-income tax credits to finance the purchase and renovation of the Times Square Hotel—that same empty building she had passed so often. With her vision, the Times Square reopened in 1993, transformed into a state-of-the-art apartment building with 652 homes for homeless and low-income residents. It had on-site counseling services to help residents turn their lives around—but it also had a garden roof deck, a computer lab, a library, and an art studio. These amenities weren't luxuries; they were all part of a therapeutic and holistic approach to restoring someone's health and dignity after years on the streets.

Homeless residents moved in directly from streets to home and case managers worked with the new tenants on mental health treatment, addictions, and disability payments. All tenants paid 30 percent of any income as rent, cooked for themselves, and abided by a code of conduct. Residents could be evicted, but Common Ground understood the fact there was literally nowhere else to go. Second, third, and fourth chances were available to try to prevent someone from returning to the streets where they would most likely die.

Above all, Roseanne and Common Ground believed in the right of every human being to have the dignity of housing restored.

By 2007, when I was learning about Roseanne from Louise, Common Ground had already opened several more buildings, including another renovated hotel called The Prince George. Now considered a worldwide expert on permanent supportive housing, Roseanne and others were spreading the Housing First philosophy to cities across the country—it just hadn't made its way to Charlotte, yet.

When I finished reading every online article I could find, I was amazed. I couldn't believe a proven solution existed. To my knowledge, we didn't have any abandoned hotels in Charlotte, but there had to be a way to make this idea work. I started dreaming not about magical beds but Common Ground buildings. If I could just tour one of their buildings to see how it worked, it seemed possible to believe we could actually build one in Charlotte.

Three weeks later, I was standing in front of Common Ground's property, The Prince George, on 27th between Madison and 5th Avenue in Manhattan. Every December, Charlie and I went to New York for an annual meeting with his company. Normally, I was happy to holiday shop for the girls while he was in meetings. For this year's visit, however, I planned to skip Christmas shopping and tour a building instead.

The week before when I had dialed Common Ground, I felt as much an imposter as when I had emailed Ron Hall asking if he could speak at an event that hadn't yet been planned. No one from UMC had any idea I was asking for a tour of a permanent supportive housing program—least of all Dale. I had no authority to be exploring housing options for Charlotte, just a growing sense of obligation to keep my promise to Denver. Over the phone, the Common Ground staff person knew none of this so she took my request seriously, promising an in-depth tour.

It was early December as I headed for The Prince George for my tour. Honestly, I couldn't have been more excited if I was heading to a Broadway show. What they had accomplished was better than a Christmas miracle—housing thousands of the hardest to help in only a decade. They were *doing* something and it was motivating.

When I finally reached East 27th Street, I hesitated in front of the doorway marked 15 and triple-checked the address. It certainly did not look like a place for formerly homeless people. There was no outside evidence to suggest this building was any different from a standard apartment complex. Stepping inside was an even bigger surprise—it looked like a cross between a bank lobby and a hotel. Dark wood paneling provided the background to soft sofas on my right, with turnstiles straight ahead. It all looked too clean, too *normal* to fit my stereotyped vision of what might be homeless housing.

Beginning in the lobby, a Common Ground staff member took me through the multistory building, including individual apartments. We went up the elevator and knocked on an apartment door.

An African American man with light brown skin and glasses opened the door and smiled warmly at us.

"Frank, this is Kathy. She is here from North Carolina," the staff person told him. "Do you mind showing her your apartment?"

"Of course," Frank said, extending his hand. "Welcome!"

Stepping inside the small home, I saw an efficiency apartment with a galley kitchen, bedroom, and cozy living area with the TV turned to the local news. On Frank's walls were typical New York memorabilia: A Giants poster featuring Plaxico Burress, a Mets pennant flag, a Knicks team poster. I don't know what I had been expecting but it was all so *normal*.

"You like sports?" I asked, attempting conversation as I took it all in.

He nodded. "Knicks are my favorite. Used to sleep outside the Garden so I could watch them go in and out. But now I watch every game on my TV." He pointed proudly to the small set.

"How long were you homeless?" I asked, not sure if it was okay to discuss his former life.

Frank didn't mind. "About eight years. These people, this place, saved my life."

It was a story that was repeated over the next hour as we walked through The Prince George. Not only were there individual apartments, there was a computer lab, art studio, and music rooms.

"You'd be surprised how many talented people we have moving in off the streets," my tour guide said as we passed a music practice room with sounds of a saxophone coming through the door.

On each floor, we passed social workers' offices. Tenants could be seen talking comfortably with counselors, and often it wasn't obvious who was a staff member and who was a resident. In fact, throughout the entire building I didn't see anyone who looked obviously (formerly) homeless.

Up the hall, a clean-shaven man in a striped shirt, jacket, and blue jeans was leaving his apartment. He carefully locked his door behind him and nodded cordially as he passed us on the way to the elevator. I stared at him as he passed us. The clean building, the *average*-looking tenants, I could have been in my New York hotel, not a Common Ground building.

The realization hit me hard: once homeless people are housed, *they are just people.*

"Homeless" is an adjective that defines an extreme situation, not a description that defines a human being's character.

Common Ground had perfected the way to change that circumstance and eliminate that stigmatizing adjective. The Prince George didn't just suggest a different way of looking at this population, it demanded it.

I was still trying to understand all the terminology. My guide had talked about this building serving *chronically* homeless, but I still wasn't sure what that meant.

"You have told me chronically homeless have disabling conditions. What exactly does that mean?" I asked.

"It can be anything from mental illness like schizophrenia or bipolar; physical issues like amputations, HIV, and diabetes. It can also mean substance abuse issues with alcohol or drugs. That's what makes the *chronically* homeless different from someone who might be *situationally* homeless because they lost a job. That person can get a job and get off the streets. But someone with a really serious untreated mental illness plus addictions is not employable until they get real help. With those kinds of limitations it's impossible to navigate the system and get off the streets."

My guide had told me everyone pays rent but I wasn't sure how that was possible. "You say these chronically homeless who live here now pay 30 percent of their income for rent, but if they are mentally ill or disabled, how do they have income?"

"Exactly, that has been the problem," she nodded. "Because of their physical and mental impairments, each tenant is eligible for disability income from the federal government, but most have never been able to complete the paperwork without the help of a case manager when they moved in. That's why Housing First works. To get off the streets, chronically homeless need a lot of help, but that can best be done when they are not starving and sleep-deprived on the streets."

I thought about all the Neighbors I had served in Charlotte, the marks of homelessness consistent and easy to define: dirty layered clothing, matted hair, red, tired eyes. Serving soup I had become accustomed to this haggard appearance but never analyzed why. Seeing this group of formerly homeless so transformed the answer was obvious. Days, weeks, months, years on the streets with little sleep, sporadic access to showers, clean clothes, and healthcare all take a dramatic and visible human toll. Once people are housed, however, they are indistinguishable from everyone else.

Their weariness and their wounds move to the inside to heal.

It had been less than a month since Denver challenged me. My desire to keep my promise to him had been fading in those weeks. But seeing The Prince George and the tenant transformation reignited the belief. The solution was right in front of me and we didn't have to just *lock them out to the bad at night.*

Better still, I didn't have to invent a solution. Roseanne Haggerty had already done that. I just had to help bring it to Charlotte.

When I returned from visiting The Prince George in New York, I could not stop thinking about what I had seen.

How would we pay for it? Who would build it? How could we staff it?

Each night as I tried to sleep, those questions and the reasons not to do this kept me awake for hours.

I have no experience in housing.

I have no idea how to finance an apartment complex.

I own a graphic design business not a real estate development company.

I don't even work for the Urban Ministry Center.

The obvious answer was clear: **walk away**.

It was a big, impossible problem. It was not something I caused. But because of my promise to Denver, I now felt personally responsible for doing something about it.

As crazy as it felt, it was already feeling crazier not to try.

13

Million Dollar Larry

Miracles are a retelling in small
letters of the very same story
which is written across the whole
world in letters too large
for some of us to see.

C. S. LEWIS

IF I WAS REALLY GOING TO CLOSE MY GRAPHIC DESIGN BUSI-
ness to work on housing the homeless, I was going to need to convince Dale of two things: to add housing to the UMC mission
statement, and to hire me to do it.

As a board member and volunteer, I had worked with Dale
enough to know he listened to new ideas. Months before, he had
listened to my fledgling True Blessings plan. Hopefully, that success
also gave me some credibility for this second pitch about The Prince
George and my growing obsession to bring the Common Ground
model to Charlotte.

Unlike when I approached him for True Blessings with no real
plan, this time I would be armed with facts from my visit to New
York. I was ready to convince Dale that UMC *must* begin housing.

I was unaware he no longer needed convincing.

While I was learning about Housing First in the Prince George lobby, another man named Moore, unrelated to Denver, was powerfully influencing Dale in a Charlotte living room because of a newspaper article.

A few months before Ron and Denver came to town, the *Charlotte Observer* ran an editorial written by the UMC's assistant director, Liz Clasen-Kelly. While Dale's strength in leading the Urban Ministry Center came from his ministerial background, Liz's skill was with numbers and public policy. Liz was a wide-eyed student intern from Davidson College when she first stepped on to the UMC campus in 1997.

Raised in predominately white Kingsport, T.N., Liz remembers only one homeless man, "Mr. Jack." In her southern town, everyone lived with someone—except Mr. Jack. As he roamed their streets, the small town took care of him—meals, shelter on cold nights, spare change. That kind of generosity didn't happen in big cities where problems become anonymous, not personal like in Mr. Jack's case. As a result, when Liz first saw the overwhelming number of homeless people at the UMC, she was shocked. Along with never seeing this many people needing homes, Liz had never even seen dreadlocks. Her amazement over this hair phenomenon led a staff member to tell Liz, "You are the most naïve person to ever come here."

That changed as Liz's four-week summer internship evolved into a lifetime passion. Liz switched her intended major from math to religion in order to better understand all she witnessed at UMC. Later, she would pursue a master's degree in public policy from Duke University. Liz believed communities didn't just need to manage people's homelessness; they needed to change the policies that contributed to it in order to end it.

While I was newly introduced to Housing First, Liz had been studying it for over a year and had tried at least once to convince Dale that UMC needed to try it. His concerns were overwhelmingly financial. Pursuing housing would cost a lot more than running a soup kitchen and right now, the UMC was struggling some months to make the bread budget.

Liz was not going to give up. She had read a persuasive article in 2006 by Malcolm Gladwell called "Million Dollar Murray." Gladwell wrote that homelessness was an issue that was easier to solve than just manage. Gladwell personalized the fact by writing the true story of one homeless veteran living in Reno, N.V., named Murray Barr. In it, Gladwell argued:

> If you toted up all his hospital bills for the ten years that he had been on the streets—as well as substance-abuse-treatment costs, doctors' fees, and other expenses—Murray Barr probably ran up a medical bill as large as anyone in the state of Nevada. It cost us one million dollars **not** to do something about Murray.

That was what shocked Liz the most. Even after *a million dollars* spent on services like hospitals, drug treatment, even jail, Murray was *still* homeless. The system was not working for anyone, least of all the chronically homeless. The surprising fact Liz realized was this: *it is less expensive to house chronically homeless people than let them die on the streets.* That is how Liz decided to write her own op-ed piece for the *Observer* newspaper.

In her essay, Liz used the cost of a Charlotte jail cell ($110 per night), an ER visit ($1,029 average), and a hospital bed ($2,165 per night) to show a certain Charlotte homeless man had similar costs to Gladwell's Million Dollar Murray. In Charlotte, like other cities, the chronically homeless were only 10-20 percent of the homeless population but used more than 50 percent of the resources dedicated to the homeless. By housing people like Million Dollar Murray, the shelters would be freed up to serve the remaining 80 percent of the homeless population, who are more easily able to transition out of homelessness with much less intensive support.

The Charlotte man whose life and costs Liz traced to make her argument for our city was Chilly Willy, who I now knew was William Larry Major. Liz knew if the UMC could help Chilly Willy, we would really have changed the conversation about homelessness in Charlotte.

Liz's article and argument were powerful and started Dale thinking about the UMC's mission. *What if he could do more? What if they tried housing some people?*

Dale and Liz had explored some preliminary costs but it seemed too daunting. After the article ran, Dale got a call from John and Pat Moore, local activists and philanthropists, asking for a meeting in their home. Although John and Pat shared the same last name as Denver, there was no connection between the families.

"Liz's article made a lot of sense to me," John told Dale.

"It's a very commonsense argument when you think about it," Dale said.

"Someone should do something about it," John said.

"I absolutely agree," Dale said feeling a little uncomfortable and wondering where this conversation was going.

"So why aren't you?" John asked.

Dale probably looked over his shoulder like I did when Denver spoke to me.

"Me?" Dale said.

"Well, yes, you and the Urban Ministry Center. Isn't that what you do? Help the homeless?" John said. "Seems like this housing idea is the best help you could give them."

"Well, that's true but it would be an expensive undertaking. And besides, we are a soup kitchen, not a shelter," Dale countered. "We weren't really planning on getting into housing."

"Well yes, but if you *were* going to do something, what would you do?" John asked not giving up.

"Uhm, I'm not sure," Dale hedged. "I guess we'd start a pilot program?"

"How much would that cost?" John probed.

Boy, this guy isn't giving up, Dale thought and he took a wild guess that he hoped would throw John Moore off, "$200,000?"

John looked at his wife, Pat, and she nodded.

"All right," John said. "We'll fund it!"

Dale was speechless. No one donor had ever given that much money to the Urban Ministry Center, much less for a program that didn't even exist. With a full promise of funding, Dale had no excuse not to try this Housing First idea. Liz was ecstatic but Dale left the Moore's home unnerved.

It was an incredible opportunity, but Dale didn't really know where to start on this pilot program idea.

How was he going to keep his promise to the Moores?

Who would run it? What if it didn't work?

It was early December 2007, as I listened to Dale tell me this story about John and Pat. I had no idea that as I had been lying awake at night the past month thinking about The Prince George and my promise to Denver, Dale and Liz were already tying into this cause for different reasons. Now I realized half my problem was already solved. I had gone into Dale's office to convince him to start a program like Common Ground.

With the Moores' gift, Dale was already motivated to start just such a program, I now only needed to convince him to hire me. So I confessed to Dale my own story, reminding him about Denver telling me to build beds, and what I had witnessed at The Prince George.

As we sat together in his office, Dale and I realized we were in the exact same position only for different reasons. We each had made a promise to a man named Moore. Each man had charged us to do something more to house the homeless. One had given what felt like divine inspiration and one had provided the most divine gift: the money to accomplish it.

It was impossible to imagine how these two events had taken place independently and yet were intricately linked.

Improbable.

Incredible.

What were the odds?

Dale didn't dismiss it as coincidence. He readily assigned our little miracle to the Almighty.

"It's a God thing for sure," he laughed, shaking his head.

Dale might have learned to accept this sort of divine occurrence in seminary, but I couldn't go there. I could only admit it was a remarkable, astounding coincidence. Dale and my sister Louise seemed already certain I had received some sort of a divine call. That was unfathomable to me. Dale and Louise believed in "callings," not me. God whispered to people like them, not me.

"So we have two job openings right now," Dale informed me. "The first one is in the development office, maintaining relationships with donors and event planning. We have a lot of follow-up after True Blessings, and I think we should make this an annual event."

I nodded. True Blessings was certainly worth repeating, but I wasn't interested in taking up event planning as my profession. Maybe Dale wasn't willing to take a chance on me for something as important as the housing project. "And the other one?"

"Well, I need Liz to help run the Urban Ministry Center so that means I need someone to start this housing pilot program," he finished with a deadpan expression.

"I want that job," I said.

We both smiled.

The thought terrified me but in my bones there was nothing I wanted more. I needed Dale to be clear that where this job was concerned what I brought was passion but no actual experience.

"You know I am completely unqualified for this position, right?"

Dale didn't hesitate. "The good news for you is, neither is anyone else."

The rest of my holidays that December were spent winding down my graphic design business. As I called my clients to explain my job change, I was giddy. It was thrilling to finally feel unstuck. I felt that my life was in motion again. I was ecstatic to start doing something that truly *mattered*.

My mom had given me a "Thought for the Day" calendar in my Christmas stocking. Thumbing through it, I laughed out loud when I saw this one on Day 218:

> *Start some big, foolish project like Noah.*
> —Rumi

I tore out the one page, and taped it to my computer screen.

On January 11, 2008, I drove to the Urban Ministry Center for the first time not as a volunteer but as a paid part-time staff person. My official contract was twenty hours a week, but Dale and I both understood I would be working much more than that.

Finally, I was no longer Graphics Girl.

I didn't know who I was exactly or what I was going to do all day, but I was making a change. In my mind, I was clear that I was doing this not because of a calling but because I had finally found my purpose. At the time, that seemed like an important distinction.

Liz Clasen-Kelly greeted me on my first official morning with her ash-blonde hair pulled back in a low ponytail and no makeup. Liz was always 100 percent authentic. I cringed, realizing I was over-dressed. While I was perfectly attired for a boardroom in black pants, jacket, and low heels, Liz was dressed to actually help someone in a simple, approachable wardrobe of jeans, blouse, and her only fashion accessory—a dazzling smile.

"Can you believe it?" she gushed.

Liz was more excited than I was, and I felt even more nervous about all the expectations riding on this program. Since Dale had made a fairly unorthodox choice in hiring me, I didn't know how my colleagues, who actually had qualifications for their jobs, might react. I would quickly learn that with Liz, there was never any judgment.

Everything about Liz was welcoming. While I served soup to Neighbors and tried not to get involved in people's lives, Liz was the exact opposite, opening her office door and heart to whoever entered. Although hundreds of men and women came to the UMC each day, like Dale, Liz knew a remarkable number by name. More importantly, she readily earned their trust to learn their personal stories of how they had become homeless. Her small office on the first floor of the former train depot was constantly filled with Neighbors and the bags they carried—physical and emotional.

I looked at Liz with equal parts envy and terror. I had no idea how to handle all the tragedy here. Liz seemed to know how to listen to people's burdens without being buried by them. No wonder she could argue so passionately for housing. For Liz, it wasn't policy, it was personal. The hundreds of homeless at UMC were her extended family, and she ardently believed each brother and sister deserved a home.

On this my first day, Liz wholeheartedly welcomed me to the cause and invited me to a meeting that afternoon.

I was thrilled to have something to actually write in my Day-Timer.

"This guy from the bank called me. He read my article, too, and said he wanted to do something about homelessness," she explained.

Neither of us was sure what that meant, but we went late that afternoon to meet Bill Holt.

Bill's office was in one of three Wachovia bank buildings in downtown Charlotte. For years, Wachovia and Bank of America were euphemistically called Charlotte's rich uncles. If you needed something done in Charlotte, you asked for the help of one of the "uncles."

Casually dressed for a banker, Bill had his coat off and sleeves rolled up when we arrived. His assistant was there to take notes, and a large, blank white board was propped at the head of the conference table.

It was laughable that Bill, a bank executive, was presenting to Liz and me, and I had only been on the job six hours. Bill was a senior vice president used to making much bigger pitches but he seemed nervous about this one. When he started talking, however, he grinned broadly and bounced on his feet with enthusiasm. If this were a movie, I thought, William Hurt with no facial hair would play Bill.

"I have been reading Liz's articles," he began. "We just *have* to do something about this homelessness mess."

While he was pitching, Bill began drawing a giant square on the white board. "I think I have an idea."

Now he drew circles indicating people in his square. "I think we should build apartments for these homeless people and then, here's the thing," he continued, adding a square within his square and tapping excitedly on the inner square as he spoke. "We put the social workers and the other people that can help the homeless *in the building with them.*"

He finished with an excited flourish and an expectant look on his face. "What do you think?"

Liz and I looked at each other, stunned.

How could this random banker we had never met be dreaming about housing the homeless at the exact moment we were poised to start?

"Bill, that is called permanent supportive housing, and I started *this morning* to do just that," I told him.

He broke out into his huge boyish grin.

As he continued, we realized he was also dreaming much bigger than the pilot project we were planning on starting. With the Moores' generous funding, Liz, Dale, and I were still trying to figure out how we would implement a test program for a few people.

Bill wanted to build a brand-new apartment complex—now.

Being a banker, he was already projecting the revenue streams and capital campaign to make it happen. Bill finished the presentation with one final revelation.

"I think we can get each of the banks to kick in $3 million."

That was ridiculous.

Dale, Liz, and I were passionate about housing but Bill was obviously a little delusional. John and Pat Moore's $200,000 was the biggest single gift in UMC history. We had not even launched the pilot project and Bill was thinking of buildings and capital campaigns?

*He expected a bank, no **two** banks, to give $3 million—**each**—to help homeless people?*

As we left, we promised Bill he was on the team—whatever that meant. In the elevator on the way down, Liz and I looked at each other and laughed. *"What was that?"*

As the elevator doors opened, Denver's words came back to me.

The people who are going to help you, they already know they are coming.

14

Wing and a Prayer

If I look at the mass I will never act.
If I look at the one, I will.

MOTHER TERESA

THE NEXT DAY, I WENT TO WORK WITH THE MEMORY OF BILL and his multimillion-dollar plan on my mind. An apartment complex was at least two years away. I couldn't begin to think about raising money for a building yet; we still had to figure out how to test this idea in Charlotte. At the entrance to my new office, a vinyl plaque on my door announced our new program title:

Homeless to Homes
Kathy Izard

It was official—I really had signed up to do this. I had a desk, a chair, a computer, a window, and no idea where to start.

That first month of work, I spent digging through research and trying to understand the landscape of homelessness in Charlotte. To my surprise, there were almost thirty agencies in the city involved in some aspect of helping those in crisis. But just like the issue of education, homelessness is a large topic with complex problems and solutions.

I finally understood the difference among the homeless. *Situational Homeless* meant a person or family who was in temporary crisis from a lost job or a sudden hospitalization. These families were the easiest to assist because they just needed a little help with rent to get back on their feet and into an apartment. If this happened more than once to a family, they were considered part of the *Episodic Homeless*. In this case, one or both of the parents most likely had an issue such as mental health or addiction, and assigning a caseworker might keep the family out of constant crisis, preventing future homelessness.

Our program would target the *Chronic Homeless*. These were street homeless with layers of issues, mental and physical, resulting in addiction and disability. There were few families in this group. Usually chronically homeless referred to individual men and women who most likely had been estranged from their families and had nowhere to go. They were by definition the hardest to help and the most likely to die on streets. I was shocked to learn that the previous year thirty-seven homeless people had died in Charlotte. That was a number equal to the murder rate of some cities.

How did this happen? It was difficult to understand how someone could stay on the streets for years. In that first month, I took a class on understanding poverty to try to connect how a person who has become homeless thinks and feels.

"Okay, imagine a time when there was an ice storm or power outage," the instructor said. "You have no power, no hot water in your house, and no way to cook any food. The refrigerator doesn't work and you can't use your computer or charge your phone."

That wasn't too hard to imagine. When Lauren was nine months old, Hurricane Hugo hit Charlotte and we had no power for ten days. It was miserable. I had to take her to the YMCA for baths and every meal was an ordeal.

"Now imagine this has gone on for a week or more," the instructor said. "You can't sleep at night because it is so cold in your house and you spend all day trying to figure out where your next meal is coming from or even how to do something as simple as make a phone call."

The class nodded in agreement, many recalling their own Hugo stories.

"It's rough, right? All the things you take for granted like eating, sleeping, just staying in touch become the focus of your day. You spent all your energy on just getting those things done, plus you were exhausted from not sleeping and clearly not thinking well, right?"

He paused as we all nodded, remembering similar experiences.

"So what would have happened if during that time someone would have tried to talk with you about your IRA account?"

"I would have hung up on them if I had a phone!" a man said.

The class laughed. "Right!" the instructor said. "How could you possibly listen to something about your long-term future when your immediate situation was so overwhelmingly bleak? You wouldn't have cared what happened in the future, only this moment, right? You could only care about the next twenty-four hours."

We all agreed.

"*That* is what homelessness is like," he said. "Except for many people it lasts years not days or weeks. And no one on the streets wants to talk about getting their high school degree that will get them a job some day. All they need is something *right now*. Not next year."

This understanding was a revelation for me.

A homeless person will never tell you what they need is a treatment program, a class, or a life strategy.

All homeless people need one thing right now: a home.

That is the only thing that will solve their immediate, overwhelming, all-consuming crisis.

Our Homeless to Homes program would be the first time any agency in Charlotte attempted to offer the chronically homeless the one thing they truly needed right now—a home.

Dale and I met to strategize. Based on best practices in other cities we knew one social worker could effectively work with fifteen people. From the hundreds of Neighbors, we would choose fifteen men and women, move them into existing apartments, and have one full-time case manager like at The Prince George to work with tenants.

Dale and I discussed doing this test pilot program for two years, and then we would have the data to show other potential funders the idea worked. That meant I had two years before I needed to worry about Bill, his $6 million plan, and building all those beds I promised Denver.

"First we need to hire that case manager," Dale said. "And then I am sure we can find some empty apartments to rent."

Both turned out to be much harder than we thought.

Out of dozens of candidates for the social work position, Joann Markley was the only one who seemed to understand that this job would be 24/7—with no road map.

When I asked one applicant what he would do in a middle-of-the-night emergency with one of the pilot program residents, he looked confused. "Call 911?"

By contrast, in her interview, Joann said without hesitation, "I'd get out of bed and go help them."

We hired her on the spot. Joann had worked for the county social services for years and was intrigued to help develop a new program. From the interview process, it was clear Joann was fearless and as we started on the next task of finding apartments for our potential tenants, I needed her courage.

Like any city, there were neighborhoods in Charlotte we could afford and those we couldn't. Inevitably the neighborhoods where we could potentially afford to rent had obvious signs of gangs or drug deals occurring on the corners. Neither bothered Joann. Where I saw danger, Joann saw opportunity.

As we roamed neighborhoods for vacancies, she would fearlessly march up to rental offices as I locked the doors waiting for her in my car. I was beginning to see that driving to the Urban Ministry Center campus was as far out of my comfort zone as I had ever gone. Not only had I hid behind the counter when I was there, I hid in my own neighborhood once I left. Charlotte had more than seventy-four zip codes, but until that month with Joann, I had probably been in only ten of them. Beyond my insular world was an extended city I had lived next to for almost twenty years but knew nothing about.

"Don't you get scared?" I asked Joann.

"At first. But you learn not to be. Sure there are bad people, but there are a lot more good people than bad," she said. "Mostly you realize being poor isn't the same as being violent. It's just TV that makes us think that. Poverty might cause someone to do something desperate but they didn't start out that way."

In those first few months of learning on the job, my best teacher was Joann. As we toured neighborhoods we discussed the program, how she would work with tenants, and what we hoped would be the outcomes.

Together, we drove through neighborhoods I never knew existed, looking for vacancies that met our unique requirements of low rent, low utilities, and a kindhearted landlord willing to take a chance on *formerly* homeless people. We were slowly realizing that combination was impossible to find in Charlotte.

I came home from one of these frustrating rental searches to a voice mail from Lynn Pearce Tate, who used to live across the street from us. Her message said she had heard what I was doing with Homeless to Homes and wanted to get together for a prayer session.

I listened to her voice mail and deleted it.

A *prayer session*? Not likely. I had always felt uncomfortable when people said they were praying for me.

Religion was something in my adult life I had actively chosen to avoid. Those forced Sunday mornings and unanswered prayers of my childhood were not something I wanted to revisit. It was nice of her to want to help, but prayers were not what I needed. I needed apartments.

But like Denver's words, I kept hearing Lynn's voice mail in my head. Worse, I felt guilty for not returning the call. In an effort to clear my conscience, I finally called her back, agreeing to meet. I arrived early one morning after taking the twins to school, having told no one about this meeting.

Lynn is chatty, perky, and has chin-length dark brown hair. She led me into her living room as if we were about to start book club.

"So how is Homeless to Homes going?" she asked.

I started to say "Fine," but the honest answer slipped out. "Over-whelming."

It felt good to admit the truth. It had only been a few months but I was beginning to fully realize the magnitude of this assignment. I had been so excited to start this new job but honestly, it had not been what I thought. It was hard, much harder than I had planned on, and we had not yet helped a single person.

Lynn nodded as if maybe she already knew this.

"I have found I have a gift of prayer," she said with no hesitation or discomfort. "I kept thinking about you and what you were trying to do and just thought I'd call to see if I could help."

Her words "gift of prayer" made me shift uncomfortably on the sofa. Lynn seemed confident about this gift, and I couldn't under-stand how or why she knew she had a direct line to God.

"So we'll just start by holding hands," she said calmly and reached over to hold my hands in hers. Lynn then closed her eyes and began praying out loud.

Our hands were loosely connected but I couldn't close my eyes. I was trying to get comfortable with this whole thing. Lynn and I had known each other for years but not like this. Our prayer meeting was definitely a different dimension in our friendship. For a minute or two, I wasn't really listening, just studying the calmness in her face as she spoke aloud. Giving in to the moment, I finally closed my eyes and tried to be as serene as Lynn.

By the time I was really hearing her words, she was finishing. "God, help Kathy find strength and wisdom for her work. Amen."

That was it. Just minutes and it was over.

The funny thing was, it seemed my anxiety was over as well. I felt enormously relieved. I had worried this prayer get-together would feel cultish but truly it just felt calming—like the end of a great yoga class. There was nothing scary about it and honestly, it seemed I needed all the help I could get on Homeless to Homes. I had to admit there was no way it could hurt, so I might as well let Lynn and her prayers try to help.

Several times that spring we got together yet I never told a soul. Not even Charlie. I was afraid he'd laugh at me for believing that a prayer was going to help me do this impossible job.

Really, I didn't understand what was happening to me or why I kept returning to Lynn's condo when clearly I didn't believe in the God she was praying to. But I loved that feeling it gave me. It was like my private confessional booth where I could truthfully admit things weren't going well. I could say this job switch was not what I had bargained for, and Lynn would nod in understanding and she would confidently pray for me.

It helped to me lessen my grip on pathological self-reliance just a little and begin to believe maybe, just maybe, I wasn't in this alone.

<hr>

It was mid-April, and I had spent weeks working with a landlord to finalize a deal. Joann and I had finally found some apartments and they were perfect, a small cluster of one-story one bedrooms in a quiet neighborhood with huge oak trees out front. We would be able to house up to twelve tenants in the same complex. I was thrilled, already envisioning the tenants gathering on the lawn or having barbecues outside their new homes. It had been three months since I started work, and *finally* we were going to be able to bring the first Neighbors off the streets.

Finally, we were actually going to *do* something.

Right before we signed a lease, however, I'd asked a lawyer friend to run a check on our new landlord, and he came back with terrible news: the apartments were in foreclosure. The guy I had been dealing with was running a scam, trying to finagle a huge check for rent on four apartments before the bank took his property.

I was crushed—months of work and we were back at the starting line. It was all feeling like a giant dead end. Worse, it felt like a huge failure. I was never getting this pilot program going, which meant I had no shot at building something like Common Ground's Prince George program.

That week, I went to my prayer session with Lynn, demoralized and unsure of my next move. She listened, and then held my hands.

This prayer I remember.

"God, please help Kathy know that every time you close a door, you open a window."

I left feeling agitated. I didn't need prayers, I needed apartments.

Later that week, I was meeting with another friend I used to work with at my first ad agency job. It had been at least a year since we had talked and I was surprised when she called. After catching up on ad agency gossip, I mentioned the difficulties in getting the program off the ground.

Unexpectedly, she offered, "There is a guy at my church who has a foundation, and I think he may have a heart for this type of program. You should call him."

She thought he might help with buying furnishings if we ever found apartments and wrote his name on a scrap piece of paper: Mike Boyd.

Since I was much more focused on actual apartments than furniture, it took me a couple of days to unearth the paper and call. On Monday, April 28, 2008, Mike answered my call.

Not very practiced in asking for things, I rambled an unprepared explanation of how I got his number and a little about the program, Homeless to Homes.

"So are you looking for apartments or money?" he asked.

Startled, I sat up in my chair. "Well, both. Why?"

"Well, I thought that was why you were calling," he said. "I have apartments."

I could not believe what I was hearing. "And you would consider renting to us?"

"Sure, let's talk."

I met Mike the next day at his apartments, but at first look, I was not optimistic. On one hand, they looked like the perfect complex I had just lost, due to the landlord's foreclosure, with single-story buildings and a small grass courtyard. Most of the one-story units, however, had huge, plywood boards covering the doors and windows. It looked like Mike thought a hurricane was coming and was overly prepared for a storm. Over the past few months, Joann and I had been to several boarded-up properties. In every case, behind the boards were rats, gang graffiti, and cockroaches.

Prying the boards loose, he apologized, "Sorry for the plywood. This is the only way I can protect the apartments from break-ins until tenants move in."

When we stepped inside, I wanted to cry.

The walls were freshly painted, carpets in pristine condition, modern appliances, and, most unbelievable compared to other apartments we had considered, they actually had heating and air conditioning. Not only were these ten times nicer than the foreclosed apartments I had agonized over losing, Mike was asking less in rent *and* he was eager to take a chance on us. It seemed he had a deep faith and helping people get back on their feet was something he felt called to do.

Leaving our newfound homes, I phoned Dale to tell him the good news about the ideal landlord who had just landed in our midst. Dale was thrilled but not surprised.

"God works like that," he laughed.

Did he? How could Dale be so confident? I remembered my dad and his confidence in prayer leading up to Maddie's heart surgery.

God might not send you exactly what you expect but he's always with you.

It felt like this time God or someone had sent exactly what I needed.

Homeless to Homes finally had homes.

15

Trash and Treasure

It often seems, looking back, that the
unexpected comes to define us,
the paths we didn't see coming and may
have wandered down by mistake.
The older we get the more willing we are
to follow those, to surprise ourselves.

Anna Quindlen

IT HAD TAKEN ALMOST FIVE MONTHS TO FIND THOSE HOMES, so with all that time to plan, I should have been more than ready. But on Saturday, May 17, 2008, Homeless to Homes inaugural move-in day, I was a wreck. It wasn't the truck, the boxes, or volunteers I was worried about, it was the four people we were moving in.

Four lives now on my watch.

Choosing those lives had been more difficult than I could have imagined. After working at the UMC every day, the Neighbors were no longer just a sea of gray clothes and anonymous faces. Now, along with Chilly Willy, I knew many of the Neighbors' names and a piece of their stories. Should we offer a home to Tyrone, who had been homeless since aging out of foster care three years ago? Or should we help Dianne, who was schizophrenic and had cycled in out of the shelter for the past three years? To accept these two might rule out a spot for Patrick with epilepsy, who always had his head bandaged from falls on the concrete sidewalks when he suffered seizures.

After weeks of agonizing debate, Chilly Willy was not offered one of the first four apartments, even though his story had been the central argument to this Housing First program getting started in Charlotte. Dale, Liz, and Joann agreed Chilly Willy was too unpredictable, and these first four tenants needed to prove that housing could work here just as it did in New York. In the end, we selected three men and one woman, each at risk of dying on the streets from health issues and each highly motivated to be housed.

Ruth would be the first woman we would bring home in Charlotte. Her story was compelling because she was over fifty years old and living on the streets with uncontrolled diabetes, severe neuropathy in both legs, and recently diagnosed gallstones. Standing barely five feet tall, Ruth's tiny figure had a large presence at the Center. She worked in the UMC job program cleaning and keeping order in the showers. Ruth usually reported for work in an oversized T-shirt and baggy jeans after spending the night under the Sixth Street highway overpass bridge. With little sleep and in chronic pain, Ruth was surly to Neighbors who lined up at the counter waiting patiently for their turn to take a shower. When she wasn't snapping orders, Ruth was slumped over the counter sleeping.

Joining Ruth that first move-in day was Raymond, who had been living in a barn; Samuel, who had spent seven years in the men's shelter; and Jay, who had completed a twenty-eight-day alcohol treatment program but was about to be released back onto the streets because he had nowhere else to go.

All four had been grateful but skeptical about being offered a place in this new program. They each desperately wanted to come off the streets, but I am not sure any of us understood exactly what we were offering them along with their house key. Joann would be their case manager, connecting them to services and working on medical, mental health, and substance issues. I would keep expanding the program, finding more apartments to match with tenants, and ultimately I was responsible for the success or failure of this idea. In two years, I needed to be able to say not only were these four still housed, they were an example of what we could do for hundreds more. *That* was overwhelming. It was impossible to distill that goal down to a single To Do item and check it off my list.

The logistics for move-in day were easier to organize than this long-term goal, and my yellow legal pad was filled with notes on getting everything accomplished: four apartments—four kitchens, bedrooms, and bathrooms to stock. Our new tenants owned little beyond clothing, so this move required buying everything from toilet paper to forks to clothes hangers. I had organized a registry at a Target store and friends bought bedding and bath and kitchen goods, fully stocking each new home.

I had drafted Charlie and my girls along with twenty volunteers from the United Way to serve as the move crew. The moving truck with dozens of donated furniture items and each of the new tenants were going to meet us at the apartments. That morning, I was frantically throwing things in my car I thought we'd need. Trash bags. Paper towels. Windex. Brooms. *Did we need shelf-lining paper? Would they care?*

Lauren watched me, shaking her head. "It's going to be fine, Mom, really!"

I pulled out of the driveway and Charlie was following behind in another car loaded with more boxes. I was going over a checklist in my head when Lauren reached into the glove compartment and pulled out a CD. She put it in the player and searched for the right song. When I recognized the first few bars, I turned to look at her, my mouth open in astonishment.

She smiled at me and turned it up. "Perfect, right?"

The lyrics to "Amazing," a Keb' Mo' song, started playing and Lauren and I sang along loudly. I had used this song to make a slide show for True Blessings. As the one thousand guests had entered the ballroom, it had been playing as background to photos of the UMC and all the amazing things that happen there. The soccer, the art, the gardening. All the things I had thought had been enough. More than enough. Now, today, there would finally be more. Four people would no longer be homeless. *That* was Amazing.

I teared up as Lauren and I belted out, together with Keb' Mo':

And I'm grateful for the simple things
That we take for granted every day

I was so grateful for this new path that had gotten me unstuck in my safe world. I had no idea what was ahead but I knew that today felt *Amazing*.

"Thanks, Lauren. I needed that."

"Of course!" She smiled.

No one could stop smiling all day, least of all me. As volunteers helped Raymond, Samuel, Ruth, and Jay move in, it was eye-opening how few possessions each owned and how they carried them to their new homes. No suitcases or boxes. Just green plastic garbage bags holding all they had in the world. Salvaged clothes and shoes, a few toiletries, maybe a wrinkled four-by-six photo. Each new tenant was over forty years old, yet from four decades of living, these few plastic bags were the only evidence of that life.

Ruth, Raymond, Samuel, and Jay moved through their new homes with disbelief. Mike's apartments were simple two-bedroom apartments with front doors opening onto a grass lawn. The new tenants kept coming in and out in astonishment.

"This is my *own* garden?" Raymond asked. "How about that! I am going to plant me some tomatoes!"

"Y'all come see *my* house," Ruth invited each volunteer.

"I can't believe I will be able to watch movies and not have to fight with all the other guys in the shelter." Samuel shook his head in wonder.

Watching Raymond talk about planting tomatoes and Ruth welcoming volunteers in her new home, it finally felt like we had **done** something. It was four people out of the hundreds who needed help, but it was a beginning.

After an all-day move in, I checked on each new resident before leaving. Joann would be on duty that night and through the weekend in case any problems arose.

At bedtime I was exhausted but I couldn't sleep. At first, the day's happy images scrolled in my head like a Disney movie with the Keb' Mo' soundtrack playing in the background.

Raymond marveling at his own bathtub.

Samuel opening and closing his refrigerator door.

Ruth testing the softness of her couch.

It really had been a remarkable day.

The happy scenes rewound in my head over and over as I tried to get comfortable in my own bed. I wondered how each of them was sleeping this first night in *their* own bed. The more I could not sleep, the more a sense of dread began pushing down on my chest.

What if right now there was a giant party going on at the apartments?

What if someone broke into Ruth's apartment tonight?

What if Raymond or Samuel, unfamiliar with using their new stoves, caused a fire?

How would I explain to Mike Boyd that we had burned down his complex?

How could I tell the Moores that this pilot program was a huge failure?

We had focused so much on getting the right apartments and the right people, I hadn't had time to think *what's next?* What if this didn't work? There was no road map for this program in Charlotte. Common Ground had started with a $40 million building and 24-hour security. That was very different than Joann and me monitoring four people who had significant challenges. Maybe Joann was confident in what to do but I certainly wasn't. It was like I had just adopted four new children into my life but I really didn't know anything about them. I wasn't brave enough to move them into my home like Ron had with Denver, but these four tenants were clearly in my life now. I was responsible for them. We had promised the Moores this would work. *I needed to make it work.*

My worries mounted all the next day, which happened to be a gloomy, rainy Sunday. It seemed to forewarn of disaster ahead. I checked my phone a hundred times, looking for a call from Joann in case something was wrong. No calls.

Monday morning, I arrived at the UMC early and full of dread. *Where was Joann?* I needed a full report on what had happened the past thirty-six hours but she wasn't in yet. I could see Ruth, however, in her usual place monitoring the shower counter. She waved at me.

That was a little weird. Ruth never waved at me. She was also smiling, wide-awake, and neatly dressed in a clean shirt with a necklace. *Necklace?* I had never seen Ruth with a fashion accessory.

Cautiously, I walked over to talk with her.

"Hey, Ruth!"

She gave me a huge, unprompted hug. "Kathy!"

"How were your first two nights?" I asked.

"Did you see how it rained yesterday?" she asked.

I nodded, not sure why that mattered.

"It rained yesterday and I didn't get *wet*!" Ruth marveled.

I wanted to laugh, not just at what Ruth said but also at myself. I had worried all weekend, thinking we hadn't done enough, couldn't do enough. And here was Ruth telling me the bar was only as high as staying dry. How could we fail if that's all we had to do? *Keep people dry at night.*

I found out there were no parties and no worries that first weekend. Raymond confided to me that he had taken multiple hour-long baths over the first two days in awe that he no longer had to stand in line or restrict his water usage like when he took showers at the UMC.

Looking at the photos from that move-in day, I framed one to keep on my desk. In it, all the move-in volunteers surround Ruth and her smile is electric. It was a constant reminder that whenever it rains, at least now, Ruth doesn't get wet. And Raymond gets wet by choice in his own bathtub.

I made a silent vow to myself that in two years, 2010, there would be a picture on my desk of dozens more smiling, dry Ruths and freshly showered Raymonds with places to call home.

The same month I helped move Ruth and her two garbage bags into her home, I moved dozens of garbage bags out of my mom's. We had a week to clean out our family house and move Mom into her new senior-living apartment. I had come early for the clean up, and my sisters would be joining for the actual move later in the week. Organizing and sorting were my strengths. When faced with the mounds of possessions stored during forty years in our home, I was sure I could be the most efficient in sorting trash from treasure.

When I had arrived the night before, it was easy to see Mom wasn't happy about this move she had agreed to months ago. She had promised to begin the process of cleaning out, but looking around the kitchen, it was clear that nothing had been done. Closets still full. Mail still stacked.

I sighed, looking at it all and wondering how we were going move and clean it all in the allotted week. Mom admitted, "I just didn't know where to start."

My mom loved this house and everything in it. It had stayed relatively unchanged since 1969, even the kitchen appliances, which were still avocado green, because over the years Mom found someone to custom paint when she need a new refrigerator or dishwasher.

One of the few things that had changed in our house was my room. Both Allyson's and Louise's bedrooms down the hall were basically untouched from the time they were thirteen. There were the same 1970s color schemes, with prom pictures and high school posters still taped to the walls. My room had been turned into Dad's office shortly after I was married. As a result, I stayed in one of my sisters' rooms when I came to visit Mom. It had always bothered me that my room was sacrificed for this purpose. Why not use Louise's room? She had been out of the house longer than I.

This visit, the last visit to my childhood home, it mattered even more.

As I walked around wondering where to begin, it struck me that this place had stopped feeling like my home, my haven, a very long time ago. Within these walls, I didn't feel safe. I felt trapped in the sadness that had begun that confusing summer and lasted for the sixteen Lost Years. To me, everything from the den couch to the dishes held memories I was more than happy to forget.

Wandering into what used to be my room, the bed under my window had been replaced with a huge wooden desk. Dad's tennis trophies and accomplishments had been moved from the den to this upstairs office. I leaned against the desk, taking it all in. I wanted to sit in the chair across from his and tell Dad about the last few months. About Denver, my new job, about my momentous moving day the week before.

I am doing something, Dad, I am finally doing something.

I hoped somehow he knew. My closet door was open and I stepped inside. My seventh-grade cheerleading uniform was hanging next to my old tutus and my high school letter jacket. I stepped up on the shelves so I could peer up at the secret fort in the top of my closet. My baby pillow was still up there and Snoopy smiled back at me.

I felt a wave of homesickness. This was it. This was my safe place, my haven. Hidden in what used to be my bedroom. Here was what was left of my childhood. I reached for Snoopy and brought him down with me to hug his neck. It was time I took him home—to Charlotte.

Snoopy accompanied me down to the kitchen to start the serious work of cleaning out. Maybe he could remind me that while I was not sentimental about many things in this house, my mom was. She was very worried about what I was going to throw away that might be important to her. I had given her a drawer of photos to sort through so she could not protest about what I was purging in the kitchen.

Opening a cabinet by the telephone, rolls of wrapping paper, ribbon, and bags of cards spilled onto the floor. Here was my mother's Hallmark addiction on full display. Andrea now owned the card store in El Paso and my mom was her best customer, shopping there at least twice a week. For each birthday, anniversary, Easter, Mother's Day, Halloween, and Valentine's Day, Mom sent a separate card to each of our girls, Charlie, and me. That was about twenty-five cards a year to my family alone. Then there were my sisters, my aunts and uncles and their children, and now their children's children. There were dozens of bags of cards from Andrea's store. Mom loved buying extras just in case. She was a like Holiday Girl Scout—always ready.

This habit always annoyed me. Why did she spend so much time on it? She spent hours every week buying, writing, and mailing these cards. Her dedication to this habit baffled me.

I knew she would want to take every card and ribbon but I was going to be ruthless. There was no way we were boxing all this and moving it. Mom would just buy it all again anyway.

Sort. Sift. Save. Discard.

Sort. Sift. Save. Discard.

I got more frustrated as I opened more drawers and cabinets. More Hallmark paraphernalia poured out. Some rolls were brand-new, never opened. Some were half used and bunched. The half-used rolls I stuffed in trash bags and the brand-new I set aside.

The bags piled up, and I dragged them past Mom to get to the garage.

"What's all that?" she said, alarmed.

"Oh, you know, kitchen junk," I said vaguely.

It was amazing to think each tenant in Charlotte had only two bags of treasure, yet I could fill two of those same trash bags in only one room of my mother's house.

I moved upstairs to Mom's bedroom and began cleaning out the bathroom vanity. There were only two drawers, a His and Hers. I knew my dad's things were still in the His, even though he had been gone for nine years. I opened Hers, my mom's drawer, first expecting to quickly *Sort, Sift, Save, Discard* the contents. When I opened the drawer, however, my father's handwriting stared up at me from the corner. It stopped me cold. His neat script was unmistakable. Dad had very precise penmanship for a man, and it was always measured and slanting right in even sure strokes.

I reached down to touch his handwriting on the top card and then picked up the stack of cards bound with a rubber band. I didn't count them, but I knew there had to be over thirty cards. They were the standard two-by-three-inch innocuous white cards the florist sends with flowers. In this case, I knew at one time, a dozen red roses had accompanied each card. The same flower, the same color, and the same dozen my dad had been sending my mom every year on their anniversary, just like he had since college. Each card read:

All my love, Leighton

Each card written by my dad. Each card saved by my mom. *For over thirty years.*

I sat down on the stool at my mom's vanity. Each action was remarkable. That my dad had handwritten each card. *Had he driven by the florist before they delivered them?* That my dad never wavered and sent the same dozen red roses each year to remind my mom of his steadfast love, even through their most difficult years. That my mom saved each card, now a two-by-three-inch record of their love story.

Charlie sent me flowers on our anniversary, my birthday, and Mother's Day, always from my favorite florist. Different arrangements each time—hydrangeas, tulips, roses—different colors and different buds according to the season. I love that he did that. I loved the surprise of not knowing what would show up on my door, but always certain that he wouldn't forget. Charlie's cards were always different, too. They would be typed from the florist with different messages that Charlie dictated over the phone. For our first anniversary:

That wasn't such a bad year, was it? Love moi

Or another favorite, harkening back to our first date story:

You wouldn't want to have a beer with me would you?
Love moi

We had over fifteen anniversaries now, but I had not saved one of those cards. My girls would never open a drawer and find the witness to our love story. It would be only ours to know. Charlie and I both easily threw things away. Our house was neat and tidy. No stacks of anything anywhere. Looking at the sweet stack my mom had saved, I regretted throwing away Charlie's cards to me. I regretted some of the other things I had discarded over the years. It made me sad to know that I had made something trash before it had the chance to be treasure.

I thought about our girls and their future love stories. Would they be romanced by flowers and cards? Or would they only have texts as witness to their stories? They couldn't say to their kids: *Look at the first text your dad ever sent me.*

I held the cards in my hand, the thirty years of love radiating from them. I may have had enormous uncertainty in my life growing up. I may have had sadness in never knowing the mom I could have had. But I had always been surrounded by a love that was truly rare. And that love had made this old house a home.

I carefully placed the cards back in the drawer. Mom would want to pack these herself.

16

Praying to a God You Don't Believe In

Man is born broken,
and the grace of God is glue.

EUGENE O'NEILL

"HEY, JAY," I SAID AS HE GOT IN MY CAR.

Jay nodded shyly at me as he put on his seatbelt in the passenger seat. He was freshly shaved and wearing a knit shirt. This wouldn't have been remarkable except I had never seen Jay this clean or this calm. Before moving in with Homeless to Homes, Jay had difficulty conversing with others. His struggles with alcoholism made him drink to oblivion. But on this day, he was sixty days out of treatment and a serene, grateful passenger in my car.

Joann had asked me to take Jay to buy groceries. While I was happy to help, I was uncomfortable at the same time. Jay and I didn't know each other, and this shopping trip was going to stretch the limits of our conversational capabilities. Jay probably would have been fine to just ride quietly, but I felt the need to talk in order to break the awkward silence.

"How's your place?" I asked.

"Fine, ma'am," Jay said with the sweetest smile, one that made him look like a happy kid bursting with the best secret. "Real nice."

Jay's apartment was next door to Samuel's so I thought that might be a line of conversation. "How's Samuel?"

"He's fine."

"A good neighbor?"

"Yes, ma'am, real fine."

I wasn't really sure what else to ask him so we drove in silence the rest of the way to the grocery store.

Frank's Supermarket was not like the grocery store in my neighborhood. There was no mini coffee shop as we entered, no delicatessen with fancy cheeses, no café tables. The produce section was not overflowing with exotic options like kiwi and passion fruit. Just the basics like apples, oranges, onions, potatoes, and tomatoes. The shelves were not bulging with products and the aisles did not have colorful promotions encouraging the consumer to stock up for the latest holiday. This was a utilitarian grocery store in which many shelves were actually bare. I had never seen such an empty store in my neighborhood, except in the aftermath of Hurricane Hugo.

Jay pulled a wrinkled list from his pocket and began methodically filling it. I was a little self-conscious tagging behind him in the aisles, but it got easier as I asked him questions about his purchases.

"Are those collards?"

"Yep," he said looking at me funny. "You didn't know that?"

"No, Jay, I'm from West Texas," I admitted. "I have never seen or eaten collards."

"What?" he laughed. "You fooling me?"

"Nope. My mom didn't cook them and I've never made them. Never ordered them either."

"What? You are missing something!" he said and started to explain how he cooked them just like his mama used to make.

We continued through the aisles, getting other things I never shopped for. Black-eyed peas, ham hocks. The whole meat cooler was a revelation. *Beef tongue? Did they sell that in my store?* What was most eye-opening was the way Jay shopped. When I went to the grocery store, I always just hurried through, throwing things in my cart as fast as I could, not checking prices or even caring if it was on my list.

Jay was deliberate and thoughtful. It finally occurred to me he was painstakingly doing the math as we shopped to insure the total would match the dollars in his pocket. At the checkout counter, he added cigarettes almost as a reward for staying in budget.

We loaded his things and got back in my car.

"Jay, you seem to be doing really well since you got out of treatment."

"Yes ma'am, I think I am," he said, making that pleased secret smile again.

We rode in silence a minute.

"You know growing up my sister told my mama that she heard voices in her head," he said. "My mama let them send my sister to the state hospital. When she came back, I didn't even recognize her. I don't know what they did to my sister in there, but I never told my mama I heard voices, too. I just started drinking. That made them quieter."

I glanced over at Jay, but he was staring out the passenger window. That brief window on his world said everything about poverty, mental illness, and homelessness. A drink might drown the voices until they drowned you. I knew my mom heard voices, but I never considered the fact that she had never turned to a bottle to escape. Thankfully, she had turned to the pages of her bible instead. Our lives would have been much more complicated had she chosen differently.

Jay's newly achieved sobriety was a marked change and each Homeless to Homes tenant that summer was going through similar transformative changes. Just as the Prince George tenants didn't "look"
homeless, our residents were returning to "normal" in those first
weeks, too. Ruth's necklace wasn't the only noticeable difference.
Each resident, once they had a solid month of sleep, food, and showers, looked remarkably well. Clear eyes, groomed hair, clean clothes,
and reduced drinking softened each into four surprisingly average
tenants. Joann and I weren't the only ones noticing.

The metamorphosis of Samuel was one of the most dramatic.
After living in the men's shelter for seven years, he had a long list of
health problems. With Joann's help he received much-needed medical care and could finally take his medicines consistently for the first
time in years. His diet improved as well now that he cooked for himself and took nutritional supplements. Samuel was the first of the four
tenants to express an interest in doing something more productive
with his days. Now that he was no longer in survival mode wondering where his next meal would come from, Samuel had time to
reflect and imagine a different life for himself. Samuel imagined he'd
like to go back to school.

Joann helped him enroll at the community college in a math
course that would be the beginning step on the path to get his GED,
the high school equivalency degree. Samuel regretted never graduating and he was going to take care of that now. He had been in a class
a few weeks when I saw him at the UMC.

He was in the dining room at lunch, sitting at a table talking
with some Neighbors who had obviously known him a while. Samuel was clean-shaven, wearing a white knit shirt, knee-length plaid
shorts, and basketball shoes. He casually slung his backpack over his
shoulder and for the first time, it wasn't full of clothes or food—just

a couple books for his math class. Samuel was clearly enjoying the positive attention and his almost celebrity status.

"Man, look at you! You done alright!"

"You got your own place now?"

"You in school!"

I smiled as I watched him. Samuel was a sweetheart. Easygoing. Quiet. Grateful. His apartment was impeccably neat. He was the model tenant. A longtime UMC staff member who had known Samuel for years came up beside me.

"I cannot believe that is Samuel," she said, shaking her head.

We watched him together a minute more before she spoke again.

"I always thought he was someone who was a lost cause."

That was the lesson that summer. No one was a lost cause.

When we started this program, we had all believed we needed to complete two years of this pilot program in order to have the data to plan a building like The Prince George.

At the time, I know I never fully envisioned that housing could so quickly produce such radical change. In promising Denver beds, I think I only imagined more comfortable living for the street homeless—a more humane circumstance. I didn't have the faith that people really would change given the chance.

Every day I was being proved wrong. This wasn't just about comfort, it was true conversion. Just as Denver had transformed from thirty years homeless to a best-selling author, possibility awaited in every single life we could touch.

Samuel and each of the Homeless to Homes tenants were demonstrating that housing represented hope. We didn't need to wait two years to "prove it." We had our proof.

It was like having the cure for cancer but waiting two years to give it to more people.

Dale and I decided we should move up the timetable with a two-tiered strategy. We would continue to fill the pilot program, but with only thirteen tenants not fifteen, saving some money so we could also move ahead with developing our own building.

Scaling back from fifteen to thirteen pilot-program tenants made each choice even more critical. Only nine more people would receive the gift of hope and housing Raymond, Samuel, Ruth, and Jay now shared.

We tried to be systematic about it, considering specific factors for each potential candidate: years on the street, health needs, background. But the truth was, so much emotion was included in all those harsh facts. There were so many layers of stories that we couldn't know until we met with each potential candidate. Joann did most of the interviewing and tried to select the neediest cases.

After one particularly heart-wrenching interview, Joann sat down heavily in the chair across from me.

"I know I don't really get a pick," she admitted, "but if I had one, this would be my guy. Something about him, he's special."

She was talking about Eugene Coleman, and he had been coming to UMC since it opened in 1994. I am sure I served him dozens of times in the soup line, but because I was trying to hide behind the counter, I hadn't noticed that he thought he was invisible, too.

"Got a cigarette?"

Eugene Coleman looked up from his sleeping bag in his campsite, a filthy hole of a place under a highway overpass near downtown Charlotte. He had a cigarette, but he wasn't about to share it with this guy.

"Sorry," he said and turned his back, trying to rest his head on his arm. It was the middle of the day but Coleman needed to get some sleep now. The nights were brutal: trains rolling by, cars overhead. The worst was trying to sleep with one eye open so that in the middle of the night nobody took what little he had. Coleman had been beaten more times than he could remember defending his campsite. It was what you did on the streets to survive and it had been his life now for longer than he could remember.

Coleman had been one of twelve children growing up in Winnsboro, South Carolina. He had been the first-born male after five daughters, but somewhere in the exhaustion of a dozen mouths to feed his exalted status wore off. With no father and bored with school, Coleman left home at fifteen to live with his Uncle Leroy, traveling the South working a series of construction jobs. Along the way he became a father to a son, Elkin Eugene Smith, but he drifted out of his boy's life, moving from one construction job to another.

Eventually, he worked his way up as a supervisor at a carton company. Coleman loved the physical labor, and when the forklift was too tedious he oftentimes used the quicker method of just lifting shipments with his strong back. Through this manual labor, Coleman developed a hernia, which required a simple surgery. But that operation was the beginning of a long, dark slide for Coleman.

When he came out of anesthesia from the operation, he knew immediately something was wrong. Coleman couldn't feel anything below his waist, and doctors confirmed he was temporarily paralyzed. The spinal tap used to anesthetize him had gone horribly wrong. After three or four weeks in the hospital, he could finally sit up without pain to go home, but his life was forever altered.

Along with drastically limited mobility and dependence on pain medication, Coleman took home an intense distrust of doctors. He swore no one would ever operate on him again.

Back at work, Coleman was not the hardworking supervisor he was before. The pain dogged him and he took more medicine than

prescribed to try to numb it. Months later he developed a new problem—a cyst had started to grow on his left shoulder. At first, only
Coleman noticed it, but each month it doubled. Soon, his employers
questioned what was on his shoulder and each time Coleman promised to get it looked at but didn't. There was no way he was going
back to a doctor and risk another surgery. It was starting to become
painful and using his shoulder was more and more difficult.

As the cyst grew, so did Coleman's lies to himself and those
around him. He missed days at work to stay home and relieve his
pain by drinking and smoking pot. Escaping with substances also
numbed the fear of going back to a hospital to remove the cyst,
which was now the size of a baseball on his shoulder.

The spiral that began with a botched hernia procedure was complete when Coleman lost his job, his income, and then his apartment. He became homeless sometime in the early 1990s. After that,
Coleman came to the Urban Ministry Center every day for food but
rarely talked to anyone. He resigned himself to his homelessness and
living under a bridge; the place he called, "The hole I lived in."

Coleman thought things couldn't get worse until he read a newspaper obituary—just a random copy of the paper picked up on the
streets he wandered. The death notice was for Elkin Eugene Smith,
his son, shot dead at seventeen.

The hole got blacker and deeper after that.

With no calendar, no family, and no purpose, the years bled into
each other. It changed that day the stranger asked him for a cigarette. As Coleman was turning away, trying to get comfortable in his
sleeping bag, he heard the man say, "I got a train to catch."

Minutes later he heard that train start rumbling through—a noise
he had heard every day, several times a day for years. But this time it
was different. This time over the deafening roar of the train he could
hear screaming. Coleman ran down the tracks but now wished he

hadn't. The man who had wanted to borrow a cigarette and had "a train to catch" had been cut in two after falling on the tracks. That bloodied, dead body was a startling wake-up call for Coleman.

Lying awake that night, Coleman prayed to a god he didn't believe in. "Lord, I don't want to die out here like this."

He wasn't sure how to get himself out of that hole, but he knew he was going to need help. And he didn't like asking for help. He'd heard the rumors at the soup kitchen that the UMC had started housing homeless people. He'd been going there for years and never heard anything like it. Sounded like a scam to him. *They probably want something from me. Probably rich people trying to make money off the backs of poor people.* But he took a chance. He wasn't going to die out here.

"Excuse me, ma'am, you got a minute?" he said to Joann. "Are you the lady that gets people off the streets?"

I still have a photo of Coleman taken the day he moved in to his Homeless to Homes apartment. In it he has short dreadlocks and is wearing a baseball hat and T-shirt. After twenty years on the streets, his eyes were wildly bloodshot but his grin, missing many teeth, stretched across his entire face. Joann had just handed him a key. Nothing fancy, just the standard silver key that looked like any other on a plain stainless steel ring.

Coleman stared at it in his palm in amazement. "I can't remember the last time I had a key to anything," he said.

He held up the key with two fingers in his right hand and smiled as I took the photo.

The camera didn't capture his words but I will never forget them.

"This is a Kodiak moment!" Coleman said.

He meant of course, Kodak.

Coleman's story was one of the first that helped me truly understand how homelessness might happen to someone. I think before I met I him, I believed the myths that some people chose to be homeless or that they liked living outside or that they had done something to deserve their situation. Coleman had been rising above the home he grew up in, just a working guy, when a medical mistake altered forever what his life looked like.

Certainly, there were twists in his story, different choices he could have made, but it began with a blindsiding collision with the unexpected. *That*, I understood.

17

Home Alone

Perhaps home is not a place
but simply an irrevocable condition.

JAMES BALDWIN

AS I WAS BEGINNING TO UNDERSTAND OUR NEW TENANTS
and their stories, I found that the Neighbors at the Center no longer felt like strangers now that I was there every day. Chilly Willy
regularly greeted me in the parking lot, sometimes remembering
my connection to his brother, Jimmy, but more often not. He was
a regular fixture in the UMC yard and depending on his mood, he
either welcomed or harassed visitors.

On a good day, he would proudly tell you that he was going to
try to quit drinking and enter the UMC substance-abuse program.
But on a drinking day, Chilly Willy could keep you tied up in his
dysfunction, a complicated entanglement where you felt bad walking away, even though self-preservation required it.

Like Jay, Chilly Willy used alcohol to drown voices and memories. On this particular day, it was clear Chilly had been attempting
some serious drowning but the buzz was wearing off.

As I approached him, he whimpered like an injured dog. "I am
not having a good day."

"If I have some time after my meeting, I will come back to talk with you," I told him.

He looked away and shook his head in disgust. We both knew I was lying, and I was really hoping he would be gone by the time I got out. I hurried inside, glad to have dodged Chilly Willy for the day.

Liz Clasen-Kelly met me at the door. "Did you get my message? I am so sorry, I left you a voice mail—we need to reschedule the meeting today."

Sigh. I had no reason now not to go back to Chilly Willy. I looked at my watch and decided to give him twenty minutes of attention and then get on with my afternoon.

I went back out and said, "Hey, Chilly, you still want to talk?"

He perked up immediately.

We sat on one of the outside benches. I didn't really know where to start with Chilly Willy but I knew he just needed to be heard. His signature white hair was in braids the way he liked and he had on a dusty black shirt and frayed jeans. He could almost be mistaken for Willie Nelson and had about as many wrinkles in his tired face as the legendary singer.

The only details I knew about Chilly's life I had learned in pieces from his brother, Jimmy, and Liz. I had heard that Chilly once had a girlfriend who was killed, but I didn't know the details. That day, Chilly Willy willingly filled in those blanks and many others with unnerving honesty. My questions slid out in no particular order, and I started by reminding him of our connection.

"You know I know your brother, Jimmy—he's my plumber."

"He is?" Chilly looked off to one side as if to find the answer in the garden. "That's right. I knew that."

"Do you have any other family?"

"I have five sisters and two brothers. One's a lawyer. One works at the local college. I got a nephew who is a fireman" he said and then finished with the most surprising fact. "My daddy was a preacher."

I was stunned. "Really?"

"Yep, right here in Charlotte," he said proudly. "He built a church over on First Avenue."

I wasn't sure what to say to the fact that Chilly Willy was the son of a preacher man. "Did you two get along?"

Chilly looked away again and shook his head. "He didn't know what to make of me."

We let that sit a moment between us.

"You had a girlfriend at one time, right?" I asked.

"Crystal was my wife. She was two months pregnant when she was hit by a car and died." Chilly looked to be replaying that nightmare in his head, and I was sorry I had brought it up.

"That's awful, Chilly. I am really sorry."

He nodded and continued to stare down at his hands.

"What exactly are you drinking all the time?" I tried distracting him, truly wanting to know how homeless people with no money could afford to get drunk.

"Cisco!" he said surprised at my naiveté.

"What?" I had no idea what he was talking about.

"Cisco," he said clearly.

Later, I Googled Cisco to learn it is a "fortified wine" product known on the street as "liquid crack" that can sell for less than a dollar a bottle. The article I found mentioned that a hundred-pound person who consumed two 375-milliliter bottles of Cisco within one hour could die due to acute alcohol poisoning.

Chilly Willy continued on about his Cisco habit. "I get banned from everywhere. I am banned from every liquor store in the city. I am even banned from a funeral parlor because they found me in a casket passed out with a bottle of Cisco in my hand."

We laughed and were silent a minute.

"Some days, all I want is a good Christian woman and a guitar [pronounced *gee*-tar]," he said with a thick southern accent and a laugh. "But look at me, what good Christian woman would marry me?"

We were quiet a moment. It was hard to imagine this gentle bear of a man tenderheartedly seeking love could also be the same guy who had gone to prison at seventeen. It made my stomach hurt to think of that teenage kid, whether guilty or innocent, thrown into a general prison population.

"Mom!"

Maddie and Emma, my own teenagers, were headed towards us from the parking lot. Their summer job was volunteering for the UMC, organizing mail, filing records, and serving during lunch. Today, they were finishing up a mural they had painted in my office. The entire wall facing my desk was now a giant kaleidoscope of color leading to these words in the center:

Amazing!
Keb' Mo'

So I would never forget that first True Blessings and that first move-in day.

"Hey, pretty girls!" Chilly Willy said. "Can I have a hug?"

Maddie and Emma smiled and dutifully gave Chilly Willy a one-arm hug with one twin on each side.

"This your mama?" he asked.

"She is!" Maddie told him.

"You do like she tells you," Chilly Willy told them solemnly. "I didn't listen to my mama at your age and look how I turned out."

Sadly, Chilly Willy was not one of the final tenants chosen for Homeless to Homes. We worried that he was still too unpredictable to live in an apartment without twenty-four-hour security like we still hoped to have in our own building someday. Gradually we filled all the remaining spots in the pilot program. Coleman, Teddy, Johnny, Edna, Chuck, Debra, TJ, James, and Christine all moved off the streets and came home.

The program operated quietly in Mike's apartments and two other units in another part of the city. We didn't announce our presence in either neighborhood for a reason: all thirteen were no longer homeless—they were housed. They were now just people who had finally lost the stigma of that word "homeless" and were trying to quietly rebuild their lives.

They ate, they slept, and they tried to remember what it was like to feel human again.

Raymond did a radio interview with a local radio station.

"What's your favorite part of your new home?" the reporter asked.

"The mailbox!" he said. "I love getting mail in my own mailbox! I even love getting junk mail. It makes me feel like a human again."

I think I somehow believed it would be that easy. *Move in. Start life. Get mail. Live happily ever after.* It was Raymond who let me know it wasn't that simple.

He was on his front porch tending his new tomato plants when I stopped by the apartments. Sitting on his concrete steps he clearly looked lonely.

"You okay?" I asked.

Raymond shrugged, his lack of words saying volumes since he always had something to say. Joann was busy with another tenant so I tried my best to help.

"You want to talk?"

Raymond hesitated, but decided I would be an acceptable substitute for Joann. "I just miss the Center is all."

That was surprising to say the least. I couldn't imagine why Raymond missed all the people, the lines, and the struggles of street life.

"I had friends there," he said simply.

"Raymond, you can go to the Center anytime," I assured him.

The Urban Ministry was about a mile-and-a-half walk from his new apartment or an easy bus ride. We assumed tenants might go for the art or gardening programs—another reason the proximity of these apartments was so perfect.

Raymond shook his head. "I can't be there anymore. I feel too guilty."

I was confused. "Why do you feel *guilty*?"

"My friends are still on the streets. I have a home and they don't," he explained. "I can't help them either."

Now, I understood. In essence, Raymond had gained a home but lost his family.

As difficult as life is on the streets, homelessness creates camaraderie. People who have nothing share something with each other. Even if they don't share their true identity, they are well known to each other by street names: *Chilly Willy, Dancing Bear, Peanut.* On the streets, just like in high school or a workplace, natural groups form and friendships develop. They share things as small as cigarettes and as big as campsites.

From this "street family" we had only housed thirteen men and women. There were dozens of their friends and, in some cases, even actual blood relatives still left behind on the streets. Raymond and the other twelve Homeless to Homes tenants had all signed the same lease agreement, which stated no one could come live with them. It was a requirement to keep order in Mike's apartments. If our tenants allowed others to move in who were not part of the program, Raymond and each resident in our program risked losing his own housing.

We had chosen thirteen people to win this housing lottery. While they all might have known each other on the streets, they weren't necessarily friends. Each was also struggling with his or her own readjustment to normal life. In selecting tenants, I had never considered the community that we would disrupt or the new one that needed to be built. Raymond was living housed but other than those in our program, anyone else he might befriend could never understand where he'd been. How could Raymond explain that his residence before this had been a barn? How could he make new friends with people who had no frame of reference for what he had endured the past few years?

Raymond had made steady progress since being housed, but now that he didn't wake up every day frantic about survival, he had time to consider his life.

Right now, his life was decidedly lonely.

Just as I had not envisioned our tenants' quick progress in some areas, I had not imagined the depths of their struggles moving beyond the stigma of homelessness. Although Raymond was now safe inside, he carried a tremendous shame of how he got there. His euphoria of move-in inevitably had given way to isolation and depression.

I was beginning to fully appreciate that while it was remarkable progress to save thirteen people from the streets, housing and living were two completely different matters.

"Hey, Mom," I said in my weekly phone call. My sisters and I each tried to call at least once a week since we lived so far away.

"I signed up for the trip to China with the museum!" Mom said.

"Really?" I asked. The idea made me equally proud and terrified. It was impressive that she was going to fulfill this lifelong dream, and ever since my dad died Mom had become increasingly independent. We had all worried that when he was gone Mom would struggle but it hadn't happened. Even though Mom was doing well, her intermittent battles with mania and depression still plagued me. I had never shaken the worry that a hospital stay was around any corner. What would we do if the long plane ride triggered a chemical imbalance while she was in Shanghai?

"There's a nice group going from El Paso, and we are even going to see the Terracotta Warriors!"

"Wow, Mom, what an adventure! That's going to be great," I said, while secretly worrying how long it would take me or my sisters to board an emergency flight to Beijing. "What are you doing today?"

"Well, I need to go to the store and get some more supplies for my bags," she said. ·

Ever since Mom read *Same Kind of Different,* she had started her own campaign to help the homeless. She kept plastic bags in her car that had a bottle of water and small cans of food. When she saw someone at a stoplight asking for help, she would give them a bag.

"And then I'm probably going to my office."

I smiled. Her office was Andrea's card store. Mom would go in to buy her cards and then set up on one of the back tables intended for customers who were picking out wedding invitations. Mom sometimes even brought her "lunch" with her—a smoothie or milkshake from Baskin Robbins. It's not like she didn't have a desk in her new apartment. It's just that she still didn't feel at home there. Ever since we had moved Mom into senior living, she spent most days trying to leave it. Not running away, just spending every minute she could somewhere else.

Mom still drove to the same beauty shop fifteen minutes away even though there was a service in her building. Her routine became fixing herself breakfast and then leaving midmornings for the beauty shop, the bank, the nail salon, the grocery store, the post office, the card store, the church—whatever errands she could do, and tried to take all day to do them so she'd be gone from her apartment. Pretty much anywhere but there suited her.

Our weekly phone calls usually began with news of her book club or bridge group before a side comment about her new living arrangement.

Mom constantly dropped subtle hints that she was the youngest, most active person in her new apartment community. "I went to visit my ninety-two-year-old friend down the hall yesterday."

She rarely told me anything about someone except their age. I accused her of age profiling.

"How is your program going?" she asked.

"Well, pretty good," I said. "A few tenants are having a hard time adjusting, you know. Even though it's better than being homeless, I think getting used to life in a new apartment is really hard. Nothing feels familiar."

"I know," Mom said.

I hung up the phone, feeling humbled. It seemed my mom and Raymond were both teaching me some hard lessons about housing. It takes more than four walls and a bed to make a place feel like home.

18

Five Guys

Sometimes beautiful things come into our lives
out of nowhere. We can't always understand
them, but we have to trust in them. I know you
want to question everything, but sometimes
it pays to just have a little faith.

LAUREN KATE

ALONG WITH HARD LESSONS, I WAS SLOWLY REALIZING THIS
was all much bigger than I had planned. When I began in January,
I agreed to start a pilot program funded through the generosity of
John and Pat Moore. Now we were thinking about raising millions of dollars that Dale and I would have to somehow find. The
deep conviction behind my promise to Denver and the excitement
of taking a dream job from Dale was being smothered by the very
real-world practicalities of keeping that promise and doing that job.
I kept showing up every morning, but I had less and less idea of what
exactly I should be doing all day.

Seven months into this housing experiment, we were committed
to the idea of an apartment building owned by the UMC, but we
both knew that to buy land, build a complex and run a program for
almost one hundred people was going to take expertise neither Dale
nor I had.

"This is going to take more than a graphic designer and a minister," I told Dale.

In order to turn this pilot program into an apartment building, we were going to need some development and business expertise. So far, our team consisted of just Bill Holt, the $3 million–dreaming banker. Dale and I brainstormed about friends we knew with the skills we needed. Matt Wall (real estate), Jerry Licari (business), Downie Saussy (construction), Hugh McColl III (finance), and David Furman (architecture). Throughout the next few years I would refer to them as my Five Guys.

We invited them all to a meeting in August 2008 to begin strategizing—or fantasizing—about building an apartment complex designed for the chronically homeless.

Matt came to the meeting prepared with printouts of available properties. In researching proper zoning for our residential building, Matt had learned that our planned apartment for homeless would be allowed only in the middle of a commercial business district. There is nothing "homey" about industrial parks, so it would be difficult to find a piece of land with this zoning that was still near grocery stores and a bus line and had a remotely neighborhood feel.

At the end of the meeting, we determined we would divide the strengths of the group into a Property Team and a Finance Team to move forward. We would delay raising the money until we had an actual property to build on.

For our first assignment, the Property Team went on an exploratory mission to evaluate all the possible sites. It was a Dream Team expedition to be sure. We were shopping for land that cost hundreds of thousands of dollars with absolutely no way to pay for it. However, we carefully considered each parcel as if we already had the cash to purchase in our pocket. Matt would slowly drive by a site and we'd all comment on the merits.

"Well, it's close to the bus line."

"Yes, but it's next to a funeral home."

"Is there a grocery store within ten miles of this place?"

David, as the architect, carried the most weight. In my mind, we would go with what he liked, until I realized which one he liked. We were evaluating two acres of rusted cars surrounding two nondescript cement buildings that advertised tires and auto repairs. Obviously, it had been a long time since business was booming, and the property sat neglected on the edge of a small neighborhood. Worse than all the decaying junk was the massive radio tower bordering the lot and looming hundreds of feet in the air over the mounds of scrap metal.

I drew a line through the property marked "929 Moretz." David was on my right circling it.

"Are you kidding?" I asked him.

"No, I like it!" he said enthusiastically. David has huge round eyes and unruly blond curls. He was very animated as he spoke. "Look, it backs up to a neighborhood, the bus line is right around the corner, and you can walk to Frank's Supermarket."

Dale agreed. "And it's right near our Homeless to Homes apartments so we know the neighborhood."

We had been driving around in circles, so I hadn't realized we were in fact only two streets away from Mike Boyd's apartments, where almost all of our tenants lived.

"What about the cars?" I asked.

"Well, we would need to budget for a huge cleanup for sure," Matt said. "But it is worth keeping on the list."

"But the radio tower?" I reminded them.

"I love it!" David said. "It's like yard art."

We ended the day narrowing our focus down to three properties, with the junkyard high on the list. Matt was charged to investigate them all and get ready to make an offer.

Returning to my office, I saw the quote still taped to my computer screen from my first week of work: *Start something big and foolish like Noah.*

It seemed we were doing just that.

Our Finance Team had put together a preliminary budget with land, construction, and some start-up operating costs: $10,000,000. *Ten million.*

There were donors in the community who could and had given six-figure gifts for colleges, hospitals, or museums. These were the type of community projects civic-minded donors regularly supported. But we would be asking for the homeless, a group many felt simply were unworthy. We were going to have to change perceptions in order to raise our millions.

I wasn't sure which was more improbable, the junkyard or the budget.

It was the fall of 2008 and the recession was starting to sink the national psyche. Even if we could dream about raising $10,000,000 some day, we needed $500,000 right now so we could buy land and have a site ready to build on. We had hoped some money might come in from Bill Holt's work with his bank and the Wachovia Foundation, but a recently announced merger with Wells Fargo had sidelined any progress on that front.

Dale and I brainstormed in his office.

"What about one of the big churches?" I asked. "Wouldn't they have a heart for this?"

Dale shook his head. "Not that kind of heart. There's not a church in Charlotte that has half a million dollars they aren't using for something already."

"The city of Charlotte? Isn't there a line item in the city budget for this?"

Dale shook his head again. "We've never gotten any traction with the city. We could apply next year to the city's Housing Trust Fund but to do that we need to own the land."

"And to buy the land we need the money!" I finished his sentence for him. "To raise money from donors we need a site and to buy a site we need money but to get money we need..."

"A miracle," Dale finished my sentence for me.

We sat for a while in frustration before Dale offered, "You know, maybe I could call Dave Campbell."

Dave headed a family foundation, and he had been the True Blessings table guest sitting next to Dale when Denver had announced, *"What are y'all doing? Y'all need to build some beds!"* Dave had leaned over and asked Dale if we were launching a capital campaign at True Blessings but that day we had no intentions of raising money. Now, we absolutely were.

Dale set up a meeting with Dave and when we arrived I was so nervous I could barely speak. I had never asked anyone for money, much less a six-figure gift. We came prepared with a sketch David Furman had created of our three-story dream, which would fit that two-acre junkyard property. Along with the drawing, we took Liz's cost data on the business case for housing and success stories of the pilot program.

Dale led our meeting with those compelling stories from Homeless to Homes: Samuel going to community college, Jay and Coleman getting clean and sober. We presented the data that it was actually cheaper to house the chronically homeless rather than let them die on the streets or cycle endlessly through the jails and emergency rooms.

Our potential donor seemed impressed and nodded along until Dale got to the ask: $500,000.

"I love the work you do, Dale, but we can't do that," he told us. "It's almost the end of the year and we are fully committed."

It was crushing to us both. We had secretly hoped Dave would somehow answer a prayer. This property might not be there next year. Even though it was a junkyard, David Furman was right. It was in a great location, near a grocery store, and properly zoned on the edge of a residential neighborhood. Because of the cleanup that would be needed to remove all the auto junk and the looming radio tower, Matt had negotiated an extremely low price. We had an option to buy but not forever. We truly needed a miracle.

Nine days later, my computer blinked an unlikely message.

I called Dale's office immediately, "Dale? I just got an email from Dave Campbell. He wants more information!"

"You're kidding!" Dale said. "Why does he want more information if he told us no?"

"I know, right?"

My heart raced as I re-read the message three times. Maybe we still had a chance. Dale and I verified all our numbers before writing him back.

We waited nervously for a reply and a few days later, more questions. More emailed data and answers. A few weeks passed, nothing.

Dale and I assumed the answer was truly a *no*. I am not sure I could blame them. This wild idea really was a leap of faith.

"Kathy, you sitting down?" Dale called my office. "I just got off the phone with Dave."

I gripped the receiver and stared at my desk. *Oh, please. Oh, please* I thought. *Please give us something. Anything. If they pledged even a $100,000, maybe we could take it to another donor and get them to match it.*

"They are sending a check for $500,000."

"What?"

"I know! Can you believe it?" Dale gushed. He was laughing. "I just wanted to jump through the phone and hug him!"

"Me, too! That's incredible! That's..." I was laughing and tearing up and having trouble speaking. I looked up and saw the mural on my wall that Maddie and Emma had painted for me. The vibrant rainbow of colors surrounding Keb' Mo's song.

"That's... Amazing!" I smiled.

Dave said the check would be in the mail, but Dale asked if we could pick it up to thank our miracle makers in person.

It was November 11, 2008, and almost a year exactly to the date of the first True Blessings, when we walked into a conference room to receive the very first check for the capital campaign and a housing dream we didn't even have a year ago. With absolutely no fanfare, Dave Campbell walked in and graciously handed us a plain white envelope.

We felt there should have been a band playing, a full chorus singing, and confetti falling from the ceiling. To us, this was the moment of a lifetime, but they obviously passed out these kinds of gifts all the time. Dale and I gratefully gushed, but they were quietly humble, deflecting any grand gesture of thanks. They had no idea just how much this meant to us.

Leaving, Dale solemnly held the sealed envelope until we were standing together on the front walkway. We were trying to be strictly professional since their offices had huge plate-glass windows, and we knew they could still see us. Dale and I agreed to drive around the corner before inspecting the check.

Dale was waiting for me as I parked and got out of my car in the church parking lot behind the foundation offices. Carefully, he opened the envelope and we looked in awe at the Pay to the Order of line.

Five Hundred Thousand Dollars and no cents

"Have you ever held anything like that?" I asked.

"Never," Dale said. "I hope it doesn't bounce. I'm calling Matt right now and telling him to make a deal."

19

Dear Santa

Christmas doesn't just come in neatly
wrapped presents. It comes in our beautiful
messy attempts to love each other.

REVEREND BECCA STEPHENS

EVERY YEAR, MY DAUGHTERS WROTE LETTERS TO SANTA. EVEN
when they were old enough to know who Santa really was I made
them write their Christmas wish lists.

"If you don't believe you don't receive!" I'd tell them.

The main reason I kept insisting they write every year was because
the letters were so entertaining. I had a fantasy that one day I would
make a book of them all to give the girls when they got older. This
idea of making a keepsake book was becoming less likely but each
year I saved them anyway. More than once, Kailey wrote on her list:

Dear Santa,
For Christmas could I please, please have
1) Baby Brother
2) Pink Barbie jeep

Kailey was always very disappointed each Christmas when neither
of these items ever appeared under our tree. Maddie's and Emma's

lists were always suspiciously the same. I had long suspected that Maddie wrote Emma's for her, thereby doubling her own chances of receiving what she wanted.

Lauren, being the oldest, had the most experience appealing to Santa and used the most hilarious techniques. This was one of my favorites that Lauren ever wrote:

Dear Santa,
This Christmas, Lauren wants:
#1 To be shrunk to the size of Thumbelina
#2 Muzzles to put on the Twins
#3 Industrial Solvents
#4 Cookies
#5 iPod. Please give this one *serious* consideration

Lauren was wise enough to know I always got her at least one thing on her list, and she was betting of those choices I would go for the iPod over the Industrial Solvents. She was correct.

In my first year as director of Homeless to Homes, I asked the Homeless to Homes residents to make a Santa wish list as well for Christmas 2008. This was the first Christmas many of them had been housed in years and some, like Coleman, had spent holidays on the streets for decades. Usually the Urban Ministry Center had a huge turkey dinner for the hundreds of homeless.

Instead of going to the UMC, Joann and I planned a special Christmas dinner for just our tenants. Ever since we realized how lonely tenants like Raymond were, we had been working the past few months to build a community. Joann and I organized birthday lunches, picnics, and even fishing trips to a local park.

Christmas would be the first big holiday for our new family and we wanted to make it special. We received a donation of thirteen three-foot trees, and a book club hosted an ornament-making party so each resident could create their own decorations. Everyone's apartment was made festive with purchases from the Dollar Store and we promised a Santa delivery on Christmas Eve with presents from the tenants' wish lists.

As we stood in the men's department of Target, Emma and Maddie helped sort through the thirteen letters. The tenants' lists had been achingly simple.

Socks. Underwear. A warm jacket.

"Mom, we can't just give these guys underwear!" Emma said when she saw the requests. Joann had told each resident they could ask for one "Special Wish," and these were the items where we could have a little more fun.

An NFL Carolinas Panther sweatshirt. A James Bond DVD. A pair of earrings.

"Mom, do you think Samuel needs XL or XXL?" Maddie asked, holding up a Panthers jersey. That had been a popular wish item and we already had several in the cart.

My mom called while we were deciding.

"Hey, Mom, I'm shopping so I can't talk right now."

"What are you shopping for?'

"Christmas. I'm with Emma and Maddie and we're getting all the Homeless to Homes folks gifts."

"Ooh, how fun! I'll help! Let's tell your sisters and make this our family service project this year!"

As we all got older, my sisters and I didn't really need much. So each year, Louise, Allyson, Mom, and I agreed on a charity that we all contributed to in lieu of gifts to each other.

"You get everyone something special from all the Green Girls," my mom said. I smiled. I had been married over twenty years and I was still a Green Girl.

With the extra funds from my family, we bought each resident everything on their lists plus a grocery gift card to make their own special dinner. We piled all the purchases on our dining room table, where the twins wrapped thirteen sets of presents, careful to make each pile equal.

"Mom, I think we need to get something more for TJ and Chuck. Their piles don't look the same," Maddie said.

"And Edna really got more than Ruth, so we need to go back for her, too." Emma added.

Kailey made trays of Christmas cookies for each resident and on Christmas Eve day, we caravanned in two cars loaded with four girls and presents to take to the apartments.

When we pulled up, Raymond was already waiting.

"Welcome! Welcome!" he called to my girls as we got out of the car. As we approached his apartment, we could see he had wrapped his entire front door with silver foil and taped holiday greeting cards to it.

"Merry Christmas!" he called out.

"Merry Christmas, Raymond!" they said, giving him a hug as they entered his home.

"Did you see my tree?" he asked.

We all admired his small pine bending from the weight of the homemade ornaments. The tree was so small it barely came up to his waist but to Robert, it was better than the one in Rockefeller Center.

"Look at that!" he said, pointing at the festive display in his living room. "I can't believe it, no sir." He choked up as he spoke to my girls. "Last Christmas I was living in a barn. I am blessed," he said, wiping his eyes. "I am blessed."

That night at my home, we opened one present each. It was a tradition started when Lauren and Kailey were young and exploding with excitement unless we allowed them to open *one* gift before going to bed on Christmas Eve. In accordance with the Izard tradition, we each selected one present and waited until it was our turn to open as everyone watched.

"Open ours, Mom!" Kailey said handing me a small box.

The girls gathered together in anticipation, watching me as the ribbon fell to the floor and I struggled with the tape. Maddie bounced with excitement like Tigger, her nickname. She was terrible at keeping secrets and finally it was too much.

"It's for your building, Mom!" she said.

"Maddie! Hush!" Lauren and Kailey scolded.

"Let her open it first before you tell her!" Emma cried.

Inside was $200 cash—their Christmas money from my mom. She always sent them money so that they could do an Izard Girl service project for Christmas just like the Green Girls did.

"We know you are raising money, and this won't buy a room or anything but we figured we could buy the door knob!" Lauren explained proudly.

I grabbed them all for a group hug. I had the best family. Ever.

Four days later I had the second-best Christmas gift. On December 29, 2008, we became the proud owners of that junkyard beneath the cell tower. Matt had made a deal with the sellers and we closed before year-end.

It was official. We were *real*. We actually were going to build a home for homeless people.

<hr />

Two weeks later, I wished that holiday gift of a junkyard could be exchanged.

During negotiations, we had factored in a low purchase price and a cash reserve for the massive debris removal. The piles of rusting auto parts, however, camouflaged a much larger underground problem that our prepurchase inspections couldn't detect. When our cleanup crews started to dig, they found barrels of oil that had been leaking into the ground for years. Apparently, one section of our newly purchased property was an environmental nightmare.

Along with the cost of the land, we would be adding legal fees and the very expensive process of environmental remediation. We were still under our total budget for land, but we were using money we had hoped to spend on construction.

This extensive cleanup was only one of the headaches that winter. While we had been quietly celebrating a real place to build, we did not imagine converting a junkyard to a new apartment complex would be so unpopular in the neighborhood.

Our property was in the Northside neighborhood and another of those 74 zip codes in Charlotte I had never entered before I started this job. It was on the far side of downtown outside the interstate. The south side of Charlotte where I lived had neighborhoods like Myers Park and Eastover that had been planned by the Olmsted brothers, who designed Central Park in New York. Years before in these more affluent Charlotte neighborhoods, oak trees had been planted, which now rose sixty feet in a green canopy that still covers sections of the city.

The Olmsted brothers had not been hired to meticulously plan Northside and the surrounding streets. Any green that existed had been lovingly planted and tended by homeowners. In Northside, large manufacturing warehouses bump up next to simple one-story brick homes struggling to create community in their industrial midst. I did not know until I met the neighborhood president that residents had been working for years to create a residential sanctuary in this very industrial neighborhood.

Daniel Grier represented the Northside Association, and he met me in the same neighborhood diner where we had our holiday dinner with Homeless to Homes residents. I had brought David Furman's construction drawings, which showed how the new three-story building fit nicely into the corner lot, dramatically improving the rust yard of autos and trash. The color renderings depicted a modern apartment complex with twenty-four-hour security, landscaping, and even a community garden. Inside there would be an art room, library, and computer lab just like I had seen at The Prince George.

I pointed out all the features I thought Daniel and the Neighborhood Association would appreciate.

Daniel was a quiet, thoughtful man, and he kept his hands folded as I spoke. He had enormous brown eyes and they oozed gentleness. I expected they might mirror my own wide-eyed enthusiasm for the project but Daniel was my first big reality check.

"They are *never* going to go for it," Daniel said, meaning his colleagues in the Northside Neighborhood Association. In fact, he was sure they would mobilize to fight it every step of the way.

I was stunned. Why would Northside not want a new, well-staffed community apartment building over this neglected mess of a junkyard? How could this not be seen as an improvement?

Daniel carefully explained. It wasn't the building they didn't want; it was the *people* in it.

The neighborhood had worked tirelessly to improve itself, and they wouldn't want eighty-five chronically homeless people moving into the area, undermining this progress—even if they were *formerly* homeless.

I certainly understood his concern but tried to get him to see it another way.

"But they won't be homeless anymore once they are moved in. They will be **housed**," I argued. "And they will have case managers to help them be just as stable or more stable than anyone else in the neighborhood."

What Daniel didn't know, and now I was afraid to tell him, was that thirteen homeless, or formerly homeless, were already dwelling in the midst of Northside and had been for almost a year. Raymond, Samuel, and others lived only blocks from where we were having coffee and where Daniel was plainly telling me they were not wanted.

Daniel gestured at the drawings, "You think anyone would let you put this in Myers Park or Eastover? They always put the shelters only in the poor neighborhoods."

I started to argue that this wasn't a transitional shelter where hoards of people came and went. This would be a permanent home. The residents would be good neighbors like Raymond, Samuel, Ruth, and Coleman. But I stopped myself from making the point.

It really didn't matter. Daniel knew, and I knew, he was right. This wouldn't fly in most areas of town. Neighborhoods designed by the Olmstead brothers didn't plan for homeless housing, on purpose. Charlotte was just like any city that experienced NIMBY—Not in My Backyard. Philosophically, people might agree with low-income housing but no one wanted it next door to them. They worried it could bring crime or lower property values.

This was the exact reason we could buy a junkyard without a zoning change and without permission in this neighborhood. Someone in city politics and planning figured out a long time ago that if housing for low income or homeless was zoned for industrial land, then it could only ever be built around poorer neighborhoods away from high-end residential. It would never be in *their* backyard.

Now, whether Daniel and Northside liked it or not, we could build.

We were both silent for a moment, realizing I had not gained an ally as intended but maybe discovered an enemy.

Daniel with his gentle demeanor didn't feel like an enemy. I didn't want Daniel to think I was his enemy either. I didn't want him to think I was trying to go from dumping cars on that lot to dumping people into his neighborhood. I wanted him to know that I cared as much about the people we were trying to house as he cared about his community.

Desperately, I began confiding about Denver and why I had this crazy compulsion to do something more for the homeless. Daniel was the first complete stranger I had ever shared that story with. Other than Louise and Charlie, it may have been the first time I said it out loud—that Denver made me do this.

He listened and looked at me earnestly, "I won't fight you, Kathy—but *they* will."

Over the weeks and months ahead, we would try to gain neighborhood support, but the damage had been done. The sentiment was simple: the neighborhood residents would rather have the junkyard than formerly homeless people. It did not matter how pretty or safe the building was. They didn't ask for the project to be in their neighborhood and they had enough shelters in their district already. This was the line in the sand where the city needed to stop "dumping" in their neighborhood, and our project was the battle they were determined to win.

Each time I drove home from one of those neighborhood meetings, I felt a little more conflicted. I had a safe secure home in a vibrant, monied part of the city. I never worried about gunfire at night or drug deals a block from my house. My daughters had played safely on the sidewalks without any worries. I had no idea what it was like to live in Northside. I had no idea what effort it took to pull up a neighborhood. But I knew that if I thought someone was threatening my hard-earned peace, I'd probably try to fight it, too.

Our residents were feeling the pressure in Northside, as well. Raymond had been at Frank's Supermarket, only blocks from his apartment and our newly acquired junkyard when a woman in front of him in the checkout line turned around to speak.

"Did you hear?" she asked him. "They are trying to move a whole building of homeless people into our neighborhood!"

Raymond just nodded, feigning his dismay.

20

Papers and Prayers

What is it you plan to do with
your one wild and precious life?

MARY OLIVER

BY APRIL 2009, THE RHETORIC HAD GROWN NASTY. LUCKILY,
our home phone number was unlisted, but my email was distributed
to the Northside Neighborhood Association. One member took to
sending me late-night rants, copying the entire Charlotte City Council about her extreme opposition to our project in general and me in
particular. One especially disturbing email ended with telling me,
"You are not Jesus Christ."

I stared at my computer screen in shock. How did it get to this?
People hating this cause and me? I had never wanted to be a crusader
on any issue and certainly not for the homeless. I was just trying to
fulfill a promise, do some good, and "build some beds."

This was all pushing my "Quit" threshold. There was a distinct
probability of failure. Reason number one to quit. This was no longer fun and required an incredible amount of work. Reason number
two to quit.

I didn't want to tell anyone, including Charlie, how ugly things
had become because I was afraid he would urge me to give it up, and
I didn't need any encouragement on that. My friends were nervous

for me—one even gave me a Taser for self-defense, fearing I might need it in the neighborhood.

On top of the neighborhood struggles, the economy was getting worse, making the idea of raising $10 million completely unrealistic. Since that miracle $500,000 gift, no other donors had magically appeared in almost six months. Dale, Hugh, Downie, and I had gone on several calls to corporations and foundations but nothing was promising. Because we were not the typical civic project, school, or museum, it was difficult to convince a corporate funder that their dollars were actually for the greater good. Our heart and mind argument was not gaining much traction.

With the expense of buying and cleaning up the lot, our funds were dwindling with no real prospects for more grants. Our best hope was Bill Holt's dream of big-bank giving, but the Wells Fargo buyout of Wachovia had made that idea much more complicated. Wells was still shifting employees and job titles, so no one was sure who could authorize a large corporate gift.

Some of the residents were struggling as much as I was that spring. Although the pilot program was proving successful, it was also exposing more weaknesses. Without the money to build our own building, our program had a huge flaw—we couldn't actually protect tenants. Programs like The Prince George had a security guard to monitor who came and went. The turnstiles I had seen in the lobby weren't designed to keep residents *in*. I now knew they were to keep dangerous people *out*.

Joann and I were learning that those most at risk in our apartments were women leaving violence on the streets and those who were trying to break away from drug activity. Abusive boyfriends and drug dealers inevitably found where our tenants were living, even if we tried to move them to different apartments. We needed that security for tenants to be safe at home.

My biggest heartbreak that spring was a resident named Christine, who had become a darling of the program. Christine was barely five feet, almost as round as she was tall, with black hair badly dyed auburn on the ends. When we first moved her in, Christine was a teary mess of hugs for everyone, incredulous that the modest square footage belonged just to her. With a bellowing laugh and a husky smoker's voice, Christine was always the rowdiest and friendliest at our Homeless to Homes community gatherings.

It was this very same friendliness that had enabled Christine to survive on the streets by attracting imposing male boyfriends to become her protectors. Unfortunately, this also came with physical abuse. Christine determined it was better to be beaten by a boyfriend than by a stranger.

When she first moved in, Christine confessed, "You don't know how glad I am to be done with that life."

Christine was a model tenant, helping cook for her neighbor next door and giving up her heavy drinking. After a few months, however, Christine started to slide back to her old habits and we weren't sure why.

"I am worried about her, Kathy," Joann said. "She's hiding something and, really, she looks terrible again."

Clear-eyed Christine had once more become red-rimmed and bleary-eyed, and often wouldn't answer the door before noon.

"She's got someone in there with her," Raymond told me. "I let her know we don't need her messing up."

After more than a year together, the thirteen all looked out for each other. Joann and I rarely had to enforce the apartment rules—the tenants did it themselves. Several residents had confronted Christine about the man sneaking in and out her back door.

With the experimental nature of the program, each tenant was afraid of making a mistake that would jeopardize everyone else's housing. We let them know that proving Housing First could work meant expanding to a building that would help dozens more. We all were nervous that an arrest or something similar might disrupt this experiment. Most often, I worried about a front-page article that would end every feel-good moment of the last year. One drug bust, fight, or apartment fire might make the UMC board members vote to shut down the program.

Christine was looking like that one problem that could have huge repercussions.

Joann finally solved the mystery of Christine's change in behavior. "It's her old street boyfriend."

He was no small problem. The first time I saw Christine's secret man, I was at the apartments looking down at my phone, unaware he was approaching me on the courtyard sidewalk. All of a sudden, 6'6" of muscle was brushing past. I turned around to see his immense back disappearing around the corner. Our little enclave of apartments didn't get many visitors, so I was sure he was the man the other tenants had been complaining about. He was huge—terrifyingly so. I could see why no one, including Christine, was doing much about him setting up residency.

Christine swore to us that he was not living there; he was just "a friend who dropped by." Unless Christine was now wearing size 13 sneakers, the clothes in her closet told a different story.

"Can we call the police?" Dale asked in our summit about the situation.

Joann shook her head. "Not unless we can get Christine to swear out a warrant against him and she won't."

"Should we evict her?" I asked.

"This program is about second, third, and fourth chances," Joann said. "I want to give her the opportunity to do the right thing. But she is so afraid of him I don't think she will."

Christine didn't.

Joann called me one morning with the news. "She's gone."

I didn't need to ask. "Christine?"

"Yes, but there's more," she warned. I could tell from Joann's tone it wasn't good. "The appliances are gone. A truck came in the middle of the night, took them out of the kitchen along with Christine."

Not wanting to believe that Christine would do such a thing, I drove to the apartment to see for myself. The bare and damaged sheetrock in the apartment Mike Boyd entrusted to us confirmed the truth. Christine and her muscle man had forcibly removed the stove and refrigerator, along with all her possessions.

I dreaded the call to Mike letting him know the bad news, but he was remarkably understanding. We agreed the UMC would replace the appliances and he was still willing to take a chance on a new tenant. With this, the best outcome, I should have been happy. But the thought of what was happening to Christine haunted me.

Was she alive? Was she dead?

Had that 6'6" of muscle beaten the life out of tiny five foot Christine?

For the next few months, I kept an eye out at the Urban Ministry Center, hoping Christine would show up in Joann's office. Maybe she would finally take out a warrant on the guy, and we could get her back into housing.

I never saw Christine again. It was a brutal reminder that we needed our own building with twenty-four-hour security if we were ever going to provide lasting change.

Losing Christine was also the reason I realized I could no longer quit before achieving that goal. This new job I started had all the hallmarks of why I would want to quit—it was probably going to fail and it was too difficult. But now I realized there was another dimension: it was personal. I cared too much. The issue of homelessness was no longer anonymous; it was personal.

Denver changed me. I could no longer *not* see the problem. I couldn't walk into the UMC parking lot without being overcome by what had been invisible to me. I couldn't walk through that parking lot and *not* worry what happened after the gates closed at 4:30.

If I quit, I'd be backing out on Raymond, Coleman, Jay, Ruth, and nine others.

What would I tell them if I quit? Would they become homeless again if I backed out? Would they be lost to the dangers of the street again like Christine? Would Dale cancel the program, and tell John and Pat Moore this pilot program was just too difficult?

I couldn't live with that because as difficult as this job was, I had learned too well it was easy compared to being homeless.

———

"I'll take the fried chicken with hush puppies and collards, corn-bread, sweet tea, and two pieces of sweet potato pie to go," Raymond said. "But just the pie to go. The rest I'll have here."

Joann looked at me and smiled. We were gathered with all the Homeless to Homes residents around a long table at a Greek diner in our neighborhood for the monthly Birthday celebration. Gigi had taught me the best way to build family was to eat together and talk together, so we now planned at least one group lunch a month. The first outing we organized had been eye-opening. I realized most of our thirteen tenants had not eaten in a restaurant in years. One or two had trouble reading the menu, and the idea of sitting together at a table was incredibly awkward. The waitress had looked at our uncomfortable, unusual group of mixed ages, ethnicities, and genders and wondered how we had wandered into her diner. But like most southerners, she was polite.

"Can I get y'all something to drink? Honey, you want sweet or unsweet tea?"

Eventually we became regulars and the staff greeted us warmly. They still didn't know who or what kind of group we were but they welcomed us anyway. As we waited for our food, we would discuss local and national news stories, sports, and, of course, weather. Everyone had a TV in his or her apartment and they watched a lot of it.

Did you see about that forest fire in California?

Who'd you pick for the Final Four?

It's going to be 97 today!

At first, just the birthday person would get to order extra pie, but eventually, everyone ordered two pieces to go whether it was their birthday or not.

Our little group started to be more than members of some housing experiment. They became friends. Raymond teased Teddy because he never talked. James ribbed Ruth that she talked too much. Chuck was the intellectual who read *The Wall Street Journal* and knew more about foreign affairs than I did.

Everyone lived in Mike Boyd's apartment complex except Coleman. When we housed Coleman, there had not been an open apartment at Mike's place, so we had rented one about ten miles away. Coleman was excited about it at first because it was in a nicer neighborhood but eventually it became a problem.

He was lonely. Lonelier than Raymond had been. Coleman needed a friend.

The answer to his loneliness came in a phone call from a church that had heard about Homeless to Homes.

"We have a group of volunteers who are trained as Stephens Ministers," the pastor explained. Stephens Ministers are church members who have not gone to divinity school but are trained to give support to their fellow congregants. "Problem is, we don't have enough people in the church who say they want help. I have all these folks wanting to give help and nobody who will say they want to receive help."

Coleman became the first tenant to be paired with a church member named Scott Mercer.

Scott had moved to Charlotte in 1992 with his wife, Julie, and their four children. Working full-time for a large corporate insurance company, he devoted himself to family and church. When he found his true calling it was not during a church service, but on his front porch.

Scott loved reading the morning newspaper and thought they must have the most accurate paperboy because the paper was always folded neatly on his front steps. Scott truly believed someone with perfect aim threw those papers that landed on his porch every day. One morning around 5:30 a.m., Scott noticed a figure on his lawn. Looking closer, Scott was surprised to realize it was his neighbor, an older man, stooping softly to place the paper with great care on Scott's porch before quietly moving on to the next house. The man wasn't actually delivering the papers, Scott realized, he was just moving them from driveway to the front door as a service to his fellow neighbors.

It was a few years later when that same Good Samaritan developed cancer and ended up in the hospital that Scott realized the paper route wasn't just a neighborhood courtesy, it was a ministry.

Scott went to visit his cancer-stricken neighbor with a particular way to help: he offered to assume the paper route—or paper "placement" until his neighbor was well again. The man was immensely thankful but admitted moving the papers to the front porches was only part of the assignment.

In order to deliver the papers correctly, Scott learned he must do something else. Before he placed the paper on a front stoop, Scott had to pray for each family.

Scott was a little taken aback. He didn't pray for himself, much less others.

"Well that's the gig," said the neighbor, who had learned this quiet method of mission work while attending divinity school. One of his professors had encouraged his seminary students to try this random act of kindness and blessing as an act of gratitude each day.

Since he had already committed to assuming the route, Scott agreed to this second, unwanted task.

It was awkward at first, but over time, the morning ritual began seeping into his soul. As he delivered each paper, Scott loved the connection he felt to his neighbors and to God. He had always thought the ultimate act of service was a foreign mission trip but this simple act of kindness occurring on his own street changed his mind. Maybe Scott didn't need to go to a third-world country to help people when there were plenty who needed help in his hometown.

As he prepared to meet Coleman, Scott didn't know what to expect. Would he and Coleman be so impossibly different they couldn't connect? How would he talk to someone who had been homeless over twenty years? But Scott and Coleman found more in common than he expected.

They shared a love of sports, a commitment to people, a passion for good food.

Each week they met, whether to attend a baseball game or to have Sunday dinner with Scott's family. It wasn't long before Coleman became part of the Mercer family.

In learning to trust Scott, Coleman shared a part of his story that few knew. It was true that Coleman had met Joann right after witnessing the man who got cut in half by the train. But Coleman told Scott the real reason he had the courage to approach Joann almost a year ago was meeting a man who had been as much of an angel in his life as Scott.

A year before, after Coleman had prayed, "God, I don't want to die out here," he had been at the UMC getting lunch. A volunteer came up and touched the huge cyst on his shoulder that was now as big as a small melon.

"Son, you need to do something about that."

Maybe because he had just witnessed the man killed by the train, Coleman was starting to believe this growth might actually kill him. Coleman did what he hadn't done before: he admitted his fear to this UMC volunteer.

"I know, but I can't go to a hospital again," Coleman said, and confessed the whole story about the pain and paralysis from his hernia operation.

"Tell you what, how about you help me with some odd jobs and I will help you get a surgeon who will take that thing off and do it right?"

Skeptical, Coleman agreed, but secretly planned to miss the appointment, even as the kind man promised to make one.

Coleman began meeting the man each morning to help him with odd jobs. One day after finishing early, they stopped for lunch at a fried chicken restaurant. His new boss went to order while Coleman went into the restroom. As he was coming out, an African American woman in her fifties was standing right outside the door almost blocking his exit.

"Ma'am, this is the men's room. You don't want to come in here," he said.

"No, I know. I was waiting for you," she told him. "I have a message from God for you."

Coleman had no idea why she would say that to him, but he wanted to get away from her. He tried to move past but he was trapped in the tight hallway. Her next words, Coleman remembered with certainty.

"*Go ahead, everything is going to be all right,*" she cryptically assured him.

Every hair on his body stood up. *Did she mean the surgery? Had his new friend put her up to this so he would let a surgeon look at the giant growth on his shoulder?*

"If you allow me," she went on, "I'm supposed to pray for you."

And there, in the cramped restroom hallway of a fried chicken chain, she put her hand on his arm, bowed her head, and prayed. By the time the prayer was over, Coleman said it was as if the weight of his enormous cyst lifted and he felt light as a feather.

No sooner had she whispered "Amen" than she was gone, leaving him in the hall alone and astonished. Coleman walked slowly to join his friend, who had been watching the unusual sight of him holding hands with a strange woman in the back of the fast-food restaurant.

"Who was that?" the man asked Coleman.

Coleman didn't know himself. He was starting to explain when the man's cell phone rang. It was the hospital. They had a cancellation and could see Coleman day after tomorrow for surgery. *Could he make that?*

Coleman thought of the mysterious woman, her assurances and her prayer.

"I believe I can," Coleman said.

This time, there were no complications, only one more tiny miracle. The procedure was an outpatient procedure, but in Coleman's case, since he had no home to go home to, he would be released after surgery onto the streets. Coleman worried he would die of an infection, not being able to properly care for the wound in his dirty camp under the bridge. But when it came time to leave the surgery center, Coleman was told he was going to Samaritan's House—a respite care home in Charlotte for cases like his. Coleman spent three days in Samaritan's House and although he had a scar from shoulder to shoulder, he walked out on the fourth day and never had a problem with his incision.

Ever since Coleman had prayed to a god he didn't believe in it seemed good things had begun happening. First the stranger with work, then the prayer woman, then a successful surgery, then meeting Joann, Homeless to Homes, and Scott Mercer.

It was enough to make a man start believing in something.

21

The First Yes

There are only two ways to live your life.
One is as though nothing is a miracle.
The other is as though everything is a miracle.

ALBERT EINSTEIN

~~~~~~~~~~~~~~

I WAS STARTING TO BELIEVE IN SOMETHING, TOO. A YEAR AGO
if you had told me Coleman's story, I would have squirmed uncomfortably when you said the word prayer. But that was before I met
Lynn or Scott or even Coleman himself. That was before Bill Holt
had wandered into the same dream to do something about the same
problem that was keeping me up at night. I was beginning to feel
like not only was this project much bigger than I had imagined, it
was also being designed by someone other than me. It was time to
live up to the second promise I had made Denver.

David Furman's architectural drawings were complete, but we
still didn't have a name for our project. Sixteen months before when
he was leaving Charlotte, I had asked Denver, "Can I name it after
you?"

At that time, I didn't even know what *it* was. Now I did, and I
knew exactly what it should be called.

I invited John and Pat Moore to the Urban Ministry Center,
telling them I wanted to give them a progress report on the pilot

program. When they arrived, they brought their adult son, Kent, who was also a volunteer at UMC, singing in our choir.

After I gave the Moores a Homeless to Homes update, I spread the newly finished architectural rendering on the conference table. Our architects, David along with Steve Barton, had dreamed big: three stories of glass forming an L shape around an interior courtyard with a pavilion. Their plan showed all the features we had imagined: a computer lab, a library, an art center, a community garden, secured entrance, medical room, and counseling center. Natural light would fill the building through windows in each apartment and the dining room would feature three-story glass panels on two sides. There would be eighty-five apartments, each a modest 366 square feet, with their own galley kitchens and bathrooms.

Going through all the drawings with John and Pat, I wished it was as easy as willing it off the paper and into existence.

It was time to tell them the reason we had asked them here.

"In honor of all you have done and all Denver inspired, we would like to name this Moore Place," I told them. "After all *three* of you."

John looked shocked and Pat's eyes welled up. Their son, Kent, laughed. "I can't *wait* to see how this goes! They have never let anything be named after them!"

A minute passed and neither John nor Pat spoke. I was starting to worry they thought we wanted something from them.

"We aren't looking for more money," I assured them. "We wouldn't be this far without your belief in the pilot program. This is just a way to honor that and thank you."

They were holding hands at the conference table and tearing up looking at the drawings. I knew they were very private people; maybe this wasn't the honor we thought it was going to be.

Pat finally spoke, "I think if it is to honor Denver, too, then we could be all right with that."

Moore Place was fully born.

Denver Moore, John and Pat Moore. They were from different states, opposite ends of the economic spectrum, no relation, but they shared the same vision and the same last name.

Coincidence?

I was starting to side with Dale: *God-instance.*

With the building name decided, our last hurdle remained: the money. Dale and I approached large churches and existing donors, but were greeted mostly with skepticism that we could ever raise the remaining $9.5 million. Hugh McColl III and I went on dozens of corporate and foundation calls but were met with southern politeness when we said we had exactly one funder to date for the building project.

Expecting money from the city or state wasn't going any better. The city of Charlotte had denied our request for $500,000 because the neighborhood opposed us. The Northside Neighborhood Association and their city council representative still wanted Moore Place anywhere but in their neighborhood.

There was a long application process for city money that required a city council vote. Right now, we had only two of the eleven representatives willing to vote for us. The state of North Carolina was even more complicated, with a request for funding requiring a lengthy legislative process. We needed money *now.* The amount we needed was also so huge that even a generous gift of $25,000 still left a monumental money mountain to climb. We need a big, million-dollar kind of believer—the kind who was willing to be a little unconventional in their corporate or foundation giving.

Bill Holt had not stopped dreaming of asking his bank, now Wells Fargo, to be that big believer. Despite the merger and the gloom caused by all the banking turmoil, Bill called periodically with optimistic updates, but they would inevitably be dashed and further delayed by the reality of job losses or relocations from the merger.

None of that bothered Bill. He had faith that if we were patient, it would all work out. From the announcement of the merger in October 2008 to March 2009, Bill and others worked behind the scenes. It was clear this was one of our last chances to make this dream of a huge gift from a bank work. No other donors were going to take us seriously if all we had was the money to buy the land and nothing else.

Finally in March, the indecision ended. It became evident that whoever was named the Eastern Region President for Wells Fargo would decide our fate.

Bill called to give us the news: Laura Schulte had received the new head job and it was all up to her. A quick Google search indicated we might have a small glimmer of hope. Laura was moving from California, and one of the charities she had been involved with was LAMP—an organization that provided housing for homeless in Los Angeles.

Further reading led to more hope. LAMP was the organization profiled in Steve Lopez's book that had been made into a movie. *The Soloist* was the true story of Nathaniel Ayers, a talented schizophrenic musician who became homeless but was eventually housed in a LAMP apartment. We had just booked Steve Lopez to be the speaker at our next True Blessings luncheon, now going on its third year as a fund-raising event for UMC.

If nothing else, Laura Schulte would be familiar with our cause and we could connect through the fact that Steve Lopez was coming to Charlotte.

Twice, we geared up for a presentation and twice we were postponed due to Laura's hectic schedule. The meeting was finally set for April 15, 2009.

Dale, Bill Holt, and I rode the elevator up to the top floor of the executive offices. All of Charlotte was visible from floor-to-ceiling windows in the sky-high conference room. I thought of all the decisions that had been made in that room and wondered if any were as personal as this. Laura Schulte had no idea how momentous this day was for us. She had no idea we had done this presentation dozens of times, waiting for someone to say *yes*.

We started our pitch with Bill giving the background about Moore Place and Dale giving the history of UMC, along with the Steve Lopez connection. My part was to ask for money—the crazy $3 million part.

As Bill and Dale were talking, I tried to push down the panic. When it was my turn, I started with the remarkable progress in the pilot program and our dream to expand this solution to help more than thirteen people. I ended with hearing myself make the most preposterous request, "We'd like to ask Wells Fargo to partner with us and we request a gift of $3 million."

I waited.

The words hung in the room.

I wanted to take them back.

Say anything, I pleaded in my head, *just don't say no.*

My friend who is actually trained in development had taught me that when you ask for money, anything other than "No" was a win. If you ask for $100,000 and you get $100 that is still a win. We needed a win. We needed *something* from Wells Fargo.

Laura started speaking, but I had no idea what she was saying. My head was fuzzy and I felt nauseous with desperation. I tried to focus. She was smiling. She was nodding. She was consulting her team.

What was she saying?

What had I heard?

"Yes."

Yes? She had said *yes?*

To what? Had she said yes to another meeting? Had she said yes to $100,000?

Bill was smiling. Dale was smiling. My ears opened.

She was saying yes to it all.

Laura Schulte had said *yes* to $3 million for the most unlikely of projects. She had said *yes* to chronically homeless men and women. She had said *yes* not because she thought these homeless people would become future bank customers opening accounts. She was not saying *yes* because this decision would improve Wells Fargo's bottom line.

I finally could hear Laura Schulte, who was saying *yes* because "*this is the right thing to do.*"

She stood. We all stood. She left the room. Just like that.

Our fairy godmother left the room and had no idea that in granting our wish she had changed *everything*. I am sure she went on that day to make a hundred other decisions. But in our world, this was the only one that mattered. There was nothing bigger.

We filed out of the conference room and pushed the button to the elevator. Bill, Dale, and I exchanged glances, making a silent pact to wait until the elevator doors closed. We stood nonchalantly as the doors slowly came together.

Like we get $3 million commitments every day.

When the doors finally glided closed, we collapsed with relief, with happiness, and with the unimaginable improbability of it all. Even with his solid belief in God, Dale had not seen this coming. I started to cry and looked at Bill and realized he was crying, too. Here was the man who had predicted it. It had been 459 days since Liz and I sat in his office and Bill had announced his plan to ask for $3 million from his employer. At the time it was just an audacious dream, and today we had all been witness to it coming true.

We landed in the lobby like we had just left Oz and ended up back in Kansas. I wanted to tell everyone, to call the newspaper and make it the morning's headline. But we couldn't—that was part of the deal. As part of the pledge, we had made an agreement to fill out grant applications, go through review, and structure the terms. Wells Fargo people needed to talk with Wachovia Foundation people and that would turn out to be way more complicated than any of us imagined. It would take months but that day was the real start out of our fund-raising hole.

I didn't tell anyone our news except Charlie. Trying to recall the details of my remarkable meeting that day, it was still hard to believe. At dinner, he kindly listened to my excitement, letting it all sink in.

"That's great, Kathy," he said over dinner. "I'm really proud of you all."

His reaction was a little muted and I started to wonder why.

Charlie was in finance, so even as I was retelling my fantastic story, he couldn't help beginning to do the math in his head. As amazing as this news was, there was a harsher reality and he knew it—he just didn't want to be the one to say it.

It was about an hour after we finished dinner before it hit me. We were in our den watching TV when a slow panic started rising and broke through my euphoria.

We now had $3.5 million pledged.

Pledged.

Not in the bank.

And that left $6.5 million still to go.

For homeless people. In a recession. In a banking city where everyone worked in the two big banks, and everyone was losing or had already lost their jobs. And everyone owned bank stocks of those same two companies where stock prices had plummeted to single digits in a matter of months.

It finally hit me, and I spoke out loud the very problem Charlie had been too nice to point out at dinner, "Where are we going to get $6.5 million?"

The miracle that was the Wells gift morphed into a mountain seemingly impossible to climb. Without $6.5 million more we couldn't pay for Moore Place, and we certainly couldn't build something we couldn't pay for.

I had pinned my hopes on Moore Place: I would finally be *doing* something. Building it would be achieving my father's hope of imagining the unimaginable.

That is what hit me that night—I was very publicly the face of a project that I could not possibly accomplish, yet I could not possibly quit either. I couldn't quit on Raymond, Coleman, and Ruth. I couldn't quit before we even tried housing Chilly Willy.

A silence settled between us in the den and the TV carried on, oblivious to my distress. Finally, I asked, "Charlie, if we don't raise this money, does it mean I *failed*?"

Failure. My worst fear.

I wanted an out.

I needed an excuse.

Charlie may or may not have known it, but he gave it to me. He looked away from the television and directly into my panic. "Kathy, if you raise that money in this economy, it will be a frigging *miracle*."

And, for some reason, that was exactly what I needed to hear.

Charlie was right. This dream was improbable. The goal of $10 million in a recession for an "unworthy" group, impossible.

No one could blame *me* if a miracle didn't arrive.

22

Crazy or Called

How precious did that grace appear,
the hour I first believed.

"AMAZING GRACE"

WITH THE WELLS FARGO PLEDGE OF $3 MILLION AND CHARLIE
providing the release from failure, I could wake up each day and
keep moving. But, really, I had only been a year and a half on the
job and I was exhausted. At night, I counted tenants instead of
sheep.

Was Raymond still lonely?

Was Samuel going to his classes?

*Was anyone making any notable progress I could sell to donors to prove
this idea of Housing First works?*

Dale and I met weekly to talk about Homeless to Homes and
Moore Place. There was always a long list, starting with tenant issues,
progress on the environmental cleanup of our lot, construction drawings, and last but always: the never-ending issue of fund-raising. I
kept a running list of donors to meet with, grants to write, churches
to call, advocates to partner with and we would divide them up hoping for a few more miracles.

I struggled to keep kids, grants, and tenants straight, and my lists
were endless.

Grants applications due
   Smith Foundation
   Walters Foundation
Carpool— Soccer Emma and Maddie Tuesday, Thursday
Homeless to Homes Birthday Lunch
Lauren— mail package to school
Kailey— Basketball game/snacks for team

It was becoming so overwhelming that I was not juggling very well. It had been easy to design logos and be a mom. But caring for the homeless never ended. I couldn't cross through this project and turn off the light at night. I would be working on a grant and forget to drive a carpool. Answer a call from Joann and burn dinner. Stay too long with a potential donor and miss being home to ask the girls about their day. Or be too exhausted to even remember what was happening in their lives when I got home.

I tried to hide my doubts and weariness from everyone, especially Dale. He had been doing this for fifteen years. How could I complain after not even two years on the job?

Dale had calmness that this all would work out. That God would provide. I let Dale think that, but I certainly didn't believe that. My sister Louise sided with Dale. Ever since our initial conversation about Roseanne Haggarty, Common Grounds, and The Prince George, my sister just innately believed that this was all going to happen.

Both Dale and Louise had faith. I didn't.

In my mind, there was only one way to get this done and that was the earthly way of working hard, not through divine intervention. I had no faith God was going to rescue us. God certainly didn't know we had a capital campaign that was short $6.5 million; that success or failure was resting squarely on me. I might agree there had been some little God-instances and even two tiny miracles with the two big gifts, but we had *so* far to go. I wasn't expecting God to finish it for me.

Doubts plagued me, but I couldn't admit them to anyone. I needed everyone to believe that I was one hundred percent positive we could successfully house almost one hundred chronically homeless people. I needed to appear calm, confidant, and rock-solid to persuade donors. But inside, I was dying.

My real fear, I couldn't admit to anyone, including myself.

Beyond the fear of failure was my constant fear of how this all started. I had listened to Denver and then to a voice within myself that said, despite all logic, *build beds for homeless people.* From my childhood, the fear of listening to voices was immense. Usually when Mom started hearing voices, she would go away to a hospital so I rarely witnessed her mania. But my senior year of high school, I was old enough to be shielded no longer. That experience was indelibly printed in my memory, and ever since then, I worried similar voices would haunt me, too.

⸻

My dad and I pushed against the metal door, but it wouldn't open. Dad wasn't a big guy but he was athletic. Tanned face and strong forearms were the result of his decades of playing tennis.

Here, even if he had his racquet, it would not have helped open the hospital door. My mom was on the other side blocking our entry with the dresser, and we pleaded with her to let us in. If she had cancer, the door would not have been shut. But this was the hospital psychiatric ward. When you pushed the button for this floor on the elevator, the other people stepped back, sorry for your destination. I think they also moved back in case it was contagious. No one wanted to catch mental illness. It was 1979 and no one talked openly about it.

"Lindsay," my Dad implored, "please open the door. I brought Kathy and we want to see you."

Slowly, there was a long scraping noise and a hollow-eyed version of my mother was revealed in the two-inch crack. She eyed us suspiciously, with no real sign of affection or recognition, just a slightly wild look of confusion as she whispered, "Come in, but keep your voices down."

I didn't dare look at my father. It was all too bizarre.

My mom moved back to the hospital bed, picking up her usual pile of index cards and four-color Bic pen. With the multicolor pen she could record her brainstorms in the same vivid Peter Max versions that must appear in her head. Her attention went to the corner of the room, and her hands were poised as if ready to take dictation. She looked up expectantly at the TV, obviously entranced by the programming.

I hadn't noticed when we came in but the program that held her captive on TV was *All in the Family,* a seventies hit sitcom. Archie, the main character, was legendary for his crass, unenlightened opinions. That my mother, a brilliant, well-read artist, was hanging on his every syllable for secret coded wisdom was more than a little crazy.

We didn't even try to dissuade her. There was no point. We watched the show with her and did not comment as she dutifully penned notes on her three-by-five-inch cards during commercial breaks. I guess we thought it was the least we could do to offer some quiet companionship amidst the loneliness of her delusion.

We remained quiet even when the ads were on. Finally, when the episode was over, we left in silence, getting back on the elevator and walking wordlessly to our car. Dad started towards our destination, a business dinner that seemed equally absurd to attend, given the scene we had just witnessed.

I broke the hush first. "Dad? Mom thinks Archie Bunker is talking to her."

The lunacy of that statement hung in the front seat between us for a few minutes.

"I know … " he started, but seemed unable to find the encouragement or explanation he was looking for to comfort his seventeen-year-old daughter.

And then he did something he rarely did. He burst out laughing. There was no explaining it but I joined him. It was the kind of silent laughter that makes you shake and no sound escapes, but your whole body gets the most wondrous release. It went on for a few minutes, like a long hug that neither of us would release from. My dad was laughing so hard that tears leaked from the corner of his sad blue eyes. He wiped them away slowly, making squeaky sounds as the laughter subsided and he caught his breath. We didn't say anything else. There was nothing to say.

We went on to the dinner at a restaurant and when someone asked how he was, my dad smiled convincingly and replied, "Fine. How are you?"

———

That day and years later, I knew when someone suffered from mental illness it took every ounce of will to keep crazy at bay. Mom's daily courage was a constant choice to live. Not only did my mom have to fight to stay sane, we had to fight to stay sane with her. I know if my dad had left, or my grandparents had not helped me and my sisters, all of our lives would have been very different.

Living my mom's story was part of the reason it was easy to feel tied to each Homeless to Homes resident and feel personally responsible for doing something. A part of me had always wanted to be the one to save my mom from the pain of each episode. But as a six-year-old or even a seventeen-year-old, there was nothing I could do. Only doctors could find the right pharmaceutical combination to restore her to the woman who would eventually pursue her master's and travel to China.

Yet witnessing her manic episodes was also the very reason I was afraid to admit what I was terrified of now.

If I was "listening" to a man who was thirty years homeless "call" me to this quest, was I any different than my mom?

What if this whole idea was just a manifestation of those same bipolar genes?

What if the voice inside me that said I should raise money to build apartments for the homeless was not Denver's voice but a form of mania?

What if I was just as mistaken listening to that "call" as my mom had been listening to Archie Bunker?

Was I, at the age of forty-four, finally exhibiting the very inheritable trait for manic depression? Was Denver for real? Was any of it real?

Just as I had my whole life, I hid my fear of a nervous breakdown in the same box I hid my mom's mental illness. I never talked about it. I didn't want to tell Charlie or anyone that I was beginning to crack.

Finally, in late April, I sent an email to a minister at the new church we had been attending, Christ Episcopal Church. When it was time for Maddie and Emma to start the eighth-grade confirmation class, they begged me to let them do it at Christ Church instead of First Presbyterian. All their friends were at Christ Church. I acquiesced, happy that they would go somewhere without a fight. I knew one of the ministers, Lisa Saunders, because Kailey and her daughter had played soccer together. I emailed Lisa, asking if she would meet with me that week. I had no idea what I would say, but I had to talk with someone who was not a part of the Moore

Place story so I could be honest. I had to tell someone: *I think I'm truly crazy.*

<center>~~~~~~~~~~~~~~~~~~~</center>

As I drove to the appointment with the minister, I wrestled with what I would say. Was I mentally ill or was this some sort of actual spiritual *call*?

Honestly, I didn't want either one. Bipolar or called—both seemed like the same kind of crazy to me.

Lisa greeted me in the church lobby and we walked back to her office, exchanging small talk. The collar around her neck was a little startling as I realized she actually had a professional life that was not visible on the soccer sidelines. She sat next to me in one of the two chairs that faced her desk and waited patiently as I fumbled with how to begin. My voice was catching on my doubt as I tried to explain why I was there.

I started by telling her a little about my mom's struggles with manic depression and then outlining the overwhelming magnitude of the grand Moore Place master plan that had gone from an exciting change of career to a boulder that was crushing me. As I continued with the added layers of resistance from neighbors, the politics, the obvious money challenges, she listened quietly, like a therapist, knowing I would eventually see my own circle.

Finally, she led me to it by asking, "So why are you here?"

Months of lying awake at night came sharply into focus. The question I had been wrestling with, refusing to address, was suddenly right before me and undeniable. I looked at her, afraid to speak, but she seemed to know what I was going to say.

"The problem is, I really want to do this," I began. "I *really* want to build this building."

She nodded in encouragement.

"But I am not big enough to do it myself," I finally finished.

My voice was halting and I was trying not to cry. I had always been able to accomplish something I truly wanted. My childhood had taught me to be pathologically self-reliant—work hard to achieve things without anyone's help.

"To do this, I need to believe in something bigger than myself," I said, as if that were a huge problem. When I said it to a minister, it certainly did not seem like a problem. I tried to elaborate. "If I am going to succeed, I am going to *have* to believe that there is something besides me, bigger than me, that is going to get this done."

There, I had said it. Out loud. Almost. I had avoided the G word.

Lisa smiled at me. She was leaning forward, forearms on her thighs, hands together almost in prayer. "And what scares you about that?"

"Because it feels crazy! I feel like I am crazy! To believe that I have been given some message, *some call,* to build this thing feels crazy!" Now, I was crying. "And to actually *listen* to it feels even crazier."

Visions of my mom and the voices she heard during my childhood were plaguing me. Wasn't I just admitting that I was in some form of premanic state, hearing voices of grand plans?

"And what if it is not?" Lisa asked, simply.

What if?

What if I really was *supposed* to meet Denver and he really *was* giving me a message I was *supposed* to hear?

What if I really was *supposed* to get Moore Place built?

It felt too much like a Noah kind of foolishness, but *that* was the heart of it.

"It is what I keep coming back to: to get this done, I *have* to believe in God because I can't do this myself. But to believe in God means I *have* to believe I got some kind of message that started this whole thing. And I *can't* believe that part."

"Why not?" Lisa asked.

"Why me?" I choked. "Why would someone who doesn't even believe in God get a message from God?"

"Why not you?" she responded matter-of-factly.

Because I didn't want it. Because I didn't believe that kind of thing—Dale and Louise did. I didn't even like the spiritual parts of Ron and Denver's book; when it got too preachy, prayerful, or heavenly, I had skipped those pages.

I liked reality. I believed in reality. It was fine for Denver to believe he had a prayer chain going, but not for me. How could I believe that Denver, who seemed to speak from an otherworldly place, had an otherworldly message for me?

But I was back in that circle again.

I wanted Moore Place. I didn't want to fail. But to succeed, I had to ask for help. Big help. Otherworldly kind of help. As Charlie had said, it was going to take a frigging miracle.

My immense doubt sat heavily in the room, and Lisa waited patiently to see what I would do with it.

"So how will I know?" I whispered to Lisa. Afraid someone, even a minister, might hear me even thinking of Believing.

How will I know I am not hearing manic voices but some kind of real deal? And the really crazy thing was, my mom never stopped being a big believer. From those college days of reading the bible with my father to today, church and prayer were a huge part of her life. Faith had truly been her salvation in her darkest days.

Lisa leaned back and smiled. She seemed relaxed, like she had been waiting to deliver this punch line. "You will know," she said with utter confidence. "God has a funny way of showing off."

23

Gifts from Above

We must be willing to let go
of the life we planned so as to have
the life that is waiting for us.

JOSEPH CAMPBELL

LEAVING LISA'S OFFICE THAT DAY, I WAS COMFORTED BUT
not fully convinced.

It felt good to have finally spoken about the demon that was chasing me—I might have bipolar disorder. In my mind, it was actually the preferable alternative to think I was slightly manic than to believe I had been somehow divinely "chosen" for this task.

Lisa's conviction stuck with me and I started to sleep a little better by trying an awkward prayer as I lay down at night. I felt a little like Scott trying to pray for neighbors on his paper route. It didn't really count as prayer in the beginning. After I got in bed, I would try to release thoughts. More a list than a litany.

God, help us find some donors.

God, help the neighborhood not hate us so much.

God, help me fill out that CHA grant application.

That last plea, the Charlotte Housing Authority grant application, was my next biggest worry. It could be worth $1.7 million of grant money towards building Moore Place but even more critical, ongoing assistance for the next *thirty years* in rent subsidies from the federal government.

We were not excited about asking for federal money. Dale had been operating the UMC for years without taking a dime of public money—on purpose. Dale liked to act compassionately and quickly on behalf of the Neighbors. Government money meant red tape and regulations about who you could help and how. So to build Moore Place, we were going to rely heavily on churches and individuals.

Once it was built, however, we needed government partnership. If we could partner with the Charlotte Housing Authority (CHA) to provide federal rental subsidies, Section 8 vouchers, which cover rent, homeless people could move in directly off the streets and work with Moore Place social workers to apply for income from disability payments. No longer sleep-deprived and in trauma, our tenants could make completely different decisions about their addictions, education, and life. Just like Coleman, Samuel, and Raymond.

It would change everything for almost a hundred people, not just thirteen.

But this crucial partnership with CHA and the federal government had a huge hurdle I had not been able to cross. The incredibly complicated federal application entailed completing binders full of information and providing detailed budget projections for the next thirty years. *Thirty years* of budget projections? My graphic design background and degree basically equipped me to draw pictures. To complete this task, I needed an MBA.

As I leafed through the dense list of requirements, I was clearly in trouble. This was not about wanting to *do good*. This was real business with proformas and accounting that I had no idea how to even guess at completing. If I could not fill these out, much less understand them, we had no business building Moore Place. We couldn't build apartments for eighty-five tenants who all had no ability to pay rent. The brutal truth, I knew, was that I just couldn't do it.

Working my way through the lunch crowd of Neighbors at the UMC, I was stopped by Jerry Licari as I tried to make my way to Dale's office to confess to him that I was no longer the woman for this job. Jerry had been in the car that day when we first spotted the junkyard lot and had been waiting for a task on this project ever since. I hadn't given him one because I wasn't really sure what to ask him to do. He was Dale's pick for the team and I really didn't know Jerry's skill set.

"Excited with all the progress on Moore Place," he said as I tried to pass him.

I nodded, feeling like a huge phony. Should I tell him that Graphics Girl had finally come to the end of her usefulness? That the ability to write snappy headlines was not going to concept us out of this huge hole?

"I'd love to be doing more," he said. "Is there anything I can do to help?"

My sarcasm escaped before I could stop it. "Not unless you can do proformas."

I knew so little about the term that I didn't even know if I had formatted my sentence correctly.

He looked at me strangely. "Are you kidding?"

I locked eyes with him and got a weird feeling. "No, why?"

"I *love* that stuff!" he exclaimed and started laughing. "I'm a retired partner from a Big Eight accounting firm. I can do that in my sleep."

I tried not to burst into tears. If what he was saying was true, it was going to mean more than me being able to keep my job and more than just being able to sleep again at night. It would truly be the difference between leaving people to die on the streets and finally bringing them home.

And what Jerry said that day was absolutely true. Jerry was a financial wizard who became the volunteer chief financial officer for Moore Place. We would be joined at the hip for the next year and a half. He created and endlessly revised financials for Moore Place. We attended countless meetings together and worked for months to craft the documents needed to secure public funding.

When the Charlotte Housing Authority held a vote on whether to award Moore Place not only $1.7 million in construction funds but Section 8 rental subsidies for the next thirty years, Jerry was sitting right beside me. Together, we watched the CHA Board members raise their hands one by one and vote "Yes."

What I didn't know until almost four years later is how improbable that meeting with Jerry turned out to be. We were having coffee in 2013 when Jerry confessed that the day we spoke in the hall was the first time he had actually admitted his accounting background. After retiring in 2006, he had made a pledge to himself to do something completely different with his life. He was done with the accounting world; he wanted no part of it.

Jerry had researched nonprofit agencies before his retirement, selecting UMC as one of two he would volunteer for, but he only wanted to be a counselor. When first asked by the UMC volunteer coordinator what his former profession was he replied, "I was a businessman." Even when Dale asked him to be on the UMC Board, Jerry had not admitted his vast prior accounting experience.

Jerry later confided, "That day was the first time I had told anyone at Urban Ministry what I used to do for a living."

For some reason that day in the hallway, Jerry thought differently about his expertise and had blurted out his skill set without thinking. Jerry finally realized his experience, his talent that he was tired of, was the one gift he needed to share. And it changed everything.

God has a funny way of showing off.

* * *

With Jerry leading the financial wizardry and Joann doing the day-to-day management with Homeless to Homes residents, I was left with the giant financial hill to climb. Although the Charlotte Housing Authority added $1.7 million, that left $4.8 million to magically appear. We had gone on dozens of calls to potential donors but the summer had been slow. The wonder of Wells Fargo was wearing off.

I looked at my watch and saw it was my table-wiping time. Dale insisted that one day a week all staff, no matter our job description, had to clean tables in the lunchroom. He felt it was easy to get caught up in administrative tasks and forget why we were all here—to help our Neighbors. There was something about wiping up dozens of nasty vegetable soup spills once a week that kept one humble. But inevitably, like today, I did not want to go. I really needed to finish an important grant application for the John S. and James L. Knight Foundation. We were applying for $1 million, and the deadline was looming.

I had six days to submit the application, a complex matrix of exacting questions and measurements designed to be sure we knew what we were doing. It felt like I was writing a master's thesis and in some ways I was. It was the culmination of a year and a half of on-the-job training and learning from other national programs. The Knight Foundation, like others, didn't care if we were doing good; they needed to be sure we could do it well. Budget projections, staffing models, and funding plans all had to be submitted along with answers to more probing questions.

Describe why the project is a priority in your community and how it presents an opportunity for transformational change.

What direct outcomes do you expect as a result of your activities and how will you know you have been successful?

What do you expect the broader, long-term results of your work to be?

The answers would have to wait until after table duty. The lunchroom was noisy and crowded as usual. I worked my way to the back to pick up a rag and waved across the room to Liz Clasen-Kelly, who had duty that day, too. As I started wiping down, I saw a young guy with wild dreadlocks get up from his table and sneak up behind those patiently waiting to pick up their trays at the stainless steel counter. I looked back to his place, where he had obviously eaten one lunch already. The UMC offered seconds on food but only in the last fifteen minutes to be sure everyone was served at least once. It wasn't a crime really, and I knew everyone who came here was legitimately hungry. But he was breaking the unwritten rule that everyone abided by. I moved up behind him to see that sure enough, he was grabbing an extra bowl.

"Excuse me?" I said.

He looked at me. Hazel eyes wild and red-rimmed. "What?" he replied roughly.

"We aren't serving seconds yet."

"This ain't seconds," he said.

"Really?" I said, pointing to his first tray still on the table behind us.

"What's it to you?" he asked loudly now, so that several people looked up, including a guy with a dirty brown leather cowboy hat eating quietly next to the man's empty tray.

I wasn't sure I was going to do or say anything more, but before I had the chance to decide, the young soup stealer threw the offending bowl of tomatoes and noodles on me. Immediately, the guy in the cowboy hat jumped up between the soup thrower and me.

"Hey! You watch yourself!" he yelled to the young rule-breaker.

The wild dreadlock guy looked like he might go after the cowboy, but two other men stood up and joined sides with my new bodyguard.

"You go on now, boy," one of them said loudly.

When the young guy turned to slink away, the cowboy asked, "You okay, ma'am?" He looked at me with kind, sky-blue eyes and a weathered face as tanned and lined as his hat. Honestly, he wasn't much taller than me, and I was even more surprised that he had stood up to defend me from the much larger and seemingly stronger thug.

I looked down at my blouse. Luckily, most had missed me and gone on the floor.

"Yes, thanks so much. I'll be fine."

Wiping my shirt, I realized I didn't even know this guy's name. "I really appreciate that you stood up for me. What's your name?"

"Bill, ma'am. Bill Halsey."

I held out my hand to shake his. "Thank you, Bill." It struck me I had never noticed Bill and now he was my protector at the Urban Ministry Center.

Liz had been working her way through the crowd.

"You okay?"

"Yes, thanks to Bill."

"Oh, I just love him," Liz said. "He's one of my favorites." She, of course, knew his story and filled me in.

Bill Halsey had one of the most unusual living arrangements of any street person in Charlotte. He had tried living in the men's shelter but it was too chaotic for him, so Bill created the only house he could. Along the railroad tracks, he had found a six-by-seven-foot concrete platform that once was used to unload bales of cotton from freight cars. Bill didn't pitch a tent on top of it; he dug a hole *under* the concrete. It took him two months to excavate his home underground: an eight-by-eight-foot dirt cave with just enough room to stand up in. Bill had been living in that hole for about five years.

As unusual as that living arrangement sounded, I kind of understood it. Bill's need to go underground for safety was not that much different than a six-year-old making a haven out of the top of a closet shelf.

"My dream day," Liz said, "will be to see Chilly Willy and Bill Halsey move into Moore Place."

I finished my shift and went back to my office.

It was astounding to think someone as sweet as Bill Halsey was living in a hole in the ground. It was amazing to think of men like Coleman and Samuel who had been on the streets for decades. They were the faces of this argument for housing, but I wasn't sure how to make anyone else care.

I had a lot of facts and data to put into the Knight application, but I also had these real-life stories that told why it truly mattered. Would someone at the Knight Foundation care about an argument of the heart as much as an argument designed for the head? I took a chance in the closing section. Maybe it was more appropriate to write a grant sticking with formal technical language and statistics. But maybe, just maybe, those reviewing the applications got tired of reading all that and wanted to hear what truly mattered. I wrote:

One fifty-year-old resident named Samuel who was in our pilot program was visiting the UMC after his first day of classes at the local community college. He was impeccably groomed and dressed in a pressed collared shirt, and proudly held his college backpack. Clearly, he stood out amidst the tattered crowd of 400 gathered in line for the UMC Soup Kitchen lunchtime meal. He had previously been a part of that crowd for more than twenty years. As he showed

others his syllabus and books, a UMC employee marveled,
"I can't believe it. I always thought he was a lost cause."
He and twelve others are proving daily in Charlotte that
there are no lost causes. Moore Place will offer the possibility
of transformation to 85 others. Their collective chance for
change will offer inspiration and hope not only to those
seeking housing but more importantly, to the housed
among us who once believed the homeless were hopeless.

I sent up a little prayer as I pressed "Send."

———————

Although we were focused on fund-raising, the resistance from the
Northside Neighborhood Association had not gone away. Throughout that summer, we were attending city and neighborhood meetings, trying to change sentiment, but it wasn't working. In late July
2009, I checked my computer and couldn't believe what I was reading. It was an email about a Northside church that wanted to help:

[We] recently heard that the property across the street
from us has been purchased by the Urban Ministry Center.
We are thrilled about that and hope that we can partner
with whatever is going on there in the future.

I knew the church, First Christian, and it was directly across
the street from our junkyard purchase. It didn't look like a tradi-
tional church—just a simple cement building that I had driven past
a hundred times. It felt almost too good to be true—a friend in the
neighborhood? Actually, a *group* of people that claimed to be *thrilled*
we were building?

It was a hot southern summer day when I went to First Christian but I was sweating for other reasons. I needed this to go well. After all the neighborhood meetings where people had been very unpleasant, I worried that it might be some kind of setup. Maybe they just wanted me there so the whole congregation could publicly shame me.

As promised, however, it was just the pastor and two friendly church members who greeted me. We sat down awkwardly in kid-sized chairs in a classroom with the happy voices of a children's summer bible camp going on in the room next door. After exchanging introductions, I brought out our brochures with the drawings of Moore Place in hopes of convincing them they had nothing to fear or protest. I was desperate to assure them these new neighbors would be like Coleman—good people who needed a chance.

"You don't need to convince us," the pastor said. "We already want to help. We did an all-church read of a book and it was very powerful."

I was amazed—an entire congregation wanting to work together on homelessness? It was a small church with seemingly limited resoures, so it was even more impressive that they wanted to generously give back.

"Wow—that's great," I said. "What was the book?"

"*Same Kind of Different As Me*," he replied.

Of course it was.

Both Dale and my sister Louise laughed when I told them.

"Kathy, you cannot make this up!" Louise said over the phone. "You are on some kind of cosmic journey! You better start writing all this down!"

I sent Lisa Saunders an email that night saying simply, "God showed off again today."

Once I was looking and listening, it seemed God was everywhere.

I had not talked to Scott Mercer much since we had paired him with Coleman, but we needed more help raising money. With a vested interest in one of our Homeless to Homes residents, I hoped Scott might be willing to be on the team asking for corporate and private donations. We met at a pancake house and talked so much about Coleman and their friendship, we barely got around to the Moore Place Capital Campaign.

"Coleman had dinner at our house a couple months ago and I served him some of my special BBQ sauce," Scott told me.

"'Scott, this is so good you should sell it,'" Coleman told him.

"And so we are!" Scott announced.

He proudly showed me a photo of the new joint venture with Coleman. A red, white, and blue bottle of BBQ sauce with the label reading, "EC's Home BBQ Sauce—The taste that brings you home."

They had already started bottling and were looking for retailers to carry their product. Scott told me the kicker. "Coleman wants to give the proceeds to the Urban Ministry Center for all they've done for him."

Scott told me he believed he was meant to meet Coleman. Their bond had become family in the same way Denver had become part of Ron Hall's family.

We were talking so much that I almost forgot why I had asked Scott to meet. As he was hurrying out, I put a Moore Place brochure in Scott's hands and asked if he would help raise money. The brochure had been created by two of my advertising friends, Julie Marr and Arkon Stewart. Inside the pages featured three people— a doctor, Jane Harrell, telling the story of how housing was vital to health; a district attorney, telling the story of how housing prevented misuse of community tax dollars; and Coleman, telling his story of the transformative power of housing.

Scott quickly flipped through the pages and agreed to connect later on details. That afternoon, I opened this email from Scott:

Kathy,

You are never going to believe this. When we were looking at the brochure this morning, I missed a page and testimonial from my physician, Dr. Jane Harrell. We have a special connection because due to her intuition and diligence she diagnosed me with early stage prostate cancer. At my fairly youthful age (by medical standards), most patients my age would not have been screened. In effect, Dr. Harrell saved me from a much worse outcome. The truth be known, I will always credit Dr. Harrell with saving my life. We have talked about this openly and we have talked about my "paper route" and she feels strongly that she was guided to have me screened for a greater purpose in my life.

You should have seen my face when I looked through the brochure again this morning upon returning to my office from our breakfast and seeing Dr. Harrell's testimonial just one page behind Coleman's. It really gave me chills. I can't wait to share with Jane on my next check up. She will be blown away when she finds out that I was paired with Coleman in your program!

Scotty

It was beyond coincidence. I hadn't even known Dr. Jane Harrell when we put her in the brochure. She was helping start a clinic at UMC, and Dale had suggested she present the medical perspective in our brochure. Neither of us knew there was any connection to Scott Mercer or Coleman.

I could no longer be surprised working on this project. Now, anytime there was a God-instance, I just looked straight up and whispered *thank you*.

———

It was September 14, 2009. I had been watching the calendar all month and the clock all day. Susan Patterson with the Knight Foundation had told me the vote would be today. Our campaign was stuck at around $5.5 million and we needed a boost. The million dollars they were voting on would not only push us past the critical halfway mark, it would signal to other foundations and donors that we were legitimate. All of the work on that master's thesis of an application came down to today.

I stared at the phone on my desk, willing it to ring. Willing it to bring good news.

When it did ring, I was afraid to answer because a *no* would be too devastating.

"Kathy, they voted," Susan began. I could see her bright red hair and stylish black glasses.

"The John S. and James L. Knight Foundation is pleased to award Moore Place a grant of $1 million."

I collapsed with relief. Susan and the Knight Foundation had the courage to be a little unconventional. It seemed that heart-and-head argument I had written had worked. All the meetings, all the cups of coffee and grant requests were finally starting to pay off, and we had $6,997,000 of the $10 million needed. Susan Patterson, as our newest donor with the Knight Foundation, suggested we hold a press conference to announce how far we had come and ask the public to help us raise the final $3 million.

We were already excited about announcing our success to date when the senior pastor at Myers Park Presbyterian (Scott Mercer's church) called Dale. The church wanted to contribute in a big way and they wanted to reveal it live at the press conference, Monday, October 19, 2009. Dale added him to the program.

I was helping set up one hundred chairs that morning in the old train depot. We had no idea if anyone would come, but friends and donors started arriving a little before 10 a.m., easily filling the room. The depot was buzzing with excitement when Jane Harrell, the doctor pictured in our fund-raising brochure and Scott's lifesaver, hurried over to me. Her wispy blonde hair was pulled back and under her coat she was in her physician's blue scrubs, having just finished a free clinic for UMC. I assumed she was coming for the press conference.

"Don't think I'm crazy," she began. "I just can't sleep. God keeps telling me to do this so now I'm doing it."

With that, Jane shoved a plain white envelope in my hand, turned around, and disappeared out the door. *That was strange.* Confused by what all that meant, I watched Jane as she headed to her car. Although I was incredibly curious about her message to me, the press conference was about to begin, so I slipped the envelope into my pocket for later.

By the time we got started, the train depot was overflowing and there was standing room only. The program began with Coleman and Scott each sharing a little about how they met and what a difference they had made in each other's life. Next up were representatives from Wells Fargo and the Charlotte Housing Authority before Dale introduced the pastor, Steve Eason, from Scott's church.

With an impassioned speech acknowledging the suffering in Charlotte due to the lost jobs at banks and the recession, Steve spoke as if it was a Sunday morning sermon, not a press conference. The pastor's plea was powerful, but Reverend Eason's final line was the most compelling, addressing all that Charlotte had lost in the past few years due to the failing economy and the loss of the two big banks as our civic centerpieces. Reverend Eason preached:

> *We can live in a community that has lost jobs or even lost businesses*
> *but we can't live in a community that has lost compassion."*

Then, his big finish was his surprise announcement. Myers Park Presbyterian Church was giving $250,000 to the Moore Place campaign—part of it as a challenge grant encouraging other churches to give. The church would give us $150,000 and then the final $100,000 once fifty other churches had given as well. Reverend Eason was calling upon the faith community to collectively declare that the homeless were decidedly worthy of support.

It was out-of-the-box thinking. That a church would give such a large gift, but also the idea to recruit fifty other houses of faith to join this campaign. My heart pounded as I did the math in my head: we were now at $7.25 million—under $3 million to go. Everyone in the room seemed to know this was huge news.

It was the best kind of feel-good story, one that would make the news on all four local stations and the front page of the newspaper the next day.

Leaving the press conference, I was ecstatic. This impossible dream was looking clearly possible. Reaching in my coat pocket for my car keys, I found Jane's envelope. Remembering her words, I wondered what "God kept telling her to do," and ripped open her envelope. There was no note, no further explanation.

Just a check to Moore Place for $10,000.

24

Bless and Multiply This Small Amount

Sometimes our light goes out,
but it is blown again into instant flame by
an encounter with another human being.
Each of us owes the deepest thanks to those
who have rekindled this inner light.

DR. ALBERT SCHWEITZER

THAT FALL, JANE HARRELL'S CHECK WAS ONE OF MANY GIFTS that seemed to just drop from heaven.

The good press coverage gave us a huge boost and gifts came in all sizes, from a children's lemonade stand that raised $105 to yet another check for $10,000 from a woman I'd never met without any explanation of who she was or why she sent it.

By far, the most mysterious gift, however, came from someone I began calling our Mailbox Angel.

Her first gift arrived when I was checking for mail at the UMC desk, which is a Grand Central Station kind of operation. Hundreds of Charlotte homeless people use 945 North College Street, our address, as their place of residence to receive checks or communicate with family. Thousands of letters are sorted each week by volunteers and put into cardboard boxes sorted A–B, C–D, E–H, and through the alphabet.

Staff mail is mixed in with this landslide of communication and oftentimes a volunteer, not recognizing "Izard" as an employee, would put my mail in the Neighbors' box. Because of this common confusion, I had a habit of not only checking my staff slot in the back but also sorting through the big box of Neighbor mail. Sure enough, a pastel envelope, which did look like a Neighbor letter from home, was resting in the I–L box with my name on it.

I took it back to my office and turned it over. There was a return address of Farmington Lane in Charlotte but no identified sender. Just my name and the Center address on a small pink envelope. Tearing it open, I found a greeting card inside like one a grandmother would buy: soft colors and violets. My mother would never buy this kind. She routinely went for the Peanuts and humor cards. When I opened the card, the mystery deepened when a $10 bill fell out. Under the preprinted card message there was this handwritten note:

May God Bless and Multiply this small amount.

That was it. No signature. No clue.

Who had sent it? Had they read about the campaign in the paper? Did I know them?

The next month, another pastel envelope arrived. Again, no name with the return address; just a card, a $5 bill, and the message, "*May God Bless and Multiply this small amount.*" The next month, another. Someone liked Hallmark as much as my mom. Each time a different dollar amount but each time the same blessing of the gift.

I started to profile my benevolent giver. A woman, I was certain. I imagined soft gray hair framing the face of an elderly, Oprah-like saint who saved up her dollar bills at the end of each month to send to us. I wanted to meet her and tell her that her gift gave me outsized hope each time an envelope arrived. The idea that someone I never met would save her dollars each month and give them to this cause made me feel I wasn't crazy to dream this at all. And that just maybe a higher power was spreading the message far more convincingly than Dale and I ever could.

It seemed her prayer was taking hold—the small amounts were being multiplied, and they were adding up significantly, moving us towards $8 million.

Dale took to the phones in order to meet the Myers Park church challenge grant announced at our press conference. Having been a minister in Charlotte for decades, he had an extensive network to call upon. Dale reached out to pastors from every house of faith to let their congregations know we needed them. He was persuasive. Methodist, Baptist, Catholic, Unitarian, and Jewish congregations joined the Presbyterians at every level. Some collected specific offerings for Moore Place and we received the day's collection. Odd amounts like $1,516 from St Ann's Catholic or $2,351 from Avondale Presbyterian. Others gave thousands of dollars from their own capital campaigns, including $30,000 from mine, Christ Church, and $75,000 from Myers Park United Methodist in honor of a church member who had once been homeless.

The past two years of convincing were starting to converge into a chorus of *yes*. With churches, foundations, and families donating, we had so much momentum that a friend, Jan Shealy, started helping me track it all. By November 23, 2009, only a month after our press conference, we had received checks and pledges to total $8,116,000, with $1,884,000 to go.

"Mom, get off the phone!" Maddie told me.

We were driving to the mountains for the holiday weekend and I checked my cell at every stoplight. A reporter from the *Observer* was going to call me for a Thanksgiving article he was writing on Moore Place. The lead angle was that we had raised nearly a million dollars in only one month since our press conference.

While I was glad for the publicity, I was nervous about the impact. A million dollars in one month was a huge story, but I didn't want people to think we didn't need their gifts. We still had a long way to go—almost two million dollars. It was going to take another breakthrough gift like the Knight Foundation to make this happen.

My cell phone rang in the car and Emma grabbed it away. "Mom, it's Thanksgiving!"

"I know, but this could be important! What's the number?"

She read it out and I didn't recognize it.

"Okay, let it go to voice mail," I relented.

We turned up the radio, and I focused on singing, driving, and family. The twins were right. It was Thanksgiving and I could forget about Moore Place for a few days. When we arrived, we got busy with all the cooking. Having four daughters was the best for holidays, because everyone had learned our family recipes and each had their own specialty. Lauren hand cut bread cubes for the sausage stuffing, Maddie kneaded and rolled the dough for the ham biscuits, Kailey created apple pies, and Emma made the cranberry sauce. Charlie was in charge of the turkey, so each year I focused on chopping onions and celery, mashed potatoes, green beans with almonds, like Gigi used to make, and gravy.

We spent the afternoon listening to music and bumping elbows in the kitchen until dinner. Every Thanksgiving, we always went around the table to say what we were grateful for.

"I am grateful Mom stayed off her phone and computer all afternoon," Maddie said.

We all laughed, but it made me remember that voice mail in the car I never listened to. It was three hours later when the dishes were done before I finally played it.

"Kathy, this is Tom Lawrence with the Leon Levine Foundation."

Hugh McColl III and I had made a presentation to the Levine Foundation months before and submitted an application, but we hadn't heard back. They were the most prominent local foundation, and after months of no word, we assumed we had not made their priority list for the year.

"The Leon Levine Foundation is pleased to award a grant of $500,000 to Moore Place."

I knew what I was grateful for that Thanksgiving. I saved that voice mail on my phone for three years and played it over and over. That remarkable message would boost year-end giving to just over $9 million: an impossible amount, especially considering that the Wells Fargo gift had been awarded only six months before.

With under a million dollars to go, I started getting nervous not about finishing the campaign but about delivering what we had promised donors. Moore Place was going to be a home for people like Chilly Willy, Bill Halsey, and hopefully women like Christine— men and women who had been on the streets for decades. Their lives were complicated and keeping them housed was going to be a daily challenge.

Moore Place was only going to be as good as the people running it and that needed to start with an incredibly effective Executive Director. That job was one I knew was over my head. The last two years I had been saved repeatedly by people like Jerry and the Five Guys filling in my weaknesses. Now we needed someone who was actually qualified for this twenty-four-hour-a-day job.

Dale knew we needed someone as well. "We better start advertising now because it could take a long time to find someone."

Honestly, I had no idea who would take this job. The ad would need to read:

Must be fearless and have no personal life.

I didn't put that in job description but it was true. I knew what Joann gave up on a daily basis to keep Homeless to Homes going. It was going to be her job times eighty-five. I listed the position on a national nonprofit website and hoped somebody like Mother Teresa would apply.

———

There were 115 volunteers all over downtown Charlotte wearing purple T-shirts that read "Counting on Change." Liz Clasen-Kelly and I had been working for months on this, the most important phase of Moore Place other than raising the money. Once we built the building, what would really matter was the people who would live there. This week was all about finding out who in Charlotte needed Moore Place the most.

Having gone through the agonizing process of trying to choose the thirteen for Homeless to Homes, we knew we needed a more objective, data-driven approach to choose the residents for Moore Place. We had no idea how many chronically homeless people there actually were in Charlotte, but our best guess was three to four hundred. With only eighty-five Moore Place apartments, we had to make sure those apartments were filled with the street homeless who most needed housing.

In advising us on setting up a program, New York's Common Ground suggested we conduct a Vulnerability Index study. Common Ground had developed this survey system with a researcher at Johns Hopkins University. The scientifically developed series of questions could help determine which chronically homeless were most likely to die on the streets. With this knowledge, we could systematically, rather than subjectively, prioritize men and women for housing.

We set the Vulnerability Index (VI) study for February 22–26, 2010, choosing the winter because typically more homeless people used shelters more often in the brutally cold months. The VI Survey system called for training volunteers, who would then attempt to interview every chronically homeless person in Charlotte during a one-week period. Ideally, at the end of the week, we would have a database of every chronically homeless person in Charlotte ranked by how likely they would be to die on the streets. From this we would create a priority list for Moore Place.

The system was straightforward; the implementation was daunting.

Since Liz loved data, she led the project. By enlisting the help of colleagues and agencies who already worked with the homeless, Liz organized fifteen partner organizations and over one hundred community volunteers. For four days, teams would begin as early as 5 a.m. in the tent camps around downtown and others worked as late as 9 p.m. in the shelters.

Common Ground sent three staff to help us conduct the city-wide search for every chronically homeless person in Charlotte. Becky Kanis, the lead on our project, had served in the military and still had close-cropped hair, but her wide-open personality was anything but regimented. All week she was like a talk show host guiding the 115 volunteers through the arduous survey process. Becky had led this survey in twenty-one cities and was supremely confident in accomplishing what felt like a herculean task. For four days, all over Charlotte, volunteers heard what the city's homeless had to say. Many had never actually spoken to a homeless person, so the stories of struggles they heard lingered long after the data had been transcribed.

There were revelations and a new understanding of the different ways a slide into homelessness begins. One volunteer talked about a man who confided to her. "You know I never thought I'd be homeless, but when I told my family I was gay, they kicked me out. No one will have anything to do with me. I don't have anywhere to go."

As we gathered stories and data, we realized the final conclusions were going to reveal a tally larger than we had imagined—807 people who had been homeless more than a year, almost double our highest estimate. The most startling statistic we learned was that Charlotte had more people identified as being homeless for over twenty years than even Los Angeles' Skid Row, which most considered the country's worst homeless problem.

It was a long, exhausting week, but the results were going to be powerful in convincing the community that Charlotte did indeed have a long-ignored problem of chronic homelessness and Moore Place was the solution.

Becky and one of her coworkers from Common Ground arranged to meet me for dinner Thursday night to celebrate the success of the week. I had spent so much time with logistics and Becky that I had barely spoken to Caroline Chambre, who had also flown down from New York with the Common Ground team. Caroline had been helping with data entry all week. So when I saw her, she usually had her blonde head down, focused on a laptop or deciphering a volunteer's handwriting.

That night, we had just finished ordering in the restaurant when Becky left the table to go to the restroom. With Becky gone, Caroline leaned over the table and quietly said, "I saw your ad."

What ad? With all the registry work, I had forgotten that a mere two weeks prior my biggest concern had been hiring a director for Moore Place. What she was talking about finally clicked. "The ad for Moore Place Executive Director?"

She nodded.

I couldn't imagine why she was even looking. Caroline held a prime job in the most respected agency for housing homeless in the country. Why in the world was she job-hunting in Charlotte when she worked for Common Ground in New York?

"Is it for real?" she asked. "Aren't you going to take that job?"

She had no idea how much I did not want that job, but the real question was, "Why in the world would *you* want to come to *Charlotte*?"

"I am from here," Caroline said simply. "I grew up in Charlotte, went to South Mecklenburg High. My parents are still here but my dad's been sick. I've wanted to move back to Charlotte to help my mom for a long time, but I didn't think I could find a job like the one I have now in New York."

Caroline's resume was better than I could have hoped for. Over the past few years, she had managed a portfolio of four housing programs for chronically homeless with a staff of seventy. She had even been the director at one property with 650 residents—Moore Place with eighty-five would be simple by comparison.

But there was one fact from her resume I could not believe. Caroline had not only worked for Common Ground, she had been on staff at the Prince George property—the very same one I had visited at Christmas two years before.

The same one where Moore Place began to be more than just a promise to Denver.

Caroline started as the new Director of Moore Place two months later and that's when I knew the final twist in her story.

"The crazy thing is, Kathy," she told me. "I wasn't even supposed to be on that trip."

"What do you mean?"

"That trip to come down here for the Vulnerability Index?" she said. "I wasn't scheduled to be one of the three who came from Common Ground. Someone bailed, and at the last minute, Rose-anne Haggarty told me to get on the plane instead."

It truly felt to me that Caroline was another in our series of God-instances and just one more person who Denver promised "knew they were coming."

One of Caroline's very first assignments was to go back to her own high school, South Mecklenburg High. Their service club hosted a week-long campaign each year to highlight a local social justice issue and a fund-raising walk for that cause. This year, the students had picked Moore Place.

The organizers at South Meck High wanted a UMC staff member paired with a Homeless to Homes resident speaker to highlight the issue. Caroline, as an alum, was the obvious choice and Coleman jumped at the chance when Joann offered.

Driving to the high school, Caroline had asked Coleman if he had his speech ready.

"I know what I want to say," he said.

Caroline decided not to press but hoped he was right. When they got to the school, Caroline and Coleman entered the gym filled with hundreds of teens. I'm sure like most high school assemblies, attendance was mandatory, and so those restlessly waiting were in a state of enforced compliance, not actually curious about the program that was about to begin.

Caroline spoke first, telling about her work with Common Ground in New York, the Homeless to Homes success, before introducing Coleman as one example.

Coleman came to the lectern, quietly gazing back at the fidgeting students. He continued to stare, not moving, not saying a word. Caroline began to worry. Had he forgotten his notes in the car? Was he paralyzed by the large crowd of teens in front of him?

Finally, Coleman leaned into the microphone and spoke softly, "Can you see me?"

Caroline, and maybe the gathered students, thought he meant did they have a good vantage point for the stage. Some students shifted in their seats, maybe to actually get a better view.

Another uncomfortable silence.

"Can you see me?" Coleman asked again.

This time the question was more disturbing. Was Coleman all right? Was he stalling for time? Maybe to encourage him to continue, some of the students called out, "Yes."

"That's important," Coleman said. "Because for twenty years, I didn't think anyone saw me."

A reporter from the Charlotte newspaper was in the audience and quoted from Coleman's speech in the next day's *Observer*:

"For twenty years, I cried that same song, 'Can You See Me?' but nobody could see me because I didn't want to be seen," said Coleman. "Drugs took all my pride, robbed me of every piece of self-respect, every dream I ever had. But somehow God saw fit to give me a second chance," he said. "And that second chance is people like you."

Coleman had gone on to share much of his personal story. When he was finished, loud applause erupted from the toughest of critics—hundreds of fifteen- to eighteen-year-olds. Afterward, many had come up to share their connections: a father who was homeless, a brother on the streets, time spent with family in a shelter.

All students, quietly whispering their secrets to Coleman, who had been brave enough to share his own.

Caroline and Coleman stayed for the walk held on the high school track. More than 550 kids had paid $5 to participate. That afternoon, kids walked side-by-side, lap after lap with Coleman and Caroline and others from Homeless to Homes. All together the service club raised $6,007.17.

The South Mecklenburg High faculty advisor for the event told Caroline one of the most memorable moments came when the school security guard had approached her, admitting that her own brother was a meth addict, homeless in Charleston, S.C. After sharing the story of her brother's struggles, the security guard pressed $60 into the teacher's hand and asked that she give it to Moore Place.

25

Just Listen

We do not believe in ourselves until someone
reveals that deep inside us something
is valuable, worth listening to, worthy of our
trust, sacred to our touch. Once we believe
in ourselves we can risk curiosity, wonder,
spontaneous delight or any experience
that reveals the human spirit.

E. E. CUMMINGS

GIFTS LIKE THOSE FROM THE SOUTH MECKLENBURG HIGH SCHOOL
service club, along with additional donations throughout spring
2010, inched us towards $9,500,000. We hoped the final $500,000
would come from the city of Charlotte.

In the past two years, so many had worked together on this effort
to solve the city's homeless problem—churches, foundations, corporations, even children running lemonade stands. We had also finally
received support from the state of North Carolina for $500,000 and
the county had created an ongoing partnership by paying the salaries
of five social workers for Moore Place.

Everyone but the city of Charlotte had chipped in. On June 14,
2010, Dale, Liz, Caroline, and I sat in the auditorium where the

council held their meetings. We nervously waited through the nineteen agenda items on the docket before ours. Before starting Moore Place, I was not really aware who was on the city council or that they held these meetings. Staring at the curved panel in front of me, I now knew the name of every councilperson and how they were likely to vote. The meeting started at 7:00 p.m. and at 8:59 p.m. the vote for $500,000 for Moore Place was called. We collectively held our breath as they voted.

Nine in favor. One opposed—the representative from the Northside Neighborhood voted against. We passed. It was our final *yes*.

Crossing this last hurdle of raising the money needed for Moore Place was exhilarating. All the months, all the work, all the dreaming. We were actually going to *do* this. At the office I was feeling heroic, but at home there had definitely been a cost to my single focus of working on this project. I was learning I had been so consumed with Do Good I had forgotten to Love Well.

I was working from home that day, trying to distract myself with emails. I was really focused on Kailey, who was upstairs, shut behind her bedroom door.

Should I knock? Should I check to see if she was breathing?

No, I was sure she was fine. I would give her some more time. I tried to return to Moore Place and my in-box. These days it was my go-to for busyness. When my own home felt out of control, I could try to pretend to exercise some control in the homeless world. Staring at my computer screen, I attempted to concentrate on the day's work.

There were several emails from the Charlotte Housing Authority I could start with. Even though we had all the money raised, we still couldn't begin construction. Since we were taking some government money, we had to wait for federal approval to move forward. Four months and no word from the government. An employee in the Greensboro, N.C., Housing and Urban Development (HUD) office refused to do her job and approve the application, which would release our funds. I was constantly fielding questions from donors to explain why we had not started construction.

As worried as I was about all that, I was more concerned about the problem upstairs. Kailey had been in her room for hours so I went to check on her again. Slowly, I climbed the stairs, but her door was still closed, no light from under the door.

Pausing halfway up the flight of stairs, I sat down and tried to calm the sense of dread that had been choking me all morning. Really, the dread had started the day before with a letter I found in the trash can. It had been Kailey's twentieth birthday and in typical fashion, she had torn through her presents. Discarded wrapping paper, boxes, and ribbon had left a foot-high heap on the table. Charlie, always the cleaner, had scooped up behind her, not checking to see whether all the boxes were empty or full. In the process, a beautiful pair of earrings had gone missing, and I was sure they were in the trash.

Searching the trash can, some thickly folded pages caught my eye. Four papers torn from a legal pad haphazardly shoved into the bag of giftwrap in attempt to make them disappear forever. But it was Kailey's handwriting that I couldn't stop staring at.

I took the journal pages from the trash and sat down to read the rest. It took my breath away. My daughter, who I thought was so happy, was in reality, desperately depressed. The girl who had written these words I did not know. The girl who had written these words needed help.

I don't know how long I stayed in the backyard trying to absorb it. *How could I have missed how unhappy she was? How could she not feel she could tell me the truth?* I had vowed to be like Gigi and curl up on the couch with my daughters and always listen.

From the time Lauren and Kailey and the twins were little, I always tried to be there when they got home from school. I loved being the mom who knew the lyrics to their songs and volunteered to drive the late shift from the school dances so I could be in on the gossip.

How could it be that Kailey had become so lost without me knowing? How could it be that I had spent the past two years getting to know people like Coleman, Raymond, and Chilly Willy, yet I didn't even know my own daughter?

How could I have been helping some of the hardest to help in Charlotte when it was my own daughter in my own home who needed help?

The pages stayed in my pocket all day, waiting for Charlie to get home so we could talk with Kailey together. It was hard to function with the burning shame that I was a failure. *If I had been a better mom, Kailey would be happy.* It was that simple. I had heard the saying "You are only as happy as your saddest child." Now I understood.

When we had sat down with the letter, Kailey looked first at the papers and then at each of us. She held Charlie's gaze a little longer. They had always had some sort of unspoken communication like whale sonar. I swear they could speak sentences without a sound. A paragraph of pain passed between them. A tear began to roll down her cheek and she stared at her hands.

"I didn't want to worry you," Kailey said softly. "I didn't know what to say."

We agreed she needed to see a doctor, and I thought of Jane Harrell. She had helped Scott Mercer even before he knew anything was wrong. She had magically put a check in my pocket for Moore Place. Somehow it felt like the reason we had come to know each other was so she could help guide Kailey. I sent her a text and she called right away, even though it was 9:30 at night.

"She will be fine, Kathy, I'm telling you. There are so many college kids who struggle and no one talks about it," Jane assured me on the phone. "You send her to my office tomorrow and we'll make a plan."

So here I was, pacing outside Kailey's door, waiting desperately for her to wake up so we could make that plan. I did better with plans. With lists and ways to fix things. As I stared at her door, wondering what she was feeling and thinking on the other side, I thought about my mom's bedroom door. How many times coming home from school had I looked at that closed door? How many times had I waited for that door to open?

I never remembered wondering what my mom was feeling on the other side. Only the disappointment that she wasn't awake to see me when I got home from school. Mom's door was like the twenty-four-inch barrier at the Urban Ministry Center. As long as I stayed on one side, I didn't have to feel. I didn't have to know. But this was my daughter. Her pain. Her problems. Her door couldn't keep me from feeling. I knew now that moms just naturally felt through doors, through distances of hundreds or even thousands of miles.

There was a bump and a shuffling as Kailey moved from her bedroom to the bathroom. I waited before standing and tapping gently on her door.

"Kailey?"

"Yeah, Mom."

"Can I come in?"

"Sure."

She was sitting in bed in her gray school sweatshirt that had paint splotches on it from when she went on a service project to rebuild homes in New Orleans after Hurricane Katrina. Ripped, torn, and stained, it was still her favorite. She hugged her knees and looked up at me expectantly.

What could I say? It will get better? Everything will be okay?

I didn't know how to make her feel better. Moms are supposed to be able to make their kids feel better. Normally, I had a long list of suggestions for my girls. I was the ultimate fixer. *You should do this. You should try that. Let's make a list. Let's make a plan.* I always had lots of advice, lots of words. I could talk and find a solution for any problem. Over the years, I thought this was what I wanted my girls to see and learn. I wanted to be a strong, capable example for them. Like my dad had taught me, I wanted them to know they could *do* anything, *be* anything. I never cried or let them see me quitting. If there was a problem, I didn't feel it, I just fixed it.

But for this, I had no fix. No solution. No words.

I climbed next to her in bed and pulled her head onto my shoulder. We both began to cry. Me, slow, sad tears. Kailey, heaving sobs. We didn't speak. We just cried until we couldn't anymore. Finally she spoke.

"You know, Mom, this is all I ever wanted. I didn't want you to fix anything," she confessed. "I just wanted you to hold me and listen."

With projects on hold and Caroline in charge, that summer gave me a chance to refocus on family, and we had planned a Colorado dude ranch vacation for hiking, horseback riding, and fishing. Ever since the pack trip in Wyoming with Lauren and Kailey, our family had started taking more adventurous vacations. We tried to pick remote and rugged ranches with little cell phone or Internet access; that way neither of us, especially Charlie, could be pulled into work.

All week had been so relaxing. No decisions to be made. No meetings to attend. No donors to update. That morning, Charlie had been distracted by a lengthy conference call. With no cell service, he'd had to use the phone in our log cabin so he was stuck in a chair next to the wood wall for over an hour while we waited for him to go on our last family horseback ride of the vacation.

"Charlie," I whispered. "Let's *go*."

He gave me the one-minute sign. I sighed. Sometimes I hated his job. Whatever it was, however, apparently needed his undivided attention. I heard him hang up and call quietly to me.

"Kathy, can we talk a minute?"

He looked serious.

"So there's a problem in the New York office," he began.

"And?"

"And they want me to work on it."

"Okay…" I wasn't getting it. Charlie rarely talked about work. The girls joked that he worked for the CIA because he never talked about what he did.

"So they are asking that I go to New York to work on it," he paused and looked at me. "As in *move*."

"*Move*? To New York? When? "

He nodded. "Like next month."

How could we do that? Our home was in Charlotte. Our life was in Charlotte. I had no desire at the age of forty-eight to make new friends. I was in the middle of building Moore Place. We just needed the federal approval, and Caroline had only started three months ago. How could I leave?

"I know there's a lot to consider," Charlie said. "We can talk about it."

We both knew we could talk about it, but we both knew what would happen. Charlie was going to New York. When work asked, it was not really a question.

We said nothing to the girls and headed out for our ride. I tried to forget about it the best I could, but my brain doesn't work that way. My brain generates ideas and options.

We could get an apartment. We could commute. We wouldn't sell our house. I could work on the construction for Moore Place from New York. Nothing would change. I could do it all.

We were in a huge pasture looking back at the ranch. The girls were begging the wrangler. *One more family race.* The horses took off with just the slightest nudge. I think they loved running wild as much as we did. Nose-to-tail saddle rides must be as boring for horses as they were for guests. Charlie was in the lead with Lauren and Kailey right on his horse's flank. Emma was in the middle with Maddie and me bringing up the rear. I gave my horse a kick with my boot to urge him ahead of Maddie's horse. We were loping side-by-side less than two feet apart. Maddie was laughing her full-out belly laugh. Her horse turned his head slightly to see us gaining on him, and midstride thrust out his powerful back right leg, landing the kick somewhere between my horse's stomach and hindquarter.

My horse pitched forward, and then abruptly stopped galloping. With the sudden change of speed to a full stop, I lurched over the saddle horn, trying to hold on. Successfully staying in the saddle, I thought I had saved the disastrous fall. Then, my horse unexpectedly reared up on his back legs. Screaming as I fell off, I collided violently with the ground. There was a roar in my ears as I stared at the sky, trying to make sense of how I got there. I remember staring at the clouds thinking: *that was out of control.*

By now the wrangler, Charlie, and the girls had all ridden back to help me. Charlie was leaning over me asking if I was hurt. I couldn't answer because I wasn't sure.

My head hurt, my back hurt, my hand hurt. *Were they broken? Why were there ants crawling on me?* Charlie and the wrangler moved me gently to the side as they assessed for broken bones. Apparently, in a field full of rocks, I had landed on a red anthill. A soft red anthill. A ten-inch mound of dirt that, even though filled with angry ants, had saved my spine.

After a trip to the emergency room by pickup truck, I came back to the ranch that night with a chipped bone in my right hand and a collar to support my sprained neck. It wasn't the injuries that kept me up that night, it was remembering that thought I had as I lay on the ground.

That was out of control

Really, I was out of control.

My life felt out of control.

It felt like I had just received a giant sign from the universe: *slow down*.

Live in New York *and* Charlotte? *And* lead Moore Place? *And* be a good mom to four daughters, one of whom had already tried to tell me to sit still and listen a little more?

I was on my back again, this time staring up at the ceiling as Charlie snored. We had to get up at 5 a.m. to catch the plane back to Charlotte but I couldn't sleep. It had been three years since I heard Denver ask *where are the beds?* Three years that I had woken up every day and tried to figure out how to house homeless people. Three years, and I had let everything come second to that one Moore Place Goal. We were almost there.

Didn't I want to still be in charge? Didn't I need to still be in charge?

I knew in my heart the answer. This past year had been incredibly difficult, but I had stayed because of my commitment to Dale Mullennix and my new family of Coleman, Raymond, and others. I had learned that about myself—I didn't quit on people. But now it was time to put *my* people first. Charlie. Lauren. Kailey. Emma. Maddie. They had taken a backseat for the past three years. Denver, Dale, Moore Place had all come first. I had lived the Do Good. It was time to live a little more of the Love Well.

I kept hearing a whisper and this time I didn't think I was crazy.

Tell Dale it's time.

26

The Last Best Yes

The most beautiful people we have known
are those who have known defeat, known suffering,
known struggle, known loss, and have found their
way out of those depths. These persons have
an appreciation, a sensitivity, and an understanding
of life that fills them with compassion,
gentleness, and a deep loving concern.
Beautiful people do not just happen.

ELISABETH KÜBLER-ROSS

MY CELL PHONE VIBRATED ON MY LAP IN THE BACKSEAT OF
the taxi, and I looked down at the number I easily recognized: Caroline. We talked a lot by cell phone these days. I *had* told Dale it was
time I stopped being a part-time employee but I couldn't really quit.
I just went back to full-time volunteer status. It had been six months
since Charlie and I began our new commuting lifestyle. We went
to New York on Mondays and usually came back on Thursdays to
spend the weekend in Charlotte. The office in the train depot was
now all Caroline's, and she had become the Executive Director of
Moore Place, even though we still technically didn't have a Moore
Place. Eleven months we had been ready to start construction and
still no approval from HUD.

While we waited for the government, Caroline had tried to be creative, working on everything from paint colors to collecting resumes for future employees. I realized I had never thought about all these details. Honestly, the actual construction process was overwhelming to me.

Where would the trash chute go?

Were there enough fire exits?

Did the handicap rooms have wide enough doorways?

Caroline easily answered all the questions and made suggestions based on the New York buildings she had managed. Funny that we had switched lives—Caroline for Charlotte and me for New York.

When we started commuting, I thought I would miss all the day-to-day details of Moore Place but it was just the people I missed. The program lunches with Raymond ordering two pieces of pie to go. The emails from Dale, excited about a new donor or progress on the capital campaign. In New York as empty nesters, I could go all day without talking to anyone until Charlie came back to the apartment for dinner.

The phone buzzed again on my lap.

"Are you sitting down?" Caroline asked.

"Yes, actually in a yellow cab," I said. The roar of traffic made it difficult to hear, so I pressed my hand over my other ear. "What's up?"

"It finally came!" she said. "Our approval from HUD! We finally got it!"

I screamed out loud in the taxi, and the driver turned around alarmed.

"Sorry!" I said pointing to the phone. "Can you believe it? Eleven months! Eleven months it took them!"

The last best *yes*.

"I have checked calendars with Mayor Foxx, Wells Fargo, Knight Foundation, the Charlotte Housing Authority, and the churches and

the best date for the grand opening is Sunday, January 29, 2012,"
Caroline said.

I smiled at the huge God-instance. Should I tell her?

We had always hoped to open by Christmas 2011, but with the
delays, we reluctantly pushed the move-in date to January 2012.

"Kathy? Is that okay with you?" Caroline asked.

"It works great for me," I admitted. "January 29 is my forty-
ninth birthday."

When I called Ron to let him know the date, I found out the
news was not good about Denver.

"We are excited about all this, Kathy, and would love to come,"
Ron said. "But I don't think there is any way Denver can make the
trip. He's having trouble with blood clots in his legs and winter travel
is especially hard. Maybe we can send a video for you all to play of
our congratulations."

When I had asked Denver about naming the building after him,
he had said, *You better hurry because I am old.*" He might not be there
to see it but my promise would be kept, and Denver's name would be
on the doors—forever.

"Kathy, its *so nice!*" Mom said as we drove into the parking lot of
Moore Place. "I didn't expect it to look *so nice!*"

I smiled because I knew what she meant. The light yellow siding.
The bright white trim. The red roof. The newly planted bushes. It
didn't look like a shelter for homeless people. It looked like a home.

It was the day before the grand opening and I was taking my
mom on a private tour of Moore Place. She had flown in for the big
event along with my sister Allyson.

Louise would miss the grand opening for a long-planned sabbatical in Costa Rica but her faith had gotten me here. I thought about the night four years before when I had confessed to her and Charlie that Denver had called me to "build beds" and the next day how she had directed me to Common Ground.

"Can you believe it?" Louise asked me right before she left on her trip.

Could I?

Not really. What I was beginning to believe was that this whole journey had very little to do with a former graphic designer and a minister and much more to do with something I was sure I might never understand.

As my mom, Allyson, and I entered through the glass doors of Moore Place, it felt perfectly full circle that Mom would be the first to officially tour. If my mom had not mentioned the book *Same Kind of Different* to me, I doubt I ever would have read it.

In front of us was the donor wall—everyone who had even given $5 on the display. Across the top, in gray script it read:

To those who brought us home:
Thank you.

Listed underneath were the hundreds of people who had made it possible. Most of whom I didn't know five years ago, and now every name meant something.

- 168 individuals, whose combined donations totaled $990,101
- 28 foundations, who together, contributed $6,423,000
- 60 houses of faith, with a total contribution of $479,512
- State, local, and federal funds totaling $2,700,000

Although Steve Barton and David Furman had created an incredible building, it was all the people who had made it happen that was truly amazing. Eight teenagers who had a bake sale to raise $550. Two Davidson College students who had cycled across the US, raising over $8,000. And the Mailbox Angel with all of her $5 and $10 gifts, which had continued to come in steadily and faithfully. Each a story. Each giving all they had in order to make this happen.

As we walked the halls, volunteers moved around us getting ready for the celebration the next day. Homeless to Homes residents were going to be giving home tours after the ceremony. Model apartments were being readied as volunteers made beds, hung shower curtains, and stocked kitchens. Every item in the eighty-five apartments had been donated by a family, book club, or church group in a "Home for the Holidays" donation drive led by Downie and Sally Saussy.

I gave Mom and Allyson the full tour of the apartments, each flooded with sunshine from large windows in every home. The library shelves were being filled with donated books that were now ready for the residents.

As we toured the art center, Mom looked lost in thought, surveying the easels and art supplies waiting for the new tenants. I thought she was remembering the art studio in our home, but she surprised us by saying, "You know, I wanted to be an art therapist."

Allyson and I looked at each other confused. "What? You did?"

"Yes!" she said looking up. "You didn't know? That is why I went back to school to get my master's after you girls went to college. I wanted to bring some kind of joy to those psych wards."

"Wait, what happened?" Allyson asked.

"Well, your dad got diagnosed with cancer and that was the end of that," she said, looking back into the art center wistfully.

We rarely talked about it. Those Lost Years. We still acted like none of it ever happened. Mom seemed to think it was better that way.

"What good does it do to rehash the past?" she would say.

But there in the halls of Moore Place so filled with hope for so many, it seemed the right time to examine some of those wounds that had never truly healed.

"I always wanted to be there for you girls but then it would happen *again*," Mom said with a huge emphasis on *again*. Her shoulders slumped and she looked defeated, as if she could sense another ride to a hospital.

There it was: *the shame, the secret, and the thing we could never talk about.*

Mom's version of "*again*" was so different than how it all could have been. Any one of those *agains* could have been *the end*. Each spiral into mania could have been a suicide. With each round of new medicine, she could have simply stopped taking. The pain of each lost year could have been amplified if she had coped using alcohol. None of that was her story. None of that became my story.

Mom always got up. She always fought her way back. Hers was the ultimate story of survival. Seven times down, eight times up. Yet she still didn't understand the power of her own story and truthfully I never had either.

I had spent nearly my whole life carrying a quiet grudge. Thinking about it all the time but never moving through it. I had never been able to truly forgive my mom. For going away. For leaving my idyllic childhood. For getting lost in the desert. But especially for not talking about it. For pretending it never happened. If we could talk about it, maybe I could finally let it go.

I looked at my mom and saw her maybe for the first time in over forty years. My truth was not that I didn't have a mother growing up. My truth was I had lost her. I had lost that mom who was poised to give me the perfect childhood and then couldn't. I still missed *that* mom every day of the past four decades when I couldn't find the mom whose knees I had hugged in adoration. The mom whose brain was brilliant *and* broken.

But who knows how *that* little girl would have grown up? Who knows what *that* little girl would have done with her life. *That* little girl never would have learned how strong she could be. *That* little girl never would have had to become resilient. *That* little girl never would have believed she could do anything—really *anything*.

I tried to tell her the truth. "All those years I was never thinking 'some day this is going to make me incredibly resilient.' "

Mom smiled.

"But it did, and I am. And without all *that*, I would not have moved so far away to Charlotte, or met Charlie, or have my four girls or ever attempted to help a single homeless person. *Your* story is *my* story and *your* story gave me all that."

We stood together in the moment, and the past forty years, including those sixteen Lost Years, were with us. Moments before, those years had been wedged between us, but it felt like they had just begun to compress in a time warp pulling together like an accordion of forgiveness.

We did not speak, we just felt. For the first time I could remember, we all just felt *together*. Not in secret. Not in shame. Not each in silence behind closed doors. Together. Taking in a sadness. Feeling a regret. Not fixing, just feeling.

That day, I took a photo of my mom standing in front of Moore Place, on that lot that had once been a junkyard. The sun was shining and the sky was incredibly blue for a January day. She was smiling broadly in the foreground, Moore Place a backdrop to her happiness.

At the grand opening the next day, I was in the lobby greeting the more than two hundred friends and donors as they arrived to fill the Moore Place dining room. Even though it wasn't my personal birthday party, it felt like one. Maddie and Kailey were able to come and Charlie arrived with his parents, Bob and Jean Izard, from New York. Before we had a single private donor to Moore Place, Bob and Jean had gone in with Charlie to be the very first donors to the capital campaign. They mailed their surprise pledge to Dale and asked that the lobby be named in my honor. Showing them the plaque, it definitely felt like the best birthday present I had ever had been given. Even better than an Easy-Bake oven.

Dale Mullennix began the program, recognizing John and Pat Moore with a piece of original art by an artist in the UMC Artworks program. Then, Dale called me forward and gave me another piece of art. It was a fifteen-by-fifteen-inch oil painting of a set of keys painted by a formerly homeless artist who would be moving into his own apartment later that week. I remember accepting the piece and turning around to see the audience standing and clapping.

Everyone there was part of this story. From the Five Guys to Joann and Coleman and Liz Clasen-Kelly. All the people I didn't know four years ago and who were now so much a part of this journey. All the people who Denver assured me: *knew they were coming.* Every person had a story, and now those hundreds of stories had built this home.

I should have thanked each one of them and said aloud every name, but I couldn't speak. There was too much to say and no words matched the feeling. Charlie was standing, clapping with the crowd, tears in his eyes. This had been a long road for both of us. He had been the First Believer when I told him I wanted to start this crazy project. As obsessed and distracted as I had become, he never asked me to quit. I stepped off the stage and gave Charlie a long hug and then sat down with my family—all of them.

As I pulled myself together, Caroline was speaking. She was poised and confident, describing how residents would go from a life of chaos to a life of normalcy. The new staff of Moore Place would help "create the ordinary."

How extraordinary that would be for eighty-five men and women.

As she spoke, I felt the letting go of the incessant need to get this done. It was finally finished. I had completed my promise to Denver and imagined the unimaginable for my father. Together, with all those in the room, we had *done something about it*. Listening to Caroline speak, it felt like a natural passage to me. I knew I would be stepping away after the grand opening. Caroline would run Moore Place, and I had worked my way out of a job, for which I was very grateful. I might have been the birth mother to Moore Place, but Caroline would raise the child. Our baby couldn't be in better hands.

After the ceremony, there were hugs, high fives, and home tours. In one final full-circle moment, the last person to ask me for a tour that day was Rufus Dalton, the same man who had been honored four years ago for his forty-year service to Outward Bound. That was the dinner after which Charlie and I debated what would be our "forty-year thing."

When I saw him in the lobby waiting, I was stunned.

Was this God showing off again?

I wanted to tell Mr. Dalton that this whole project started years ago with his recognition dinner and the discussion Charlie and I had on the way home. I tried to find the words to tell Rufus how unreal it was to see him standing there in the Moore Place lobby on Opening Day. But I had no idea how to make him understand all that had happened since that dinner.

27

I Feel Like People Now

And once the storm is over,
you won't remember how you made it through,
how you managed to survive. You won't even
be sure whether the storm is really over.
But one thing is certain.
When you come out of the storm you
won't be the same person who walked in.
That's what the storm is all about.

HARUKI MURAKAMI

AFTER ALMOST FIVE YEARS OF WISHING AND WAITING, ONE OF the first tenants to move in was Chilly Willy.

It took Dale, Liz, Caroline, and Chilly Willy's brother, Jimmy, all to convince Charlotte's most famous street person that this wasn't a trick. Moore Place wasn't a jail or a lock-down facility but truly a home of his own, and it happened that his move-in date would be Valentine's Day 2012.

That morning, Caroline was on high alert, waiting to welcome Chilly Willy home, finally fulfilling the promise that Moore Place could successfully house Charlotte's own Million Dollar Larry. As the day wore on, no one had seen him. Caroline called his brother,

Jimmy, to see if he knew where Chilly Willy was but it seemed he had gone missing.

Had Chilly Willy really forgotten about the big day? Or had he just decided he couldn't come inside to live?

Finally late afternoon, Caroline spotted Chilly Willy in the parking lot. She went outside to meet him and was surprised to find him completely sober.

He announced he had checked himself into the city "drunk tank" to "clean up" for his momentous day. And one more thing—he was no longer Chilly Willy. He told Caroline that from this day forward, he was giving up his street name, and he wanted everyone to call him by his birth name: William Larry Major.

A couple of weeks later, Liz Clasen-Kelly handed me a note from Larry. To this day, I carry his letter along with a group photo of the first thirteen Homeless to Homes residents. Both are tucked in the front pocket of my black meeting notebook and Larry's note reads:

> Ms. Kathy Izard
> I'm William Larry Major.
> Will you come visit me?
> I'm doing good and I feel much better.
> I love my place, I feel like people now.
> Thanks you'er [sic] friend,
> William L. Major

Also among the new residents would be soup kitchen cowboy Bill Halsey and his brown leather hat. Bill was that kind cowboy who had stood up for me in the soup kitchen and had lived in his hole in the ground for years until the day he moved into Moore Place. We were thrilled to be able to give Bill a home finally, but it turned out that wasn't the best part of his move into Moore Place.

For years, Bill's mother had been praying about him. She did not know how to help her homeless son or where to find him, but she knew he got meals and mail at UMC. Along with praying, she wrote to him using the Center address.

When Bill Halsey found out he was going to be housed at Moore Place, he proudly called his mom to let her know. Mrs. Halsey was there for her son's move-in day, with tears in her eyes.

"I always prayed this day would come," she confessed to Caroline. "I followed the stories about Moore Place in the newspaper and hoped one day my son would find his way here."

What dear Mrs. Halsey didn't admit was that she had done more than pray and send letters to her son.

Even after Moore Place was built, the pastel envelopes kept coming from our Mailbox Angel with notes of encouragement and still the words, "May God Bless and Multiply this small amount." Now they were addressed to the Moore Place mailbox instead of the UMC, yet there was still no way to thank the giver personally. Caroline would record them as I had under Anonymous, wondering who our long-time benefactor might be.

Then one day, after receiving another Angel envelope, Caroline noticed something different—maybe a mistake. This time in the top left hand corner of the pastel envelope there was a name: *Lily Halsey*.

Caroline couldn't wait to call. "Kathy, you are not going to believe this. The woman behind our God Bless This Small Amount mystery? All this time? It's been Bill Halsey's mom!"

I had not talked to Ron since I sent him the photos from the grand opening, so I was surprised to see his number on my cell phone two months later on April 1, 2012.

"Hey, Ron!" I said.

"Kathy, Denver died last night in his sleep."

I couldn't even process what Ron said. Everything I knew about Denver had been so otherworldly; I think I assumed he was immortal. I knew he had been sick and that he had blood clots in his legs, but I wasn't expecting this. Hanging up the phone, I was in shock. I had no right to be as upset as Ron. I had not taken Denver into my home and we had not been close friends. Denver never really even knew how much he had changed my life.

The last time I had seen Denver was March 6, 2008. Four months after that first True Blessings, our founding team, Sarah, Kim, Angela, and I, had decided to take a trip to Texas to visit Ron and Denver. At the time, I was just starting my new job at the UMC, and I wanted to see what kind of "beds" they had in Denver's hometown. We were excited to spend time with Ron and Denver again and tour the Fort Union Gospel Mission they had written about in their book. We arranged a dinner with the two of them, but when we arrived at the restaurant, only Ron was waiting. Denver, as customary, was nowhere to be found.

"He'll be along," Ron promised.

Ron filled the dinner hour with stories of the past year and all the places they had spoken.

"We've been approached for a movie deal!" he told us. "Denver wants Forrest Whittaker to play him!"

Dinner progressed, entrees arrived and were cleared, but no Denver. Angela's right leg shook nervously as she checked her watch and stared at the restaurant entrance, willing Denver to arrive.

"Ron, we really wanted to see Denver again and hear all his *wisdom*!" Sarah confided.

Ron tried Denver's cell phone several times but no answer.

The evening was coming to a close and we thought Denver was going to stand us up. When Denver finally made his grand entrance, he looked like a movie star dressed in a flashy new suit with pin-stripes and sunglasses even though it was 10 p.m. Restaurant guests obviously recognized the homeless man turned celebrity author and many wanted to speak with him. Denver had nodded at people and accepted handshakes from the most insistent fans.

Finally reaching our table, he shook his head, telling us, "I don't understand why they all want to shake my hand *now*. None of them wanted to touch me when I was homeless."

Denver held court with us for the next hour, telling stories and throwing out Denverisms.

Our limitation is God's opportunity. When you get all the way to the end of your rope and there ain't nothin' you can do, that's when God takes over.

Sarah had brought a small notebook and pen and tried to tran-scribe the circuitous philosophical mind of Denver Moore. Later, we all flipped through the pages and agreed there was no way to do his musings justice. There was something about Denver that couldn't be captured on paper. Being in his presence was undeniably remarkable. His words gave you goose bumps only when they were delivered with those dark eyes drilling into your soul.

I wondered what Denver saw with those eyes. Did he see like the rest of us or could he see something different? Had Denver ever really even seen me, or like Coleman, was I invisible? Was Denver ever really giving me, Kathy Izard, a message? Or, since *all white folk look alike,* was he just speaking about the injustices of homelessness, and I hap-pened to be standing there, feeling responsible for something?

I may have had a four-year obsession to fulfill a promise with Moore Place, but I am convinced Denver Moore never knew my name—first or last. All the same, I would never forget *him*. Meeting Denver had been my spiritual awakening and the beginning of making everything previously invisible, indelibly visible. It had been over four years since I had promised Denver to build beds and promised myself to finish before he died.

We had just made it.

The grand opening just before Denver's death and Larry's Valentine's Day move-in would have been a Hollywood happy ending for this story. But real life is much messier.

Six months after Denver died, on October 19, 2012, I woke to an early morning text from Caroline sent late the night before:

> Larry is dead. Car accident on 7th Street.
> Will be convening staff early in am.
> Am in shock. Just leaving building.

I was in shock, too. In the past twenty years, Larry, aka Chilly Willy, had survived prison, muggings, illness, heat waves, and ice storms. I remembered Jimmy telling me about the weekly phone calls from friends asking if Chilly Willy was dead when they hadn't seen him on the streets in a while. Always the rumors were untrue—not this time.

I called Caroline immediately.

"I thought it was a mistake again, Kathy. You know how everyone always would say he had died, but we'd find out he was in jail or something?" Caroline was having trouble talking. "But, this time, it was true," she finished.

William Larry Major, fifty-eight, was dead. A car outside a neighborhood bar had struck him. The driver was a sixty-five-year-old woman, undoubtedly traumatized but not charged.

Caroline sounded exhausted and shaky. Not only had she been fielding phone calls all night from distraught residents of Moore Place, she was blaming herself about how it could have played out differently.

"I've been trying to think what I could have done," she said.

The truth was Caroline had, beyond all probability, kept Larry housed, and very much alive, for eight months. Many times after moving in, Larry had given back his Moore Place apartment key to Caroline, saying he couldn't do it anymore. Each time, she had given it back, assuring him he could.

I hung up with Caroline and searched the Internet, where it seems the answer to any question can be found. Larry's death was no exception. There was already a *Charlotte Observer* news article, a blog post by a local writer, an RIP Chilly Willy Facebook page, and a YouTube video with 1000 hits and counting of Larry singing, all posted within hours of his death. I watched the video and smiled at Larry's gravelly voice belting out his favorite Charlie Daniels Band song, "Long Haired Country Boy," one last time.

My cell interrupted the video and I saw it was Liz. I answered my phone with, "I heard," and was surprised to find I could not speak without crying.

Liz was even more distraught. Her concern for Larry, whose addiction and pain played out publicly on Charlotte's streets, had helped write the moral and economic case for Moore Place. His story of cycling needlessly in and out of jails and hospitals had inspired John and Pat Moore to call Dale with their extraordinary first gift for the pilot program in 2008. That had changed the lives of dozens of chronically homeless in Charlotte, including Coleman, Raymond, and Ruth and, finally, for Larry himself.

At the end of our call, Liz made a comment I carry with me still.

"When I saw in the paper that they wrote 'formerly homeless,' she said, "I took comfort in that."

While this wasn't the Hollywood ending, there was, as Liz said, mercy in Larry's story. He hadn't frozen under a bridge or been beaten to death. And while Larry was so proud to finally have his own place, he was still struggling with how to begin his own life again for the first time in two decades.

In the days that followed, Charlotte overflowed with love for William Larry Major. Radio and TV stations ran stories, the *Charlotte Observer* wrote two feature articles, the online obituary guestbook had 294 entries, and that Facebook tribute page grew to more than 10,000 views. Larry, in his own wild way, was a community talisman. People wrote of his humor, wisdom, and innate sweetness. How he had offered a kind word, a song, or a joke. Apparently, he was known in neighborhoods I didn't even know he wandered.

Larry's family held a service for him on October 22, 2012, in the church Larry's father had started. Dozens of people stood in line outside the church to pay their respects. It was the most diverse crowd I had ever been with in Charlotte. Every age, every income, and every race were represented amongst the mourners, all patiently waiting to come inside the overflowing church.

While waiting in line, I stood beside a police officer, sheriff, EMT worker, and a city bus driver, each recalling how the free-spirited Larry impacted their lives. At the front of the church were photos of Larry during his days at Moore Place, winning at Bingo, flashing a peace sign to the camera at a picnic. Two handmade posters signed by dozens of Moore Place friends, one poster reading, "Ride your Harley to Heaven! In Loving Memory."

Larry's family asked that memorials be made to Moore Place and after the service they scattered Larry's ashes on the streets of Charlotte—the place he loved the most.

28

God Was in It

"WELL NOW YOU KNOW HOW I FEEL ABOUT GOD,"
said Owen Meany. "I CAN'T SEE HIM—
BUT I ABSOLUTELY KNOW HE IS THERE!"

A Prayer for Owen Meany
JOHN IRVING

NOW I KNEW THE ENDING TO DENVER'S AND LARRY'S STORIES, but I still couldn't write the next chapter of mine. With Moore Place open, I wasn't really needed. I had no idea what to make of the last few years or what I should do for the next decade. If I was no longer Graphics Girl or Homeless to Homes director, who was I? What was I supposed to do with all this newfound knowledge of building and raising money? If I had felt this one purpose so clearly, would there ever be another?

Allyson thought I could do some soul searching at her favorite retreat center, Kripalu, a former seminary, now yoga center in the Berkshires. She had invited my mom and me to a workshop with English poet and philosopher David Whyte. I agreed to go even though I had never heard of him.

I had come prepared for the workshop with pen and paper ready to absorb all David Whyte's wisdom, but I was disappointed to realize there were no handouts, no slides, and no PowerPoint presentations. It seemed there were no Life Lessons starred and highlighted in his lectures. If I were looking for takeaways, I was going to have to really listen and find them myself.

My attention had been drifting as the poet enigmatically recited his poems at the front of the large room, chanting really. It took me a few minutes to realize he was quoting everything from memory. He did not pause for effect in the natural places or even finish the entire work. It was disconcerting to me as he rolled through lines, stopping and starting like a dance instructor repeating steps. It was this one line that bolted me to full attention:

> *"Sometimes everything has to be inscribed across the heavens*
> *so you can find the one line already written inside you."*

That was amazing.

I felt like this poet, David Whyte, had pulled up a chair to my psyche and given me the CliffsNotes to my life. That one line was everything that had happened to me in the past five years. That one sentence described all the God-instance and randomness and Grace that began with a book and ended with an apartment building. But really that one sentence explained how a lost six-year-old who missed her mother could end up a resilient forty-nine-year-old able to believe she could do anything.

David Whyte was continuing on with his poem, but I could not hear him. I just stared at the words I had memorized, "already written inside you" and wondered how they got there, those metaphorical words inside me. Did it happen when my parents named me Katherine Grace or did it start sooner? Back when they were two college sweethearts reading scripture to each other.

And now these three remain: faith, hope and love.
But the greatest of these is love.

Their love had been bruised and broken and hospitalized and even parted by death but Mom was still here. Still trying to learn at age eighty. Still listening to life. Still keeping over thirty years of "*All my love, Leighton*" cards bound tightly with a rubber band. I looked over at her. Mom's hands were folded across her chest as she sat. She stared intently ahead, listening to the poet's words as he continued on to the next line.

"Someone has written something new in the ashes of your life."

Mom smiled imperceptibly. The Phoenix. Her private symbol.

My mom's password for all her Internet accounts is Phoenix and then the numbers of her anniversary. To her "Phoenix" signifies the fabled purple bird, which rises from the ashes after, legend has it, perishing in a fire of its own making.

Mom views her life, her story, similar to that legendary bird in that she was able to withstand all those fires of mania and survive. My whole life I believed my foundations came mostly from my dad: do good, work hard, change the world. Throughout our lives, Dad had given each of his three daughters a compass to search for a bigger purpose. I had almost overlooked my mother's quieter messages, which ultimately, I needed for this journey maybe even more: faith and resilience. In truth, by recommending *Same Kind of Different As Me,* my mother had given me the key to my greatest gift—my calling. That elusive purpose I had been so desperate to discover.

My Mom. The Phoenix. Rising from the ashes.

My childhood. My life. Perfectly imperfect, so I could finally see the line that was already written inside me.

As I looked back on the journey of Moore Place, it seemed all the dots had been connected except one: Mrs. Halsey. Caroline had met her but I never had. Thinking about all that had happened and all the God-instances, I needed to tell Lily Halsey that what she did had *mattered*—that a Hallmark card cradling a blessing and a few dollars had made all the difference to me.

Lily Halsey and her cards. My mom and her cards. My mom's habit that had always quietly irritated me.

Why did she buy so many cards? Why did she take so much time and put so much energy into this out-of-fashion paper habit?

I couldn't value it in my own mother until I could value it in someone else's mother. This care. This connection. This compassion. It wasn't a waste of time for Lily Halsey to send me all those cards. It had meant everything to me.

It wasn't silly for my mom to track the birthdays, anniversaries, and holidays and send literally hundreds of cards a year. Thousands in her lifetime. It was her ministry.

I was driving to Huntersville, N.C., to finally meet Lily Halsey, my mysterious Mailbox Angel, who now lived in assisted living. Driving there, I realized I had no idea which room she was in or what she looked like. A nurse helped me find her. She was sitting in a wheelchair by the front door, talking with a friend, and I came up behind her.

"Mrs. Halsey?"

A woman with soft gray hair turned to gaze up at me, two sky-blue eyes searching my face for recognition.

She clearly didn't know me, but I would have known her anywhere. Her son, Bill Halsey, had those exact same blue eyes that looked up from under his cowboy hat.

I had brought her an orchid as a small offering of thanks, and I put it on the coffee table as I pulled out one of her notes that I had saved. I thought it might help explain my visit. This one read:

Thank you for your help and love for the HOMELESS and the needy. Pray that God will multiply [sic] this small amount. Pray for me.

As I handed her the note, I could see she understood and remembered writing it. I tried speaking, "Mrs. Halsey, I'm Kathy Izard. You used to send me those notes…"

Mrs. Halsey's friend interrupted. "You need to speak loudly, dear. She can't hear well."

I realized that Lily was still searching my face but had not heard a word. I leaned down close and put my words of gratitude right next to her ear.

"Mrs. Halsey, I'm Kathy Izard. You used to send me those notes, and I wanted to tell you how much they mattered. They meant the world to me."

I tried not to cry but my throat was closing and my eyes were welling. It felt good to finally be at the end of this journey. This long road that began with Denver was now ending with a woman I had never met but who had profoundly impacted my life, too.

Lily Halsey was crying as well. A tear rolled down her cheek and she said softly, "Oh, I used to pray for you. I still do. I prayed this morning for you and Moore Place."

We visited for an hour. With the help of her friend, who I found out had worked with Lily at an advertising agency in Charlotte, they filled in the pieces I never knew about Bill Halsey.

Before he became a fixture at the Urban Ministry Center, Bill Halsey was a college graduate and talented artist. He worked for years as a graphic designer. I almost laughed when she told me. A graphic designer? Bill? The same profession I had given up to start this project.

Apparently, Bill and I were about the same age, so we had both learned how to create layouts by hand before computers became so ubiquitous in the industry. Once the profession demanded computer skills, I remember how difficult it was to make the transition. I took classes at the community college and finally hired a private tutor to teach me the more advanced software.

Bill hadn't been as lucky. Bill couldn't afford a tutor. He didn't know how to look online to see that he could take classes at the community college. Bill couldn't compete in the digital world. He lost his job, his confidence, and everything after that was a slow slide to desperation. His father died and the family lost contact with Bill when he started living in that hole in the ground. Lily never stopped worrying about the son she loved.

The newspaper articles about the Urban Ministry Center's plans for housing the homeless caught her eye. She didn't know if they would help her son, but she could pray, couldn't she?

When I asked Lily Halsey why she began sending cards to me, she replied with complete certainty, "When I read about Moore Place, I knew I had to help."

Her blue eyes looked straight into mine, and she said with unwavering faith, "*No one* would have built Moore Place unless they believed God was in it."

Trust the Whisper

Listen to your life. See it for the fathomless mystery that
it is. In the boredom and pain of it no less than in the
excitement and gladness: touch, taste, smell your way to
the holy hidden heart of it because in the last analysis all
moments are key moments and life itself is grace.

FREDERICK BUECHNER

I ALWAYS BELIEVED MOORE PLACE WAS THE END GAME. FOR
years, I thought my purpose started the day I met Denver and would
end the day we opened the doors to that dream of a building. But
just as I eventually learned everything started way before Denver,
it continues after Moore Place as well. The road keeps going, and
Moore Place was one stop on a path that stretches too far ahead for
me to see. If I keep listening, my life is still talking to me.

What was I supposed to do with all that knowledge about building and raising money? *To not be afraid to do it again.*

A year and a half after Moore Place opened, a friend asked if
I could talk to her about a project she and her husband were feeling called to lead. Their family had experienced mental illness and
had found it nearly impossible to find care. Although she was an
event planner and her husband a banker, and neither had any formal psychiatric or medical training, they felt compelled to try to

do something to help all the families in Charlotte struggling with mental illness. The overwhelming need kept whispering to them.

"Did you know there are 7.4 million people within 100 miles of Charlotte and not a single residential mental health treatment bed?" my friend asked. *"Does that make any sense to you?"*

It didn't.

I knew how difficult it was to have a parent cycle in and out of hospitals. Charlie and I had just experienced the pain of trying to get help for a child with depression.

She didn't have to ask the next question.

Are you going to do something about it?

Charlie and I decided to work on this one together, and this time I did not lead.

We just walked alongside Bill and Betsy Blue as they spearheaded a community effort to raise $25 million to build HopeWay, the region's first and only nonprofit residential mental health treatment center. It opened in 2016—four years after Moore Place.

As I was working to raise money for HopeWay, I wrote and rewrote versions of this book. Witnessing Bill and Betsy listening to their call, it reminded me of all the people who were a part of the Moore Place journey. Liz, Dale, Bill Holt, Jerry Licari, and so many more who heard that small whisper to *do something*. I didn't want all those stories to be lost. I didn't want to forget how all of this might not have happened if even a few of those people had not listened and acted on what they were hearing. No matter how crazy it seemed.

It is difficult to make sense of it all. How life seems perfectly random, yet completely designed all at the same time. Louise sent me a sermon she wrote which said in part:

> *If it's all constructed, we might as well write a story large enough*
> *to live in. An adventurous story—one where we are joyful, creative,*

and connected. One where we name ourselves as powerful,
willing and able to offer deep service, available for passionate living.
One where we thrive, instead of merely survive.

More than anything, that is the gift of the past few years—the ability to rewrite my story. One where I am connected to a community of friends willing to work for change. One where my history with my mother is not filled with resentment but with compassion. One where my life has a faith found, not forced.

And one where, when I pay attention, God definitely shows off.

I no longer believe people are called to religion. I don't think a calling is just for people like Dale or Louise who go into the ministry.

I believe, now, we are each called to life—true, abundant, purposeful life.

Each of us has a call patiently waiting and whispering. You might be hearing yours already but are afraid to admit it. It could be as big as a building, as technical as creating proformas for a nonprofit, or as simple and powerful as a ministry of sending cards.

My message to you is this:

Trust the Whisper.

Whatever it is. Whatever you feel is quietly, persistently, relentlessly calling to you. *No matter how crazy or inconvenient it might be to listen.*

Once you hear it, that one true thing, it's impossible to turn away because it will keep whispering. And when it does, you must either spend the rest of your life answering it or pretending you never heard it.

Be willing to listen.

Be willing to let go.

Be willing to take that leap of faith.

When you do, the life you can't see is infinitely richer and more significant than the life you can see and thought you had planned.

The day I took a ride with Denver, he took me to a road that was never even on my map. I hope your journey begins today on a path you never thought capable of navigating.

I can't explain Grace or God's plan, but this much I have learned. Grace is that moment when your purpose speaks to you so loudly that you can't help but hear it. Believing in it is crazy but denying you heard it is even crazier. You may not see it coming, but when Grace finds you, stop, listen, and take good notes. Everything in your life has prepared you for this.

You are ready and Grace is real.

THE LAST WORD

Although some names in *The Hundred Story Home* were changed to protect the privacy of an individual, the one name I regret I could not change was my mother's, which I know would have been her preference. After the long sixteen-year search for the right medication and treatment, Mom has lived the past thirty as many patients do—in silence and secrecy about her circumstances because of the pervasive stigma surrounding mental illness.

My mother's bipolar diagnosis did not and does not define her life. It merely became one facet she needed to manage. Mom never wanted a career because her singular goal in life was to be a mother. She wanted to expose her three daughters to each of the arts she loves so much: art, music, dance, opera.

During her struggles and after, Mom was always determined that her life "would mean something." She was instrumental in establishing the Girls Club of El Paso, and she served in several roles, including president, volunteer coordinator, and program coordinator. First Presbyterian Church has also been a main focus of her service. There, she has been a deacon, an elder, and a faithful choir member. Her passion for reading makes her a dedicated member of both the Tuesday Book Club and the Fantastiks. Her favorite activity each week, however, remains her Wednesday bridge group, with whom she has laughed and shared stories for more than twenty years. Mom has always believed that the three sustaining pillars of her life have been faith, family, and friends.

Mental illness affects one in five adults, and everyone knows someone who has struggled with a mental health issue: anxiety, depression, or addiction, to name a few. I pray that the final message of this book is to know there is treatment, and hope, available. Let's end the stigma and start talking about mental health with the same normalcy we extend to physical health. That is something we all can do.

Here are some mental health resources:

IN CHARLOTTE

HopeWay
www.hopeway.org

NATIONAL

NAMI: National Alliance on Mental Illness
www.nami.org

Bring Change 2 Mind
A nonprofit organization working to end the stigma and discrimination surrounding mental illness. Start the conversation. End the stigma.
www.bringchange2mind.org

ACKNOWLEDGMENTS

There are a hundred stories that made up Moore Place. Some are told in these pages, but countless others, and the people who are a part of them, are not. So for those stories I didn't tell, and names I didn't name, please know you are part of the fabric of Moore Place, and I am so grateful for your help and presence along this journey. I am particularly indebted to the following:

To Charlie, the First Believer. My goose.

To Lauren, Kailey, Emma, and Maddie, thank you for all your love, patience, and support from the first True Blessings to the doorknob. No Words.

To Louise, my oracle, for being there from the beginning through every otherworldly happening.

To Dad for making me believe I could do anything.

To Mom for your daily courage and for starting the journey I never saw coming.

To Bob and Jean for being the first donors to the dream and loving me as your own.

To Allyson for being my first best friend and helping me find the words written inside.

To Karen Green Pirinelli, thank you for being the first Green Girl to discover *Same Kind of Different As Me.*

To *Ann and Rolfe Neill,* thank you for bringing me to Charlotte, where this story began.

To *Liz Clasen-Kelly* for being the passionate voice that always knew what this city needed to do.

To *Dale Mullennix* for giving this Graphics Girl a chance and doing the really hard work every day for two decades.

To *Sarah Belk, Angela Breeden, Kim Belk, Edwina Willis Fleming, Paige Waugh, Karen Pritchett, and Paige James* for the First True Blessings that started it all.

To *Libba Rule, Christe Eades, Barb Singer, Mary Katherine Black,* and all those who have kept True Blessings running strong for ten years.

To *Caroline Chambre* for leaving New York and making Moore Place your home.

To *Joann Markley* for starting this journey with me and keeping the first thirteen safe.

To *the original Homeless to Homes tenants* for having the courage to be first and showing what was possible.

To *Coleman* for sharing your story and making me believe in angels.

To *Jennie Buckner* for having the courage to lead the change on our mission.

To *Rich Hoard, Megan Coffey, Liz Peralta, Lauren Cranford, Trish Fries, and Beth Galen* for your dedication to this work, which made Moore Place possible.

To *Bill Holt, Hugh McColl, Downie Saussy, Matt Wall, and Jerry Licari (the Five Guys)* for doing everything I couldn't and more.

To *Gary Chesson, Mike Clement, and Greg Gach* for your
leadership in changing hearts and minds.

To *David Furman and Steve Barton* for taking a sketch on
a napkin and translating it into an amazing home.

To *Laura Schulte* for saying the improbable, impossible,
and biggest "Yes" and *Jay Everette* for everything else

To *Mike Rizer* for being the miracle maker behind
the scenes.

To *Anthony Foxx* for championing what was right even
when people thought it was wrong.

To *Paul Walker, Lori Thomas, and Susan Furtney* for
creating the plan that would make the vision
of Moore Place possible.

To *Louise Parsons, Sally Saussy, Anne Fehring, Angela
Breeden, Tricia Harrison, and Barb Singer* for making
each room a home.

To *Jan Shealy* for keeping track of every dollar and
every name, and *Tommy Shealy* for his leadership
in the campaign.

To *Zelleka Beirman* for putting heart and soul into
city policy.

To *Tammie Lesene* for listening and showing me how
to live in the gray.

To *Heidi Rotberg* for teaching me there are no magic
wands or crystal balls and forgiveness is a good thing.

To *Chip Edens* for encouraging me to take a leap of faith.

To *Lisa Saunders* for making me Believe.

To *Lynn Pearce Tate* for keeping me in her prayers and helping me believe in my own.

To *the Schpilkies* for fifteen years of friendship and helping me imagine the unimaginable.

To *Mary Beth Hollet,* who encouraged me to write this and especially for pushing me to She Speaks.

To *Amy Carroll* for teaching me how to write my message

To *Liza Branch, Julie Marr, Renee McColl, and Kathleen Richardson* for two decades of keeping it real and always reminding Sister Mary Margaret to do the same; and supporting every dream.

To *Edwina Willis Fleming* for the words I carry in my wallet and not letting me forget.

To *Jane Harrell* for making me comfortable with this whole God thing and so much more.

To *Julie Marr* for being my spiritual director, encouraging me to Tell About It and writing a genius title.

To *Betsy and Bill Blue* for inviting me on their journey and showing me how Grace continues to lead.

To *Lisa Cashion* for showing me the new dream and where this road goes next.

To *Emily Bell* for making me dig ever deeper than I ever wanted to go.

To *Peg Robachek* for encouraging me that this may be good enough and reading my first bad drafts.

To my beta readers: Kristin Hills Bradberry, Carrie Banwell, Beth Gast, Susan Izard, Gigi Priebe, and Nancy Engen (with her canasta club: Susie Davis, Erin Lamb, and Susan Wasilauskas) for giving me the confidence to take this manuscript out of a drawer.

To Jon Valk for taking a chance on coffee, pushing me to embrace my story and creating a brilliant cover.

To Fiona Hallowell for being the final God-instance in making this book better than I ever imagined.

To Karen Minster for taking a manuscript and making the magic of the beautiful book in my hands.

To Diane Aronson for making this very imperfect manuscript shine.

To my digital marketing team: Lauren and Kailey Izard, Corrie Smith, Morgan Bailey, Susan Walker and Emily Brinkley for your creative and beautiful work that put this story into the world.

To the staff and volunteers at Urban Ministry Center and Moore Place who still show up 365 days a year to love thy Neighbor.

To the 259 donors to Moore Place: Thank you for bringing us home.

WANT TO KNOW MORE?

Photos, Group Study Guide, and Reader Resources
are available on www.kathyizard.com.

LIKE THE BOOK?
WANT TO RECOMMEND IT?

As an indie author, reviews are invaluable to me.
If you are willing to take a moment to post a quick review
on Amazon or Goodreads to let people know what
you thought of *The Hundred Story Home*,
I would really appreciate it. Thank you!

Thank you for purchasing this book.
Proceeds will be donated to Moore Place and
the Urban Ministry Center in Charlotte, N.C.
If you want to learn more or donate directly online,
please visit: www.urbanministrycenter.org.

66002050R00189

Made in the USA
Lexington, KY
31 July 2017